Gable

Biography of a Mountain and its Upper Valleys

Dedicated to Margaret Craig

Gable

Biography of a Mountain and its Upper Valleys

Dr Malcolm Craig

© Dr Malcolm Craig 2011

Dr Malcolm Craig has asserted his moral rights to be identified as the author of this work in accordance with the Copyright, Designs and Patents Act 1988.

Published by Sigma Leisure – an imprint of
Sigma Press, Stobart House, Pontyclerc, Penybanc Road
Ammanford, Carmarthenshire SA18 3HP
www.sigmapress.co.uk

British Library Cataloguing in Publication Data

A CIP record for this book is available from the British Library

ISBN: 978-1-85058-899-3

Typesetting and Design by: Sigma Press, Ammanford, Carmarthenshire

Cover picture: *Gable, south side, from Wasdale Head.*
Alfred Heaton Cooper 1863-1929

Printed by: Akcent Media Limited

Disclaimer: The information in this book is given in good faith and is believed to be correct at the time of publication.

Every effort has been made to fulfil requirements with regard to reproducing copyright material. The author and publisher will be glad to rectify any omissions at the earliest opportunity

Acknowledgements

The following people and organizations have given me considerable help while doing the research and eventual writing of this book.

Peter Friend, geologist and writer, for guidance in presenting the subject of geology to the non-geologist.

Geologists, Michael Branney and David Millward for giving me wise caution in the handling of Gable's geology. Any misunderstanding is entirely mine.

The late Peter Hodgkiss for very helpful critical reading of climbing-related parts of the book.

Generations of Editors and Contributors to the Transactions of the Cumberland and Westmorland Antiquarian and Archaeological Society from 1866 to date. A wealth of information about Cumbria and an invaluable source.

Generations of Editors and Contributors to the wonderful red journals of the Fell and Rock Climbing Club of the English Lake District for not only climbing details but a range of topics related to Lakeland.

Kate Iliffe Archivist of Sedbergh School for accessing details from the school's 1914-1918 Roll of Honour.

Peter Smith Archivist of the Fell and Rock Climbing Club for his help in gaining reproduction rights and for his searching of membership records for details I had not been able to locate.

Susan Steinberg, granddaughter of Ashley Abraham, for permission to reproduce the two Abraham climbing-related photographs.

Robert Baxter Archivist Cumbria Records Office Whitehaven, for his searching and advice.

Alun Martin of the University of Cambridge Unit for Landscape Modelling for his searching to locate the aerial photograph of the Gable Group.

To get suitable photographs, when living in Cambridge, would mean camping on Gable hopeful of getting the weather and light for quality images, possibly many days. In addition I am no photographer so am very grateful to Ann Bowker and Andrew Leaney for kindly giving me high resolution digital images of photographs appearing on their web sites, respectively: www.keswick.u-net.com and: www.leaney.org

Carrie Allen of the Westmorland Gazette Photographic Department for permission to use a photograph from Kenneth Shepherd's book, *Lakeland 50 Years Ago.*

Alastair Cameron of the Honister Slate Mine for his permission to reproduce the Abraham photograph of a slate barrow in use.

Julian and John Heaton Cooper of the Gallery in Grasmere for permission to reproduce work of Alfred Heaton Cooper and William Heaton Cooper.

Denise Noble of The Ramblers for permission to use the photograph taken by the late Tom Stephenson.

Staff at the Earth Sciences Library University of Cambridge and staff at the University Library Cambridge for their cheerful assistance at all times.

Friend and author Cyril Aydon for encouragement and helpful comments over the years.

Jane Evans Editor Sigma Press. After unfortunate experiences with Editors Jane has restored my faith in their profession with her helpful, friendly and efficient approach.

Daughter and son, Alison and Andrew for their continued interest and encouragement.

Last, but certainly not least, Margaret my wife for her patience, critical reading and use of family-history knowledge which, together, has played a major part in the writing of this book.

Contents

I Background

Love of place

This story is a personal view of one Lake District mountain and its immediate upper valleys, a mountain held in great affection by many walkers and climbers. Those who have climbed Great Gable, not once but many times could tell, in their own way, this story too. They could write possibly of rock climbs, of trips on particular anniversaries, of interesting ways to the top or rock recesses near water where brews of tea or coffee have been made. Some walkers and climbers may even write of loving this mountain. There are people who can identify with 'place' as much as with family or friends. A bond can build with a mountain or hill, the glade of a wood or a favourite stream. In mountainous country this bond can be created on a first climb or happen gradually as different images of a place are discovered. A place can appear to take on a life of its own, and can be looked upon as a friend. A good example of seeing a place in this way comes from journalist and author of well-known children's books, Arthur Ransome. As a child, he put his hand in Coniston Water at the beginning of each Lakeland holiday; this was done as a friendly greeting, half-expecting Coniston Water to recognize his return to that place.

Feelings about place and in particular mountains have been captured in a delightful book by Elisee Reclus, published in 1881 and translated from the French.[1]

'I loved the mountain for its own sake. I loved its superb calm face, lighted up by the sun while we were still in gloom; I loved its mighty shoulder laden with ice – full of blue reflections; its sides whereon pastures alternated with forests and waste ground; its routes stretch out like those of an enormous tree separated by the valleys with rivulets, cascades, lakes and meadows; I loved everything belonging to the mountain down to the yellow or green moss growing upon the rocks, down to the stone gleaming in the midst of turf .'

Many walkers and climbers can love a particular mountain in this way, with feelings similar to those expressed by Reclus. Archaeologist Richard Bradley refers to archaeology of natural places because they have significance in the minds of people at that time.

Feelings about place are not confined to wild country. Virginia Woolf thought about London and identified with the city as though it had personality and Jean Moorcroft Wilson wrote about the relationship Woolf had with this sprawling mass of buildings and gardens, describing her book as a 'biography of place'.[2] The book first triggered the idea of writing about Gable as a biography. Giving personality to a mountain can be thought of as pure whimsy, an odd or quaint habit. Seasoned climbers or walkers may see a favourite mountain as having personality; not as anthropomorphism, giving human characteristics to Gable, even though sometimes we talk about its face, foot, head or the shoulder of a ridge. The term personality and the image this creates, comes mainly from feelings of warmth towards the mountain. Often Gable is described as, 'proud and aloof'. Molly Lefebure, Lake District writer, recalls telling a doctor that man now has the power to blow these formerly eternal hills to bits, the doctor replied with conviction, 'Oh, Great Gable would never allow that to happen, you know. He would come striding down to the House of Commons and put a stop to all that'. Lefebure writes that however inanimate mountains may appear to the dull or unobservant they are without doubt alive to all who know them intimately. Professor John Tyndall, scientist who made a study of Alpine glaciers in the nineteenth century, when on a visit to Wasdale Head wrote, 'Great Gable appears to carry on a conflict with a grey cloud which assailed his summit'. Author Hugh Walpole writes of 'Skiddaw's calm self-confidence of its broad shoulders, the sturdiness, the quiet power and endurance'.

A similar theme has been followed by Peter Ackroyd in writing about London, and in a later book about the River Thames. The book *Liquid History* by Stephen Croad also chronicles this river's life in a 'biographical' way, though mainly in pictorial form. Both writers see city or river as having a life. Peter Ackroyd chooses to trace London's beginning to Neolithic time. Here I see Gable as having a 'life' going back even further; long before humans came near the mountain and indeed long before they appeared on Earth. There is great insight to be gained about a mountain by knowing of its birthplace, when it was formed, and how.

After being on Gable when a match would remain alight with barely a flicker to days when the wind was so strong we stood upright with great difficulty, we may claim to know its many moods. Experiencing the mountain's moods can lead us to believe we know Gable well, but to know the mountain fully we need the knowledge of many people, among them: geologists, meteorologists, botanists and industrial archaeologists. When various specialists have contributed their knowledge, the putting together of a biographical view appears to be limited only by our imagination.

Symbolic landscape
Gable can be seen as symbolic landscape; if not, as often claimed, the birthplace of rock climbing in Britain, certainly the main area for its

early development, and of all mountains in Lakeland it is the one most closely associated with the oldest climbing club in the area. Gable is also the central image in a symbol used to represent the Lake District National Park, and is the site of possibly the most evocative war memorial in the country.

Dorothy Wordsworth and Coleridge wrote of Gable in glowing terms, in what was to become part of a changed attitude towards wild places in this country, during what has been called the romantic period. Gable with its distinctive shape, being uniformly steep on all sides with probably more crag than any mountain in Lakeland, is easily recognizable from numerous view-points. Walkers and climbers are drawn to the mountain, time and time again, excited by its features and the experiences offered. While rock climbing in the Ogwen valley I sensed that the feelings we had for Gable in Lakeland were to be found among climbers going regularly to North Wales, whose 'special' mountain was Tryfan. Wilfred Noyce, mountaineer and author who, when in Britain, rock climbed mainly in Wales but wrote of looking up into the misty ridges of Great Gable, described it as the peak that most resembles well-loved Tryfan.[3]

Gable was once a focal point for the smuggling of valuable graphite and allegedly for the making and smuggling of whiskey. There are legendary tales about a smuggler's route around the mountain's western flanks, and about a mysterious hut placed in a most unlikely position on its steep north face. The northern flanks were also the site of mining once-valuable industrial materials. Over the past 300 years writers, artists and poets have been describing Gable's form and the influence it has upon them; at times, without ever being on the mountain. Gable in its independent central position presides over the most varied landscape to be found anywhere in the world, and there is no finer place to view this landscape than from Gable's noble head.

First view of Gable
My first day of discovery on Great Gable is still clear in memory though happening more than fifty years ago; to be remembered over many years in this way the experience had to be very special indeed. I arrived alone in Seatoller at the head of Borrowdale after a night at a Youth Hostel further down the valley. This first day on Gable came after a journey across the Pennines from Sunderland. The day marked the beginning of a lifetime among moors, hills and mountains, in Britain, the Alps and Far East. After visiting and working in many countries, I know of no place where there is such symmetry, balance of scale and beauty in one turn of the head as in the English Lake District. There had been an earlier car-bound visit to the eastern Lakes around Ullswater with my mother and father which opened my eyes to this beauty. My father would have loved to walk in the hills but

was prevented by a crippled leg and my mother would not be shod in anything but high heels.

Gable was first climbed alone, almost by accident from Seatoller. A Bartholomew half-inch map I carried was fine for cycling but rather limited when off the road, so I simply went uphill from the village, the only desire to get as high as possible, and as quickly as possible. No track was being followed only rough ground over Seatoller Fell parallel to the Honister road before moving up left, heading for a rocky ramp leading to a ridge above me. Eventually the ridge was reached just north of Grey Knotts. I was lost for words to describe what lay before me. Much later I discovered Coleridge, who described the area, in *Table Talk,* as a cabinet of beauties, 'each thing being beautiful in itself and the very passage of one lake, mountain or valley to another is itself a beautiful thing again'. These words would have summed up my feelings perfectly on that morning. Looking from the ridge on a clear sunny spring day, largely determined the course of my life; fortunate indeed to have made this discovery at a young age. Later, in the Alps, I came across less fortunate older climbers, one in particular who made the joyful discovery of mountaineering in his forties and was climbing feverishly in too much haste, making up for lost time. Soon he was dead, lost while climbing alone on the Weisshorn. In my case, on that particular day, there was the realization that all being well many years of climbing and walking among mountains lay ahead.

Standing on that ridge near Grey Knotts gave me a first full view of the Lake District: Buttermere, Crummock Water and surrounding tops to the west, then moving around to see a panorama from north to east that was awe inspiring.

The next hour, walking along the north ridge of Gable, over Brandreth, was sheer delight. Again no track but keeping as high as possible and making frequent stops to look down into Buttermere, then down to Ennerdale. The route led over rock outcrops, past small pools until suddenly I looked down into a gap in the ridge ahead. I had reached the summit of Green Gable. From here the impressive crag of Gable's Ennerdale face was very close, and seemed to me at that time un-climbable. When beginning to clamber up the rocks from Windy Gap voices were heard above. Suddenly two climbers appeared, one had a coiled rope over his shoulder and both wore clinker-nailed boots; they were real climbers. The pair of boots I was wearing had recently been given to me by a friend of my father, also nailed with clinkers; this made me feel almost one of a select group. I did not realize that before long I was to be one of the very last people to climb rock regularly in nailed boots. Climbers already skilled in climbing with nails: Jim Cameron and Gwen Moffat in the Lake District and George (Scotty) Dwyer in North Wales showed me the way shortly before boot nails were consigned to climbing history.

The sound of clinkers on rock and, later in the day, on a tarmac road has been lost to the present-day climber. 'And a good thing too', I can hear them say.

Despite the weight of nails, walking that ridge was like being on a cushion of air, floating along fully absorbed in the scene around me. There was to be another 'first' that day clambering upwards from Windy Gap; it was the feel of rock that delights so much, and which defies explanation of why this should be so. I recall that one of the two climbers said something like, 'not far now son' as both trundled down the rocks at speed. On looking back to this day I did not want it to be 'not far' the climb could go on forever, such was the joy of being in that place. The scrambling over rock soon came to an end, a first summit, a glorious unforgettable hour wandering around the rim of Gable's top.

The word adventure had a special meaning in those days when there were still places in the world to explore. Sunderland Central Library was searched for the work of writers who were having adventures: Sebastian Snow, Bill Tilman and Eric Shipton; and for those who had adventures in the past such as Edward Whymper, William Coolidge and Ernest Shackleton. They were my heroes. A day alone on an English mountain was very mild in comparison with their exploits, but surely a start? I stood by the memorial plaque on the summit thinking of those named climbers who died in war and, as every time since, saying 'thank you' which seems totally inadequate but nevertheless appropriate. In time, I would read about some of the men, their lives and their climbing, who have their names on that plaque. From the summit, it was a short walk to look down on the valley of Wasdale before wandering around the western rim of the summit to the north and being scared by the view down Gable Crag. Time on the summit was spent searching the map to put names to tops and valleys close to Gable and on the horizon. All this while still quite alone, the contrast with confining Sunderland could not have been greater.

The descent to the valley on that day was made with a heavy heart even though staying there, on the summit, was unrealistic. At times since, appalling weather has made me pleased to rush from a summit, but normally there is a strong desire to remain. When thinking of reluctance to leave a well-loved summit, lines from Dante Gabriel Rossetti come to mind.[4]

> *'And now that I have climbed and won this height,*
> *I must tread downward through the sloping shade*
> *And travel the bewildered tracks till night.*
> *Yet for this hour I still may here be stayed*
> *And see the gold air and the silver fade*
> *And the last bird fly into the last night.'*

A quiet stroll down Sty Head Pass took me to the farm at Seathwaite. In later years, after being on Scafell or Gable with climbing colleagues, Edmondson the farmer would like to say, 'see you've brought rain with you again,' showing a wry sense of humour from a man living in the wettest inhabited place in England. When local farmers were asked by visitors, often in exasperated tones, whether it always rains in the Lake District some would say, 'no, sometimes it snows'. A Whitehaven doctor, John Fletcher Miller had rain gauges put down at Seathwaite Farm and Sty Head Pass and established that at an average rainfall of 123 inches a year the farm was the wettest place to live in England, but the wettest place was around Sty Head at 170 inches. As young climbers we did wonder if there was any truth in the story that some walkers, on reaching Seathwaite after a long day on Gable or the Scafells, relieved themselves using the rain gauge.

The farm could not be passed without drinking tea; someone asked why more tea was drunk at Seathwaite than anywhere else in the world. On that day, refreshed and on the road beyond the farm my nailed boots made what was becoming a familiar clinking almost musical sound, like the closing notes of a wonderful day. My equipment on this journey was extremely basic and consisted of flannel trousers tucked into socks, worn just like walkers I had seen while cycling over moorland roads. Two pairs of socks, the outer going over the top of my boot, hopefully to keep out stones, but inviting water; again it was what proper walkers did. In a borrowed knapsack, not a rucksack, that had probably held a gas mask a few years earlier, I carried a yellow oilskin cycle cape that when rolled up stuck to itself at each turn. This cape had to be prized open, and eventually was put on over an already wet body. Grenfell was the nearest possible material to keep you dry, but on an apprentice's weekly wage of one pound ten shillings we could only dream of such protection. An ex-army jacket was brought into use but had rain-repelling qualities of muslin. Soon I became resigned to being completely wet, comforted by the comment from older climbers that skin is waterproof. Industrial lads and lasses who spent much of their spare time on rocks, on cycles or walking hills had exactly the same experience, we did not even use the word 'equipment'. That wonderful day came to an end on arriving back at the village of Seatoller. Mountaineer and writer H.E.G. Tyndale, recounting how a schoolmaster was telling him and other pupils about Vittorino da Feltra being born in a mountain village, paused, leant forward and said, 'I hope you will all be born in mountain villages'.[5] I appreciate what that schoolmaster meant; a new life can begin in a mountain village.

Gable and escape
The first experience of Gable led to other ventures of this kind either to other parts of the Lake District or moors of Durham and

Northumberland; they were great escapes from working life in a shipyard. Escape from being constantly surrounded by steel which dulled the senses. Escape from an imprisoning shipyard apprenticeship, mostly from noise, but also from the acrid smell of machine cooling water, time-clocks that had to be punched before a siren sounded at 7.30 each morning, and dirt that entered the pores and refused to move despite much scrubbing. Being afraid to get your hands dirty was a regular insult made to young apprentices. Frustratingly, we could not explain that it had nothing to do with being afraid, but simply a dislike of the oily cloying sensation. Yet all pleas were in vain. Spending a weekend in the wilds was not understood by many older colleagues in the shipyard. At a time of full employment and over-full order books, managers wanted us to work at weekends and not be cycling, walking or climbing in wild country. What do young men, groomed as factory fodder, want with mountains? Eventually, after much persistence, further journeys for walking and rock climbing were made, alone or with friends. Days were spent on Gable, Scafell, Langdale crags or nearer to home on the Wanney and Simonside crags of Northumberland; the contact with rock cleansed the body to make us feel more human again and not only an extension of a machine.

One comfort to be found in the shipyard was a small grass embankment close to the colour of green and the only touch of nature for some distance around. For a small group of like-minded apprentices there was mid-day dinnertime, not lunch, minor escapes to this oasis, where we could talk of future trips on cycle or foot. Each great escape could also be planned while working a centre lathe or putting a marine engine together. We began to realize there was as much satisfaction in planning as there was in the journey, especially as imagination could take us temporarily beyond the factory. Our minds were freed from an industry for which we did not feel suited. I was not alone among the apprentices in feeling this way, though initially like myself, their escape was gained by cycling into Teesdale, Weardale or the wild expanses of Northumberland, mainly on almost car-free roads at a time when they could find a bed in proper Youth Hostels; this was simple accommodation only for those getting there under their own steam. The bicycle I used at this time still rests in a garage, being unable to throw away this 'chariot to freedom,' and my clinker-nailed climbing boots are retired in the same way.

Venturing into the higher places like Great Gable or Scafell was different, yet for all of us this was an extension of the urge to get away from oppressive industrialization. A special delight was offered by members of the Northumbrian Mountaineering Club. We would travel from Newcastle, by coach, in mid-winter to Borrowdale and climb Great End Central Gulley when it was full of snow and ice. This was a first opportunity to practise the use of an ice axe, and provided those of us in industry with a very real sense of escape.

This is the background to the book. Writers who choose the Lake District as a subject invariably talk about Great Gable as being somehow special, I am no exception, and this book allows me to say, as best I can, what makes it so special to me, and, possibly, to explain something of the mountain's appeal to others. The reading of books about the Lake District is for me a great pleasure: Dorothy and William Wordsworth, Owen Glynne Jones, Lehmann Oppenheimer, Molly Lefebure, William Rollinson, Harry Griffin, Alfred Wainwright, Hunter Davies, Melvyn Bragg and Walt Unsworth are among those to be read more than once.

The idea for this book is quite simple; Great Gable means so much to so many people, why not write about only that mountain? I can hear people saying, 'not another book set in the Lake District, there are hundreds of books about the area'. Even in 1816, Thomas Home wrote, 'so many Tours to the beautiful Lakes of this county have already been published, that he who adds to their number may justly be charged with presumption; unless the information he communicates posses more than ordinary value and interest'.[6] Hugh Walpole had around 300 books about Lakeland in his library and if alive now would have many more to collect.

An occasional publication will devote almost a chapter to Great Gable, along with other significant tops, but at each reading we normally want to know more about a particular place. A great many books have to be read before a complete description of any one mountain or hill has been gained. Getting to know a mountain like Gable in great detail is like getting to know a great painting, well worth the research. Mountaineer and writer Wilfred Noyce wrote, 'A summer's day walk up the Sty head side of Gable, or the Chamonix side of Mont Blanc, for instance, would not give me a perfect knowledge of these mountains. I desire, feverishly almost, to pry into every nook and cranny of them that I can attain, not only to reach the summit, and consequently to climb them by every path within my powers'.

Books have been written about one mountain alone: Guido Ray's book on the Matterhorn is possibly the earliest attempt to portray one mountain, then Douglas Milner writing only about Mont Blanc, and more recently *Ben Nevis* by Ken Crocket and *Scafell, Portrait of a Mountain* by Bill Birkett. In each case, apart from Birkett's writing, these books have a strong focus only on climbing upon one mountain and it is the climbs which receive greatest attention.

A distinction is to be made between a guide book listing walks or climbs together with topography and some human history, and what should be in a biography. A biographical approach still serves as a guide, only a more in-depth guide. Guide books to a specific area necessarily have to sacrifice more in-depth coverage in the interest of breadth. There is value in having guides which seek to take a deeper more intimate look at a mountain itself and all forms of life on its slopes from the earliest beginnings. The main aim of this book is to achieve, for Gable and its upper valleys, an in-depth picture of this kind.

Practical features

One geologist of the British Geolgical Survey wrote to me that attempting to describe the birth and formation of Great Gable was an awesome task. The area where Gable stands has been extensively researched by geologists for almost 200 years, but questions still need to be answered. The first published study was by Jonathan Otley in 1820.[7] Otley identified three rock formations in the Lake District: Skiddaw Slates, Borrowdale Volcanic Series and Upper Slates. The names have changed over the years but his overall observation, of three distinct areas, is still valid. Otley wandered widely over the district and realized that these three types of rock formation provided three different kinds of landscape. Gable, sitting as it does in central Lakeland, is part of what is now known as the Borrowdale Volcanic Group. The geology is considered in more detail in the next chapter.

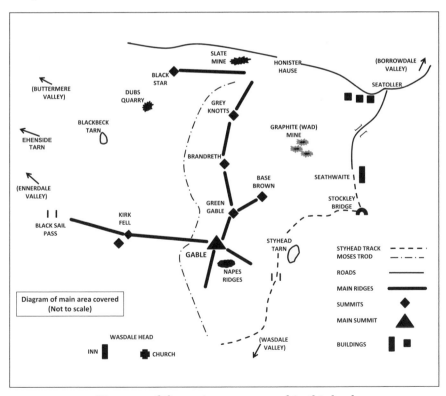

Diagram of the main area covered in this book

From time to time, looking around from the summit made me realize that Great Gable lies within a distinct boundary which includes lower adjoining summits, ridges and surrounding upper valleys. From the north side of Gable can be seen the impressive crag overlooking the Ennerdale valley, known commonly as Gable Crag. Close to the east side of this crag is the summit of Green Gable, viewed in this book as part of Gable's north ridge which leads over Brandreth and Grey Knotts, ending at Honister Hause. This ridge can be seen stretching further north to Cat Bells, but mines and a vehicle road over the Hause at Honister prevents our eyes seeing it as one continuous line of wild country. Eastward, the most prominent immediate feature is Sty Head pass with its tarn and hanging valley at Taylor Gill Force. On the south side of the mountain lie the famous Napes ridges, where some of the earliest rock climbing in Britain took place; these rocks overlook the dwellings at Wasdale Head. Finally, to the west are the twin summits of Kirk Fell and to the west again the boundary limit of the Gable group is Black Sail pass. Kirk Fell deserves to be better known and bringing it within the Gable Group may be of some help.

Great Gable and its upper valleys, within this boundary, roughly match the same land designated as the Fell and Rock Climbing Club memorial to the fallen during the 1914-1918 War. The boundary is also close to that described in the Great Deed of Borrowdale, discussed in Chapter VI. How we group summits and ridges can be very much a matter of perception; boundaries can be easily drawn on maps or by walling and fencing on the ground, but not by any means placed upon our imagination.

Molly Lefebure was expressing the same line of thought about a mountain and its subsidiary summits when writing about Scafell, 'there is no such mountain as Scafell Pike, there is a mountain called Scafell, and to this mountain is attached a chain of pikes or peaks'.[8] Wordsworth too made the same distinction between the Pikes and Scafell. He was quoting from a letter written by his sister Dorothy when writing in his guide to the Lakes, 'we resolved instead to aim at another point on the same mountain, called the Pikes'. Dorothy with a friend, and a Guide, intended to climb Scafell but short of time settled for the Pikes instead. Some local shepherds generally regard Scafell as extending no further north than the ridge of Mickledore, and they see the Pikes as another mountain. A view of Scafell being the main mountain generally holds true, even though the highest Pike is greater than Scafell by 48 feet and there is little over 50 feet drop between them where both are joined at Mickledore. Walkers may go up the mountain of Scafell or simply climb the Pikes on that mountain. This was also my initial image of Great Gable many years ago, a central mountain with ridges and adjoining lower tops, an image which has been adopted in this book.

Aerial photograph showing Gable's North Ridge and Borrowdale Valley.
Unit for Landscape Modelling, University of Cambridge

The aerial photograph above from Cambridge University Unit for Landscape Modelling shows most of the area covered by this book, only the Wasdale side of Gable cannot be seen. Gable is the highest point with to its left, Kirk Fell. Green Gable and the north ridge can be seen dropping down to Honister mine, just visible to the right of the picture. Above the glaciated upper Borrowdale valley can be seen the track going up to Sty Head, where the lake can also be seen, top left of the photograph. Note the two glaciated corries, discussed in Chapter III, the larger immediately below the north ridge called Gillercomb and one much smaller on Seatoller Fell, bottom right.

Lake District and Cumbria are used interchangeably in these pages but the two terms are not synonymous. The Lake District can be taken as bounded by Bassenthwaite to the north, Haweswater to the east, Windermere to the south and Ennerdale Water to the west. Cumbria in contrast refers to the county boundary after 1974 when Cumberland, Westmorland and the most northerly part of Lancashire were merged to form one county.

Before attempting to describe the birth of Gable in the next chapter, a note on the use of measurement will be useful. A geologist, Dr Moseley, made indiscriminate use of miles, kilometres, feet and metres, his excuse being that we should all be bilingual.[9] Heights of hills and mountains are given only in feet. Wainwright or, as he preferred to be known to friends, Alf or 'AW', writer of *Pictorial Guides to the Lake District*, said it was a disgrace that Great Gable should be demoted to under 1,000 metres instead of just under 3,000 feet. In this book at 2,949 feet Gable shall remain and not 899 metres. In Britain a hill is said to be below 2,000 feet and anything over this height is a mountain. This standard has been adopted in a book, *The Mountains of England and Wales* by John and Anne Nuttall.

In metric, Gable is a mountain more than 609.6 metres high, equivalent of 2,000 feet. As Wainwright said, you cannot apply metric measurement to mountains, not in Britain anyway and that is all he was concerned about and all we need to be concerned about in this book. Height will be given in feet, or as some early English Alpine mountaineers would write, 'English feet'. As a matter of interest, there are no 1,000 metre tops in Lakeland. Measurement of distance and area is given in Imperial with decimal equivalent in parenthesis. As a passing nod to 'progress', temperature will be given in centigrade. I feel sure Dr Moseley would be pleased.

Measurement of time is more problematic; concept of time is man's invention, once upon a time there was no time. Calendar years before AD are normally given as BC but radiocarbon dating is indicated by using lower case, bc. When writing about dates in pre-history some researchers quote calendar years and others use radiocarbon dating. I have taken the easy way out and simply used 'years before the present' or 'years ago'. In works of geology the term 'present' is normally set at 1950 but here, 2000 is the base-line used for the present. Carbon years, bc, can be converted to calendar years and then stated as years before the present. We also need to accept a tolerance when discussing years in their thousands, millions or even billions. Any date as given cannot be exact when writing of events in pre-history; there is inevitably a number of years plus or minus around the date stated.

To appreciate Gable's early years it is necessary to grasp the idea of events happening millions or even billions of years ago, this can be difficult for anyone not trained in geology, geomorphology or palaeontology. There are ways to develop an appreciation of huge time-spans. Probably the most common is to visualize the Earth's history as one day from midnight to midnight, and be given the information that dinosaurs appeared late in the evening at 22.42 hrs; humans have been on the Earth for only 90 seconds before the end of that day. Examples of this kind are fine for bar-room type chatting but more impact and understanding can come from taking yourself to a wild place where it is much easier to imagine extremely long spans of time. One method for visualizing time in this way is to stand alone on some high barren spot that has not changed significantly in millennia. Looking eastward from the summit of Gable, a remote part of the northern Highlands, northern Pennines or on the Harlech Dome are ideal locations. Think of grandparents three or four generations back who, when alive, could have stood in the same place and enjoyed the same view. Ancestors, going back even further, could also view the same scene and have the same experience. Wild places can, with some visualizing, provide a link with the past and give us a clearer perspective of passing time. The four locations recommended above have changed dramatically over time but not over what we know of as human time in Britain since the end of the last ice age, around 12,000 years before the present. Gable and its rocky neighbours provide a landscape that has remained largely unchanged over hundreds of generations. Valleys and upper valleys have changed during this period but not higher central Lakeland.

The naming of places, mountains and other features around Gable are taken from the Ordnance Survey map of the district. I prefer the traditional Norse-based name 'gill' rather than 'ghyll'. For some reason the Survey use gill, with only one exception: Dungeon Ghyll; following the map, these are the spellings used here. One deviation from the map is to use the name Wastwater, when the Survey split the name to Wast Water.

Before beginning research for this book I knew Gable well. Over a number of years, especially as a young man, I came to love it, respect it, and to feel wholesome within its shadow, whether climbing rocks in the company of others or wandering alone over the mountain in all seasons. Thinking of the place in a 'biographical' sense has led to a completely new perspective and to the discovery of ideas which have not always been easy to grasp, in particular the geology which is both fascinating and bewildering in its complexity.

References

[1] Reclus, E. (1881) *The History of a Mountain*. London: Sampson Low.

[2] Wilson, J.M. (1987) *Virginia Woolf: Life and London: A Biography of Place*. London: Cecil Woolf.

[3] Noyce, W. 1947. *Mountains and Men*, p. 56. London: Geoffrey Bles.

[4] Rossetti, D.G. 2003. *Collected Poetry and Prose*. Yale University Press.

[5] Tyndale, H.E.G. 1848. *Mountain Paths*, p.23. London: Eyre & Spottiswoode.

[6] Home, T.H. 1816. *The Lakes of Lancashire, Westmorland and Cumberland*. London: T Cadell & W Davies.

[7] Otley, J. 1820. *Remarks on the succession of rocks in the District of the Lakes*. Lonsdale Magazine, vol. 1, pp.433-438.

[8] Lefebure, M. 1964. *The English Lake District*. p.142. London: B.T. Batsford Ltd.

[9] Moseley, F. 1983. *Volcanic Rocks of the Lake District: a Geological Guide to the Central Fells*. London: Macmillan.

II Beginnings

Mountains are most worthy of deep study.
For everywhere you turn, they present to
every sense a multitude of objects to excite
and delight the mind. They offer problem
to our intellect; they amaze our souls. They
remind us of the infinite variety of creation,
and offer an unequalled field for the obser-
vation of the processes of nature.

Josias Simler 1574

A very complex geology
To know and fully appreciate any mountain, time is well spent understanding the events, and forces, which led to its birth. Where was the birthplace of Great Gable? Has Gable always been in its present location? How old is the mountain? Has it always had its very distinctive shape? How was it formed; under the sea or above? These are typically the questions I set out to answer here. Information of this kind can be seen as additional to any deep feelings you may have about the mountain, which have developed naturally.

When writing biographies of people, authors can trace back through generations, beginning with a family tree or other records. The origins of Gable are far more problematic. There is no shortage of data or information but there are also many different ideas about how the mountain could have been formed. As a non-geologist aiming to understand the birth and development of Gable I have navigated through claims, counter-claims and on-going discussions about an area that is, geologically, highly complex.

The history of geology is punctuated by many theories and serious debate about how various landscapes develop. Geologists have debated, among themselves, since the mid-nineteenth century and conflicting ideas, when they exist, have been presented mostly to geological journals; here we often find new interpretation each time further evidence is uncovered. Dr Moseley, a prominent writer on Lake District geology, when asked to comment upon a particular geological paper about an area in Lakeland, regretted that he had to make an appalling admission of complete agreement with the authors, adding that perhaps other geologists taking part in the discussion would be more imaginative. When searching for answers to the formation of Gable, full agreement, that so appalled Mosley, has not yet been reached.

A relatively young Gable

Time and place of a mountain's birth can only be discovered by going back millions of years. A claim that Gable's age is measured in millions of years, rather than thousands, will not be accepted by everyone; the idea conflicts with a firmly held belief by some people that the Earth is not nearly so old. In 1644, John Lightfoot, Vice Chancellor of Cambridge University, gave September 17, 3928 BC as the date when the Earth was finally created in six days. This 'discovery' by Lightfoot was soon contradicted by Archbishop Ussher, Primate of Ireland, when he gave October 23, 4004 BC which was taken up in an edition of the English Bible. Then aged 69, the Archbishop may have felt it was time for him to be remembered for something; a kind of legacy. These time-spans claimed for the age of the earth remained unchallenged for around 200 years.

There does appear to have been some arrogance in assuming that the age of the Earth must roughly coincide with the, then perceived, time-span of human life. The words of Hans Cloos, a German Geologist, come to mind, 'the Earth is large and old enough to teach us modesty'.[1] If, like the Vice Chancellor and Archbishop, we accept around 6000 years as the true age of the Earth, Great Gable and mountain neighbours would have been formed immediately as we see them now because it is impossible for weathering and erosion to fashion such a landscape in this relatively short period of time. We can witness for ourselves how few changes occur through weathering and erosion among the mountains in around fifty years of an active lifetime; think about how many thousands of years need to pass, before significant changes can be noted. In contrast to these earlier ideas, there is a view held on the basis of data taken from uranium-lead and other radiometric dating that the age of the Earth, from the time it reached its present mass, is 4.55 billion years, with a tolerance of plus or minus seventy million years, formed during what has been named the Hadean. This estimate of age has held firm since 1956.[2] Information of this kind about the age of the Earth helps to put the birth of our mountain in some perspective.

Surprisingly, Gable is young relative to the age of the Earth. The mountain's foundations were formed from a series of volcanic events between 460 and 450 million years ago in the Caradoc Age; Gable's birthplace had existed millions of years before that time. Working with timescales of this kind is the only way we can begin to understand Gable's early development. The American writer Emerson wrote: 'The years teach much which the days never know', to paraphrase here, we could say: 'Millennia teach much which Centuries never know'. As an added perspective, the age of Gable's rocks at around 460 million years old can be compared with the age of oldest rocks so far recorded of 3.8 to 3.9 billion years in South Africa and up to 4.4 billion years in Australia.

Southern Ocean birthplace

Around 520 million years ago the birthplace of Great Gable was close to the northern limit of the Southern Ocean. Sail beyond Africa in the South Atlantic until latitude sixty degrees is reached; beyond this point only heaving waves are to be seen, until the shores of Antarctica appear on the horizon. Where this ocean now is, Gable's birthplace lay. There is some evidence that between 1000 million and 770 million years ago two super continents lay between latitude sixty degrees and the South Pole. Eventually these large continents began breaking up into smaller continents, and even smaller micro continents or more accurately, micro-terrains. Evidence of this movement between land masses comes mainly from plant and fossil distribution shared between continents in the southern hemisphere, showing that the continents must have been joined at some time because the species could not have evolved as they have if the continents had always been separated.

During this splitting-up of land masses a new ocean developed between two continents now named Gondwana and Laurentia, these continents developed from supercontinents between 750 and 550 million years ago. The ocean, first known as Proto-Atlantic, was given the name of Iapetus as recently as 1972.[3] Steadily Iapetus widened until a maximum width of 5000 km was reached around 488 million years ago. Gondwana lay at 60° and Laurentia at 15° south.[4] What was to become the birthplace of Great Gable can be positioned on the edge of a micro-terrain, Avalonia named after the Avalon Peninsula of Newfoundland. This smaller land mass of Avalonia became a micro terrain when it broke away from Gondwana and drifted towards Laurentia. Again an Ocean opened up between Avalonia and the parent-body of land Gondwana, which has become known as the Rheic Ocean. At this time a sea, the Tornquist, was closing between drifting Avalonia and a micro continent, Baltica. Eventually these two masses 'docked' together obliquely rather than 'head on' and continued the journey northward, getting closer to Laurentia as the Iapetus Ocean closed. The coming together of Avelonia and Baltica with the larger land mass Laurentia must have been gentle in comparison with the land-mass 'collision' which resulted in the Himalayas.

The closure of Iapetus triggered a series of volcanic events in what some geologists believe to be an island-arc formation along the margin of Avalonia, similar to formations in Japan. The eruptions were caused by the ocean plate sliding below the continent; what is known as subduction.

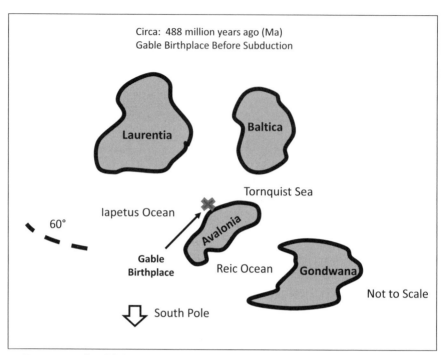

Diagram of Gable's Birthplace in the Southern Ocean before Subduction

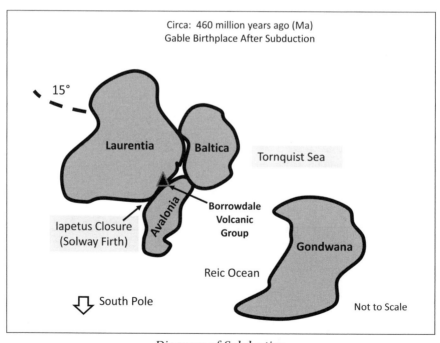

Diagram of Subduction

Movement of ocean plates has happened for at least two billion years, but is better understood by the general public since a subduction in the Indian Ocean, on Boxing Day 2004, caused a massive tidal wave. On the margin of Avalonia there were three main volcanic episodes; two taking place above sea level, or sub-aerially in geologists' words, and a third at least partially above the sea. There have been conflicting views over the past 150 years about whether the mountains of the Lake District were formed beneath the waves, subaqueous formation, or above. The sub-aerial formation of Gable and other central mountains in Lakeland has now been established beyond reasonable doubt.[5] Of Gable's neighbours only the Skiddaw group to the north of the district was formed below sea level, between 520 and 478 million years ago.[6] The Skiddaw group has the oldest rocks of the district made up of marine mudstone, siltstone and sandstone. Skiddaw was 'born' when marine turbidites built up under water to a considerable thickness on the margin of Avalonia. How Skiddaw was eventually uplifted is not clear; there has been some suggestion that it could have been caused by the early stages of the Iapetus subduction. A Professor of geology at Cambridge University, O. T. Jones, studied why geosynclines sank and concluded that they sank because they had that sinking feeling; possibly the same could be said for mountains being uplifted from beneath the sea, they had that uplifting feeling. The subduction began in the early Tremadoc around 488 years ago and finally, after 63 million years of drifting at a few centimetres a year, Avalonia and Baltica joined southern Laurentia, to become what has been called the new super terrain of Laurasia which covered an area that today is from the Pacific Ocean

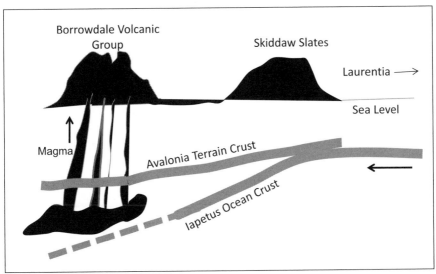

Diagram of Gable's Birthplace in the Southern Ocean after Subduction

in the west to the Ural Mountains in the east. To help visualize this slow movement, Peter Friend geologist and writer suggested thinking about the growth of our finger nails. How much growth between their cuttings in millimetres? How many weeks between their cuttings? How far, in millimetres, does the end of the nail travel in a year? Then you have some idea about the rate of land movement.

The Laurentia part of this new terrain included the lands of Scotland, eastern parts of North America and Greenland. Avalonia, included what is now England, south of the Solway Firth, Wales, the Republic of Ireland and part of continental Europe. Not only Gable is relatively young but 'Britain' also. When Avalonia and Laurentia finally came together, England and Wales joined Scotland for the first time. Britain has been united in this way for only 10% of geological time.

This movement of continents can be likened to the movement of clouds; if we choose one cloud and follow its progress for a number of minutes it will change, normally by docking with another cloud or by breaking up into smaller clouds. The timescale is around a maximum of ten minutes rather than ten million years or more in the case of continents coming together, but the simple comparison can help us visualize this breaking up, drifting and joining of land masses. Movement of land in this way, which became known as continental drift, was suggested by Francis Bacon in the early 17th Century, but was not presented as a theory until Alfred Wegener's work in 1915.[7] Now, looking at a world map, it is possible to speculate how different shorelines, as between the east coast of South American and the west coast of Africa, could fit together. This possible joining of two continents is much more believable if the respective under-water continental shelves are compared instead of only the visible shorelines shown on a map of the world.

Research was done by Alexander du Toit in 1937 but a major breakthrough was made in 1962 when the theory of Plate Tectonics became established, bringing together previous ideas about continental drift and sea-floor spreading.[8] Some years before this discovery was made a number of people believed that Britain had always been in Shakespeare's words 'a sea-girt Isle'. There now is, since the 1960s, a unifying theory within geology of Plate Tectonics which is claimed to be comparable in importance to the Earth sciences as evolution is for the biological sciences.[9]

By 425 million years ago, in the Silurian Period, the Iapetus Ocean no longer existed and in its place was a land-suture which now coincides roughly with the Solway Firth. There has been an argument within geology that identifying the Solway line as the Iapetus suture is a red herring with suggestions that the joining was further south.[10] Final word seems to be that the Solway is close to the site of the suture. Evidence from fossil distribution and regional geology either side of the join shows that the closure could not have been further south, as suggested. This 'super' continent, newly-formed to contain Laurentia, Avalonia and Baltica, has changed shape beyond recognition since this time, but the site of joining near Solway Firth has remained intact to the present day.

The Earth-movements which created Gable's northerly neighbour, Skiddaw, occurred millions of years before the sub-aerial volcanic activity which created Gable. At some stage the land mass of Skiddaw stood above sea-level surrounded by a landscape which we would not begin to recognise as the Lake District; Gable with its neighbours were yet to be 'born'. Casual comparison alone between the rocks of Gable and of Skiddaw show enormous differences between the two. Most of Gable's rock is dense and fine-grained, forming impressive crags, beloved of rock climbers, while rock on Skiddaw is mostly slate-like, friable and mainly in the form of gently-inclined slabs.

The first, partly subaerial, eruptions took place near Skiddaw around 470 million years ago in the mid-Ordovician period and in 1972 was given the name of Eycott Volcanic Group now called simply Eycott Group.[11] The Borrowdale Volcanic Group eruptions, around 460 million years ago in the Llanvirn-Caradoc age, took place near Scafell in the west of the district. Before these separate volcanic events were recognised all volcanic rock in the area was called the Borrowdale Volcanic Series. Now, three main volcanic events are recognised with the third and final set of Earth movements taking place in the south of the district, named the Windermere Supergroup, believed to have been created by the collision of Avalonia and Laurentia. All this volcanic activity was taking place while the Iapetus Ocean plate was creeping below the Avalonia plate, and it is believed that the subduction continued after the magma from volcanoes stopped flowing and until the Iapetus Ocean finally closed. Magma and ash, at up to 900°C, were thrown into the air from vents near Gable but the location of each vent has not been clearly identified. One could be near the head of the Buttermere valley while another could be near the head of Borrowdale and between Base Brown and Green Gable. Two more central vents could have been at Little Narrow Cove, immediately to the east of the Scafell Pikes, and at Cam Spout Crag to the south of Scafell. The whole central volcanic episode was over within an estimated five million years; geologically speaking 'in a flash' and very different from the building of Skiddaw which occurred from late-Cambrian through the whole of the Early Palaeozoic, around 100 million years. The formation of Great Gable had begun but anyone walking amid the smouldering ash at the time would not recognise the mountain, so easily recognisable now. The actions of ice, wind and water would be needed for weathering, and then erosion to take place over millions of years before the Gable we know could be recognised so readily.

Giant volcano

Gable was part of a giant explosive caldera volcano. Calderas are large topographic depressions and can be from 1km to 20km in horizontal extent which is always much larger than their depth. The mountain was part of the Scafell caldera volcano and would only begin to take shape when the Caldera collapsed.[12]

Calderas do not survive well and the rock scenery around Scafell is an almost unique example of caldera development. The rocks of Gable and its near neighbours are so well exposed that they allow us to see this formation in a way that is seldom seen in such detail elsewhere in the world. The form of collapse has been called piece-meal, where the process is chaotic and highly fragmented leaving a number of fault lines in the landscape, rather than the volcano floor subsiding uniformly. Faults typically lie in different directions: north to south (N-S), WSW-ESE and NW-SE.

The giant explosive Scafell Caldera had an area estimated at 220 km^2 and between 15 and 17 km across at its greatest extent. The boundary of the caldera is difficult to define but is believed to have been from Dore Head above Wasdale on the west, across to the east at Dunmail Raise near Grasmere. The eruptions were greater than any that have been recorded in historical times. Today, a complete Caldera is to be seen at Sumbawa, Indonesia called, Tambora; the Caldera is 6 km in diameter and was formed in 1815 when the greatest eruption in historical times took place. Around 200,000 people died either directly or indirectly as a result of the eruption. That the Scafell volcano was far greater than Tambora gives some idea of the violent events that helped create Gable.

Gable rests on a bed, or batholith, of granite, estimated at 1 km deep, that can be seen in only a few places directly at the foot and in places around the mountain. During the volcanic activity, around 450 million years ago plus or minus three million, a pluton of granite was formed beneath the erupting area. What can be described as granitic magma welled up to fill a space left by erupting volcanic ashes and ignimbrites and it is Eskdale granite which underlies Gable; parts of the batholith can be seen at the foot of Gable just above Wasdale Head. The pinkish fine-grained rock peeps out as outcrops like toes through a worn sock and lie around the junction of Gable Beck and Lingmell Beck. If walking past the junction of these becks above Wasdale Head, take time to ponder how long these rocks have lain there and how they reach well into the mountain itself like some great natural foundation. A place to see the Eskdale granite is at Beckfoot Quarry near the Ravenglass and Eskdale Railway line. Similar rock lies below Gable on the northwest side, but this is Ennerdale Granophyre, formed around 452 million years ago, plus or minus four million years. The age of these two types of intrusive rock, Eskdale and Ennerdale, have been debated for many years but in the year 2000 it was said that these dates should bring the debate to an end.[13] The Ennerdale granophyre reaches around to the west of Gable and joins up with Eskdale granite at only one place, the southern end of Wastwater. A good place to see this rock is at Bowness Knott a viewpoint immediately above Ennerdale Water. The rock has been described as relatively uncomplicated stuff that seemingly will stay there forever, 'firm and unmoved'. The formation of this batholith is unlike Gable which is built of distinctive layers with names, from the base, of Lingcove, Whorneyside Tuff, Airy's Bridge, Seathwaite Fell, Lincombe Tarns, and Esk Pike Formation. The rocks are: basalt, andesite, dacite and rhyolitic lavas and welded ignimbrite in a very complex formation. New Zealand geologist Robin Langford Oliver was one of the first to research the formations specifically on and around Gable.[14] In 1961, Oliver mapped the concentration of secondary minerals to be found on Gable, Brandreth, Grey Knotts and around Sty Head. On Gable, Oliver found epidote and some feldspar, and similarly on Brandreth with the addition of quartz. More quartz and some iron sulphide were found on Grey Knotts in addition to small concentrations of epidote and felspar.

Two volcanic episodes have been identified. The first of andesite lava flows, now called the Birker Fell or Lower Borrowdale Volcanic Group. The second episode was of explosive volcanism and caldera formation. When the final volcanic eruptions subsided, and the piecemeal collapse of the Scafell Caldera had taken place, faulting continued to create obvious lines of weakness in the landscape. One of the most significant and extensive is the Coniston Fault to the east of Gable, which runs from Coniston Water, north past Grasmere to Thirlmere. Much closer to the mountain an impressive fault passes through the Ennerdale valley over Windy Gap between Great Gable and Green Gable and onwards, trench-like to Esk Hause, Rossett Gill and into Great Langdale. The Causey Pike fault on an east-north-east line through Keswick and Penrith to Crossfell, divides the Eycot Group in the north from the central Borrowdale Volcanic Group, and formed between 480 and 450 million years ago.

We can only speculate about the development of Gable between the formation of the Borrowdale Volcanic Group in the Southern Ocean around 460 million years ago and the beginning of the Quaternary period around two million years ago. The Quaternary, as a period of study, provides us with an enormous amount of information about how natural landscape was formed due to the appearance of ice caps and glaciers, discussed in the next chapter. For millions of years before this time, Gable enjoyed a tropical climate as the mountain travelled from the Southern Ocean towards the Equator, reaching there around 350 million years ago in the late-Devonian period. It is possible to imagine the mountain lying in a tropical climate; not unlike Gabon in West Africa, now near the same latitude. These conditions continued until the Gable crust came closer to the present-day position; by mid-Miocene, 13 million years ago, the climate became cooler, and later ice sheets formed interspersed by warmer periods, interglacials, some believed to be warmer than today. Gable was not completely sheathed in ice until around 750,000 years ago. At present Gable is passing through 54 degrees 29 seconds latitude and in time its birthplace may complete a journey from 60 degrees south to 60 degrees north.

A major debate, still on-going, is how the landscape around Gable was formed and the mountain sculptured into its present shape. One view is that ice action over a number of glacial periods formed the landscape out of what could have been a single dome of volcanic rock, but it is very unlikely that a glacier alone could fashion a valley system from a uniform dome. A more realistic view is that the volcanic action left a landscape of peaks and valleys more or less where they are now, which were modified firstly by water and then ice action over successive ice ages, widening and straightening the valleys and sculpting rock into the natural architecture seen on and around Gable. A conclusion currently accepted is that the main watersheds and valleys around Gable existed before the glaciations which have taken place over the last two million years, these pre-existing landforms have been modified by a number of ice ages during the Quaternary; a period when significant parts of the existing landscape were taking shape.

A problem when tracing the development of a mountain across past ice ages is that the glaciers of each age removes from the landscape almost all trace of what existed previously. Very little evidence remains of what happened to the landscape before the last, Devensian glaciation and ice-sheet cover. For this reason we can only rely upon evidence from the last great ice age when ice-capping and glaciers helped in the final shaping of Gable. We can also take evidence from glaciers alone which visited the mountain during what is known as the Loch Lomond Re-advance, glaciers returned to the high ground of Cumbria during this period, when Gable had glaciers lying to the north and north-east. These two events: the last major ice age, and later, a return of glaciers, will be considered in more detail in the next chapter.

Seeing the geology today

One view commonly held, especially among walkers, is of two Lake Districts; one picture-postcard tranquil the other, while not wilderness, is certainly wildness which can be brutal and daunting. Imagine if you can, standing beside an ice-cream van in Grasmere looking around at the hills, here it is easier to accept the idea of man-modified or even 'man-made' but not when walking across Esk Hause looking out over Great Gable on a raw February afternoon. This is a place, and a time, when only an experienced climber or walker can feel confident in his or her ability to be there. From the moment when the last glaciers melted and vegetation began returning to the slopes, the scene has changed little over the past 8,000 years. The landscape has been relatively stable during this period; no classic landforms have developed and existing landforms show only minor changes[15] since the end of the last ice age. Becks and rivers around Gable have flowed along the same courses; rock faces rear up with only minor changes through erosion, or rock falls caused by local earthquakes.

An impression is often given by writers on Lakeland that man has had an enormous impact upon what was originally wilderness Lakeland. In the central area there is little evidence to support this view. When looking at Gable from a valley or from a nearby top what you see is largely what the final ice sculpting left behind. The first people, we know from evidence, to have walked the upper valleys of Gable, lived in Neolithic or New Stone Age time when they would see only the top thousand feet of the mountain rising above the tree line. The rocks and familiar dome-shape they saw at this time would be very much like what we see today. The main difference between stone-age landscape and the rather barren rock-strewn upper valleys we walk through now is that the valleys were thickly forested.

There are many references, in Lake District guide books and pamphlets, to man-made landscape but I prefer to think of Gable's surrounding valleys as man-modified. To look down upon the Wasdale valley from Westmorland cairn near the summit of Gable, is to see a man-modified landscape. To look up at the Napes ridges of Gable from that valley is to see a much more natural wild landscape. Henry Salt described these ridges on the south face of Gable as 'barrenness indeed, yet to the lover of such solitudes, is more fruitful than the choicest vineyard or cornfield'.[16] To appreciate this landscape we should try to understand the real forces which moved the rocks to the formation we see now. To see man as 'making' this landscape is to credit humans with powers well beyond what they could ever be capable of. The 'modifications' made since humans appeared on and around Gable, there to be seen in the form of dry-stone walling, scattered buildings and cattle-grazed fields have had minimum impact upon the mountain and cannot be compared with natural forces experienced by Gable over millennia. Scottish poet Hugh MacDiarmid in his work, *On a Raised Beach* wrote that, 'what happens to us is irrelevant to the world's geology, but what happens to the world's geology is not irrelevant to us' also that, 'there are plenty of ruined buildings in the world but no ruined stones'.[17] Mountaineers and sailors, as they move among mountains or sail the seas, possibly better than anyone, are in a position to recognise the irrelevance of humans. When thinking about our own relationship to wild places, the word 'humble' often comes to mind but does not fully describe the irrelevance which can be felt. Arrogance on the other hand, is not too strong a word to describe people who claim that the landscape we see on and around Gable is 'man made'.

Imagining back 8,000 years it is possible to visualize the scene walking from Esk Hause to Sty Head and into Borrowdale on an afternoon in winter. Vegetation not yet fully re-established, at that height there would be no peat or soil cover, only rock underfoot; peat is slow to develop among mountains because the steep relief and rapid drainage does not encourage growth. Just below 2,000 feet can be seen the beginning of a tree line with what would become, below this level, thick deciduous forest. The surrounding mountains are easily recognisable. Great End immediately above to your left, the Langdale Pikes behind and Great Gable rearing up not far away in front. Imagine the light fading as your footsteps move towards Gable; on your right lies the recently-vacated glacier bed, to be named Grains or Grain Gill after the thirteenth century when it was known as the 'Causey'. The descent over rough ground to where a tarn lay would not be unlike one made in winter at present. The snow-covered east flank of Gable rears up above as you turn right to pass the tarn. One day a mountain rescue box will stand here on the pass, and there will be a footpath to follow. Soon afterwards you have a problem crossing the full gushing beck, without having Professor Airy's bridge to help. Approaching the lower valley brings other noticeable missing features. At the bottom of a final steep slope there is no familiar bridge over Stockley Beck and some searching is needed to find a suitable crossing place among the large boulders lying there. Shortly afterwards there would be no Seathwaite Farm for that well-deserved pot of tea. The two bridges and some dry-stone walling before reaching the farm, followed by tea would be the only missing man-made features and event of any significance in the whole journey. Even man-made erosion, caused by many boots, is merely incidental, and as shown during foot and mouth outbreaks the paths, without use, do become less obvious in a relatively short period of time. An imaginary journey of this kind, 8,000 years ago, may help us to appreciate what little change has taken place immediately on and around Gable during these years.

The significant influences which have created Great Gable and its neighbours have occurred over millions of years and the colossal power of these influences from plate tectonics, volcanism and glacier-erosion can be difficult to imagine fully. The Victorian mountaineer, and father of Virginia Woolf, Leslie Stephen, linked these forces to how we view scenery when he wrote, 'that we could have a half-conscious sense of the power that must have been at work that a great part of the influence of mountain scenery is due'.

A simple example of a mountain's unchanging 'permanence' at least within human time came in 1992, while climbing on the north side of Cader Idris in mid-Wales. I photographed Pencoed Pillar from the same stance on the climb where Ashley Abraham, Keswick-based photographer, stood to photograph climber Owen Glynne Jones and party on the arête in 1897. The Victorian picture is included in Alan Hankinson's book on Abraham's photographs.[18] The 1897 photograph shows a rock precariously balanced on a ledge just below the rim of the Pillar; that rock was still precariously balanced in the photograph I took in 1992. The pattern of lichen coating the flat top of the pillar is the same in both photographs, the rock formation in every detail is the same; the only difference is that Victorian tweed-clad climbers are missing from my photograph. This anecdotal account of how it is possible to observe little or no change on a mountain in almost 100 years does help to see the passing of many years as though they had been no more than minutes. We may ponder beyond almost 100 years; was that block on Pencoed Pillar perched there in 1797 or 1097 or even earlier? We may think the same about the well-known Napes Needle on Great Gable; we know that apart from cracks in the rock being no longer filled with vegetation and a crucial foothold below the top being very much smaller, the Needle has changed little since it was first climbed over 100 years ago. Then ask whether the Needle was much the same when late stone-age people, 5,000 ago, struggled through the trees and across Gable's scree as they passed beneath the Napes' ridges.

References

[1]   Cloos, H. 1954. *Conversations with the Earth.* London: Routledge and K Paul.
[2]   Patterson, C.C. 1956. *Age of meteorites and the Earth.* Geochimica et Cosmochimica Acta, vol.10, pp.230-237.
[3]   Harland, W.B. and Gayer, R.A. 1972. *The Arctic Caledonides and earlier oceans.* Geological Magazine, vol.109, pp.289-314.
[4]   Torsvik, T.H. and Trench, A. 1991. *The Ordovician history of the Iapetus Ocean in Britain.* Journal of the Geological Society, London, vol.148, p.423.
[5]   Branney, M.J. 1988. *The sub-aerial setting of the Ordovician Borrowdale Volcanic Group, The English Lake District.* Journal of the Geological Society, London, 145, pp.887-890.
[6]   Cooper, A.H. et al. 1995, *The stratigraphy, correlation, provenance and Palaeogeography of the Skiddaw Group (Ordovician) in the Lake District.* Geological Magazine, vol. 132, pp.185-211.
[7]   Wegener, A. 1924. *The Origin of Continents and Oceans.* London: Methuen.
[8]   Hess, H.H. 1962. *History of ocean basins.* In Engel, A.E.J. et al. (eds.) Petrological Studies. New York: Geological Society of America, pp. 599-620.
[9]   Cocks, L.R.M. 2005. *Presidential Address 2005: Where was Britain*

in the Palaeozoic? Proceedings of the Geologists' Association, p.125.

[10] Allen, P.M. 1987. *The Solway Line is not the Iapetus suture.* Geological Magazine, vol.124 (5), pp.485-486.

[11] Downie, C. and Soper, N.J.1972. *Age of the Eycott Volcanic Group and its conformable relationship to the Skiddaw slates in the English Lake District.* Geological Magazine, vol. 109, pp.259-268.

[12] Branney, M.J. and Kokelaar, P. 1994. *Volcanotectonic faulting, deformations and rheomorphism of tuffs during development of a piecemeal caldera.* Geological Society of America Bulletin, vol.106, pp.507-530.

[13] Millward, D. et al. 2000. *Geology of the Ambleside District.* Memoir for 1:50,000 Geology Sheet 38.

[14] Oliver, R.L. 1953. *The Borrowdale Volcanics and Associated Rocks of the Scafell Area in the Lake District (England).* PhD Dissertation, Cambridge University.

[15] Boardman, J. 1996. *Classic Landforms of the Lake District.* Sheffield: The Geographical Association.

[16] Salt, H.S. 1908. *On Cambrian and Cumbrian Hills.* London: A.C. Fifield.

[17] MacDiarmid, H. 1985. *On a Raised Beach.* Biggar: V Grieve.

[18] Hankinson, A. 1975. *Camera on the Crags: a portfolio of early rock climbing photographs by the Abraham Brothers.* Cambridge: Silent Books.

III Ice

Forming of Gable's valleys

Great Gable has been described as a possible centre or hub of a so-called radial pattern of valleys in Lakeland. William Wordsworth, in his *Guide to the Lake District*, was possibly the first to encourage this idea. The guide was published anonymously in 1810, and one of the best-known editions was published in 1835 as, *A Guide through the District of the Lakes*, further editions, as in 1853, had a contribution from geologist Professor Sedgwick. The book is still one of the finest Lake District Guides available.[1] In imagination Wordsworth asked readers to place themselves upon some given point:

> 'Let it be the top of either of the mountains, Great Gavel or Scawfell; or, rather, let us suppose our station to be a cloud hanging midway between those two mountains, at not more than half a mile from the summit of each, and not many yards above their highest elevation; we shall then see stretched at our feet a number of valleys, not fewer than eight, diverging from the point, on which we are supposed to stand, like spokes from the nave of a wheel.'

This radial-pattern view leads naturally to a claim that the valleys could have been cut initially from dome-shaped rock by forces of water and ice. Around 100 years after Wordsworth's observation, John Edward Marr of St John's College Cambridge, described a sugar-spoon shaped dome.[2] He reasoned that if the dome were symmetrical the rivers would be truly radial. Marr described the dome as shaped like an upturned spoon. He placed the radial pattern of valleys around the 'bowl' portion and rectilinear valleys along the 'handle' of the spoon. Scafell and Gable he placed near the centre of the bowl with the handle running eastwards from the central area. Recently these ideas have been questioned, claiming that the valleys are not so radial as supposed.[3] If all valleys in the central district were truly radial the hub would not be a cloud between Great Gable (Great Gavel) and Scafell as Wordsworth suggested, or on a cloudless day an area around Sty Head, but would be a small central point on High Raise, further to the east. A true central hub of this kind, from which valleys truly radiate, does not exist; only Ennerdale, Buttermere (Upper Cocker) and Great Langdale come near to giving an impression of radial drainage.

To question Wordsworth's claim of radial valleys, walk around the summit of Gable on a clear day, beginning at Westmorland cairn and view, in addition to Wasdale, the valleys of Ennerdale, Buttermere and Borrowdale spread out below; to describe their arrangement as radial calls for some imagination beyond what Wordsworth was asking for in his guide. The same can be said for other Lakeland valleys, using the area around High Raise as a possible hub. There is no obvious image of a dome ever existing; unlike the landscape when walking over the northern end of the Rhinog mountains in mid-Wales, here the Harlech Dome becomes very real. There seems to be strong evidence that valleys and the high shattered tops of Crinkle Crags, Scafells and Gable, as a result of caldera collapse described in the previous chapter, were there long before the first onslaught of ice. There is strong evidence that the overall pattern of valleys, main watersheds and high places in the Lake District were established by the end of the Tertiary period 1.8 million years ago. The successive visits of ice caps and glaciers did the final sculpting work to give Gable its rock architecture, combes or cirques, and its block-field summit of numerous small weather-shattered stones.

There seems to be a general consensus that deep V-shaped valleys, developed mainly by earth movement and water action, existed before any erosion by glaciers. For millions of years leading up to the Quaternary period, which began almost two million years ago, there would be drainage channels coursing down the slopes around Gable as deep, very narrow V-shaped water-worn clefts. There is strong evidence that successive glacier periods modified these clefts by widening and straightening them into the valleys we see today. The glaciers simply followed these courses and by grinding deeper into the bed, and taking away rocks from the sides, created the U-shaped, or more accurately parabola-shaped valleys. An ideal place to see the result of this ice-action is beside Westmorland Cairn near the summit of Gable, looking down into Wasdale where a classic U-shaped valley can be seen.

Ice ages

Earth has gone through repeated cycles of warming, a green-house state, and cooling, an ice-house state for an estimated 600 million years.[4] When thinking about the formation of Gable and its valleys we need consider only local glacial periods.

From the beginning of the last great ice age, Gable was held in a frozen grip for at least 12,000 years. This period has become known as the main Devensian Glaciation, when Britain was covered by ice almost to the Thames valley. There has been a tendency in reported research for the erosion-effects of the last glaciation to be exaggerated rather than seeing the shaping of Gable as part of a very long process lasting millions of years. The last great ice age simply completed the work to date, of sculpting Gable's very distinctive shape. The cycles of fluctuating climate patterns, over thousands of years, described in this section, helped shape the mountain.

England and Wales have been totally free of ice capping or glaciers for around 14,000 years, and Gable in particular for around 10,000 years. The term 'Little Ice Age' to describe the climate between 1550 and 1700, although bringing severe hardship to many people, is an exaggeration when conditions at the time are compared with past ice ages, and with what can be expected in the future. Deterioration in climate began around 14 million years ago as Britain moved northward past 50° of latitude with ice sheets forming in the Atlantic, and later from Greenland, 3 million years ago. From this time until the last ice age, there were cycles of warm to very cold periods and it is expected that Gable would, at some time, be beneath an ice cap or be surrounded by extensive glaciers. During the last million years there has been an estimated nine glacial periods. The first full ice age was around 750,000 years ago. From this time large ice sheets grew and declined several times; temperature not only dropped but precipitation increased. Each cycle of glacial followed by warmer and relatively shorter period of interglacial could last for around 20,000 years. A long cold period has been recorded between 75,000 and 30,000 years ago,[5] possibly causing restricted glaciation on the high ground around Gable.

The coldest periods within glacials are known as stadials, and the milder years between as interstadials. Longer warmer periods between glacials are known as interglacials, which we appear to be living through at the present time. Examples of these periods during the last great ice age in Cumbria are: a very cold Dimlington Stadial between 26,000 and 13,000 years ago, followed by a warmer shorter Windermere Interstadial, 13,000 to 11,000, then the colder Loch Lomond stadial until 10,000 years ago when the present warmer Flandrian Interglacial period began.

Professor Marr, almost 100 years ago, felt there had been only one major glacier period over the district but data from boreholes sunk to the west of Gable show a succession of glacial episodes.[6] These data about cycles of interglacial, glacial and again interglacial over the past 120,000 years were collected from boreholes made by the Nuclear Industry Radioactive Waste Executive (NIREX) to discover whether the area was suitable for nuclear waste depositories.[7] Many millions of pounds have been spent in searching the area for a suitable site, an estimated 20 million going to the British Geological Survey alone. From collected data, and information about huge fluctuations in climate we can imagine our mountain going through drastic periods of weathering where rocks are prized open before erosion takes place to move the debris away. When Gable has been covered, or mainly covered, by ice there is much less chance of serious weathering and erosion because the ice cover becomes protective; a solid state where ice is frozen to the bedrock. Most of the sculpting to shape Gable in its very distinctive way took place during periods of ice build-up and eventual melting. Most ice-erosion is caused by glaciers. When sharp rocks are frozen into the bed of a glacier, a gigantic file or rasp is created which can gouge out softer land beneath by around 1 mm per year.[8] Similarly, at the valley sides a glacier is said to pluck away rocks, though this idea of plucking has been questioned, the glacier may simply carry away loose rocks after they have been exposed for long periods to freeze-thaw action. Rock can only be taken away by a glacier if its tensile strength is less than that of the ice. With melt-water at the base of ice as a lubricant a glacier can act like a truck carrying away the debris, to become a vehicle of erosion.

There is a limit to erosion which can be caused by the action of ice; glaciers take away mainly loose rock rather than prizing away solid crags. Looking around Gable today we can see large areas of rock and boulders which will be carried away during the next ice age. Current landmarks which are not too solid such as the top block of Napes Needle and the left side of Kern Knotts Crack may also be carried away, or the whole of Napes Needle could fall and be carried away along with many other rock climbs. Walkers and climbers, especially members of the Fell and Rock Climbing Club, would prefer not to think of such a possibility. There is however no valid reason to believe that glaciers and ice caps will not return, so the wonderful Needle can be expected to disappear at some time.

Today, in the Alps, a prime example of weathering and erosion can be witnessed first-hand on the east face of the Matterhorn, where after mid-day a cannonade of rocks can be seen and heard shooting to the snow field below; like watching a mountain fall down. From what we know of past ice ages it would be possible to build a speculative, physical, model of what Gable will look like after the next ice age.

Gable as a nunatak
Looking from the summit of Gable at the beginning of the last great ice age, around 26,000 years ago, would be seen not only the steady arrival of snow and build-up of glaciers but the formation of an ice-cap. There has been a claim that the approach of ice began 33,000 years ago, but the severest part of the period was between 26,000 and 18,000 years ago, when the highest point of ice-forming was reached.

There is evidence from research on weathering lines that ice reached a height of 2,600 to 2,700 feet on Great Gable.[9] The mountain along with other Lakeland tops above this height could at this time be referred to as nunataks; points of rock appearing above the surface of land-ice. The highest point reached by the ice cap was on

Bowfell to the east of Gable, where it lay at 2,850 feet. The ice movement left behind striations on rock and where these are to be seen in valleys up to 1,750 feet they follow the direction of the valley; above this level they follow a south-west and west to north-westerly direction towards the coast. In 1873, an early geologist Clifton Ward searched the area extensively looking for striations on rock and evidence of glacier cover, but he could find none above 2,500 feet and said he was not prepared to accept that the higher tops had been covered by ice at this time.[10] Since then there have been various references to ice cover being up to 4,000-5,000 feet during the last great ice age but it appears that Ward was correct in his conclusions which he based purely upon direct observation. Weathering lines are fixed by comparing glacially-eroded rocks which lay beneath the ice with frost-weathered rocks which lay above. On this evidence nine summits, including Great Gable, were above the ice cap and as a result all have frost-shattered crags and summits; quite unlike the mountains nearby which lay completely below the ice cap. The lower tops, part of a group surrounding Gable: Kirk Fell, Green Gable, Brandreth and Base Brown are all similar in appearance but very different when compared with Gable. These summits were over-run by ice moving in a westerly direction and are relatively smooth and offer reasonable grazing for sheep. The summit of Gable is typical of a mountain top that has had close exposure to glaciers. Although not covered by ice there was permafrost, at 0°C or below, on the summit throughout this period. Any changes in air temperature affected only the surface, where the block-field of small stones now lies and a shattering of side-walls down to the weathering line.

If you are fortunate enough to be on the summit of Gable, very early in the day, when a sea of cloud stretches to the horizon and the sky above is clear, you could, depending upon the height of cloud cover, see eight summits in the near and far distance around you. This was the scene from Gable's summit every clear day for thousands of years. Gable and other nunataks were the only visible parts of the land above a sea of glistening white to blue ice. The scene at that time can be likened more to the ice fields and glaciers of Greenland at present, rather than what we see now in the Alps. The ice cap and glaciers were created and maintained entirely within the central Lake District. On Gable there are no erratics, boulders deposited from another area. All existing loose rock, boulders and scree have their source on or near the mountain. Some boulders and moraine materials have been carried away from the mountain by the ice and can be found miles beyond their original position. Some of these rocks can be seen at the north end of Bassenthwaite Lake, along with boulders from Scotland which have been carried south. The ice even carried rocks over the watershed on Whinlatter pass into the Vale of Lorton. Wordsworth looked at some of these boulders from time to time on his Lake District travels, some weighing many tons, and wrote in 1802:[11]

> 'As a huge stone is sometimes seen to lie
> Couched on the bald top of an eminence;
> Wonder to all who do the same espy,
> By what means it could thither come, and whence'
> So that it seems endued with sense:
> Like a sea beast crawled forth, that on a shelf
> Of rock or sand reposeth, there to sun itself.'

The ice flowing from central Lakeland, into the Solway Firth was diverted by ice from Scotland into the Irish Sea area; no ice or erratics from Scotland reached the central area of Lakeland.

Ice action from this time has left us with beautiful hanging valleys around Gable. A short distance beyond Stockley Bridge, on the Sty Head route, can be seen the waterfall at Taylorgill Force, as Sty Head Gill drops over a hanging valley on its way into Borrowdale. Above Seathwaite Farm the white tumbling waters of Sourmilk Gill come from the hanging valley of Gillercomb. Hanging valleys can also be caused by river systems but there are strong reasons to believe that those on Gable are mainly the result of ice-action.

There are significant hollows to the north and east of the mountain which have been deepened by glaciation. Hollows of this kind can have a range of names: cove or combe are common in Lakeland, cwm in Wales, corrie in Scotland and used elsewhere under Scots' influence except in the Alps, where the name is cirque. The various names will be used interchangeably here. The hollows come in many sizes, but there is an 'ideal' ratio between height of the back retaining wall and length of the hollow's bed for it to be a proper corrie or cwm. The ratio lies between 2.8 and 3.2 to 1 so these wonderful features of our mountains are remarkably consistent in overall shape. As on Gable, corries can be found on Helvellyn, Blencathra, Coniston Old Man, and most impressively Cwm Cau on Cader Idris in mid-Wales; all have tarns within their hollows. Where are the tarns to fill Gable's combes?

There is no sign on Gable of that most wonderful sight, a high-mountain stretch of water glinting in sunlight or moonlight. The finest hollow on Gable is Gillercomb, above Seathwaite, where a steep back wall, facing east, and lower down a glacier moraine should be bounding a tarn. All there is to be seen, or rather felt, is a wet boggy area. A less well developed hollow lies to the west, over the ridge from Gillercomb, below Gable's Ennerdale Crag. The place is named Stone Cove; cove being a suitable term because it is more like a large cavern carved out of surrounding rocks by glacier action. Here also, there is little evidence of a tarn having been there. There is too a little-noticed modest cirque to the north of Kirk Fell summit, best viewed from the top of Haystacks across the valley. No glacier formed on Kirk Fell during the Loch Lomond Stadial, the last local glaciation, and this cirque with the unromantic name of Baysoar Slack, is most likely a water-eroded feature but again no tarn. On the east side of Kirk Fell lies Beck Head Tarn, from where the west face of Gable rears up; in summer this tarn is little more than a pool. On the other side of Gable, Dry Tarn above Kern Knotts crags has been well named, it lies, usually dry, around 600 feet above Sty Head and near the walkers' route up Gable; to find it a grid reference is useful (215098). How can it be called a tarn? I suppose, in the same way that Innonimate Tarn on nearby Haystacks is called this because it has no name. Below is Sty Head Tarn where now its banks provide a very good wildish place to camp. This tarn can be rather sombre and bleak. Molly Lefebure described Sty Head as always melancholy.[12] Here there is an enclosed feeling without the advantage of rock architecture which is to be experienced in most Corries. A sense of 'place' seems missing in contrast with nearby Sprinkling Tarn to the east. In the natural making of landscape Great Gable has not been well served with tarns. The only consolation is that the largest combe in the district, Hobcarton below Grisedale Pike, also has no tarn.

What we see now during a climb up Gable, or especially a complete traverse around the mountain near the 2,000 foot contour, are the remains of these seemingly destructive forces. There are tall shattered columns of rock surrounded by boulders; huge to small, pile upon pile of rock above and below where you walk. The next great ice age will continue the work where the last one finished around 14000 years ago.

Loch Lomond stadial

The last act of ice-ages in Cumbria took place during what is known as the Loch Lomond Stadial or glaciers re-advance. The last time Gable was visited by glaciers was around 11,000 years ago, they finally melted approximately 700 years later. Pollen data taken from the coast west of Gable show that before this event there was a warm period of roughly 2,000 years.[13] This interstadial began 13,220 years ago when it was as warm or warmer than today. Various forms of vegetation returned, as the tundra landscape from the previous major ice age gave way to shrub. In the valleys around Gable appeared juniper, willows and crowberry and in the lower valleys, even birch trees.[14] Around 11000 years ago colder weather returned; an average drop in temperature of only 6-8°C and increased precipitation was enough for glaciers to form on high ground, this period has become known as the Loch Lomond Stadial.[15] Data from beetle faunas as well as pollen can show deterioration of climate at this time; beetles respond to changes in temperature more rapidly than vegetation, they migrate quickly and provide ideal indicators of temperature in the past. Around 12,000 years ago the species of beetle was one preferring a temperate climate but in a relatively short period of time the beetle, then present, was of a sub-arctic species.

The return to frozen conditions happened over a period of between 50 and 100 years, during a time that the rainfall average was over 70 inches (178 cm). On and around Gable, where the glaciers formed, the amount of annual rainfall would be well over 100 inches (254 cm), and the average summer temperature was close to 4ºC. Walking north from the highest point of Gable to the edge of the northern Ennerdale crag, you would see at this time a sizeable glacier stretching from below these northern cliffs to just short of where the Black Sail shepherds' hut now stands. The shallow hollow you see below Ennerdale crag was filled by an upper glacier, which would remain there for around 250 years. This glacier was quite unusual because from very steep upper reaches, immediately below Gable, it suddenly flattened out, which caused erratic movement of the glacier ice. Glaciers have been described as either feckless or able agents of erosion; they erode some parts of a bed and deposit piles of till, that is a mixture of gravel, clay, rocks, sand and silt, at other parts.[16] Evidence of this movement is there for all to see in the upper Ennerdale valley. Walkers on Wainwright's Coast to Coast route pass the Shepherds' hut, used by the Youth Hostel Association since Easter 1932 and, at the time of writing, one of the last true Youth Hostels open in the country, before entering an area of glacier-moraine mounds. These vegetation-covered piles of till below Gable lie at a place where the Ennerdale valley begins to flatten out and the most likely cause of this rather unusual formation is glacier surge. In the lower flatter part of a glaciated valley there is a sudden build-up of melt water below the glacier which reduces friction between ice and the ground. In this case it is felt that the very steep upper reaches make the glacier surge forward from time to time, which can throw up a series of mounds of the kind seen in upper Ennerdale. In thick mist I have had difficulty tracing a track between these curious obstacles on the way to Loft Beck. This type of moraine forming is not commonly found among mountains, so take a good look if passing between them. Moraines provide indisputable evidence of glaciers and ice action so they should be of interest to all who visit mountain areas. There are similar formations in a small glaciated valley off Glen Torridon in Scotland.

There was a glacier too in Gillercomb, where from its snout would be pouring melt water, now the waterfall Sourmilk Gill. These two main glaciers on Gable at close to 1 km square were among the largest in the district; where 64 glaciers existed in total at that time. A rather unusual smaller glacier formed at the end of Gable's north ridge below Grey Knotts around the 1,200 foot contour, near what is now Honister slate mine. The explanation for this glacier is that the place on the ridge quickly gathered wind-blown snow which compacted into ice.

On the eastern side of Gable, around and below Sty Head, was a snow field but no glacier; the head collection area for snow was not sufficiently high for glacier formation. What was thought to be a moraine ridge at the northern end of Sty Head Tarn was most likely formed from a delta of scree coming from Aaron Slack, which goes up to Gable's Windy Gap. The largest of the glaciers near Gable passed down Grains Gill from the cliffs of Great End. There are some splendid examples of glacier moraines in this gill which show the course and magnitude of the ice flow. Moraines from the Grains Gill glacier are to be seen in the same way when passing from Seatoller to Seathwaite in Borrowdale, and then to Stockley Bridge on the way to Gable or Scafell. Near Seatoller is Thorneythwaite Farm which stands upon an impressive ridge of moraine debris that protects the buildings from possible valley floods, one in 1942, and in 1966 the fast-flowing water caused serious damage to Stockley bridge further up the valley. Some of the dry stone walls around Thorneythwaite are particularly wide, which is assumed to be the result of needing to clear the ground of rocks, left by the last glacial event.

Glaciers can be thought of as destructive by the loosening and removal of previously-weathered rock, but the end result is normally beautiful in a grand, dramatic way. One exception to this statement can be seen today below Monte Rosa in Switzerland where post-glacier valleys are covered in a uniform slate-grey sea of mud and rock; an area to be admired only when covered in snow. The idea that glaciers existed on Gable was stated in the first serious study of the mountain in 1855 by Dr J Bryce in a report to the British Association.[17] After studying striated rocks in the valleys and movement of boulders, he deduced the previous existence of glaciers radiating out from Great Gable. There were three glaciers on the mountain during the Loch Lomond Stadial, but no ice capping at this time. The glaciers and intense cold brought tundra-like conditions causing newly-established vegetation to die. There was also a breaking up of rock through freeze-thaw action, especially on the summit and surrounding crags. Cracks in rock gather water which when frozen expands by 10%, gradually forcing the crack wider until a breaking occurs, or more dramatically a whole section of cliff falls away. There is no evidence that ice can cause this type of weathering without cracks already being present. The rock ridges and gullies of the Napes on Gable, overlooking the south side of Sty Head Pass, are particularly splintered and show steady weathering; the extensive screes of loose rock directly below show the amount of erosion. The rocks of the Napes facing south heat quickly in summer and rock being a poor conductor of heat means that only the surface temperature increases. At night, heat is lost quickly from the rock faces while there is no outflow of heat from within to compensate for the flow of heat from the surface. There is generally more splintering of rock faces and scree to be found on south facing crags. This action could be seen as destructive, but the result is to have wonderfully impressive rock architecture standing as natural works of art.

The block-field, a surface of broken rock, covering the whole top of Gable is largely caused by the climate during this period, known as periglacial because of the effects of being within the influence of nearby glaciers.

When the last glacier ice finally melted away, around 10,000 years ago, there was a long period with the mountain still frozen into a bleak tundra landscape, when only cold-tolerant vegetation of dwarf shrub would survive. The loss of glaciers was caused by a lack of precipitation and no further build-up of snow rather than a warming of the overall climate. Eventually, warmer days arrived and the valleys filled with shrub and trees up to a level of around 2,000 feet. The interglacial, or longer warm spell, had begun and is with us today.

Gable's vegetation

Without ice, Gable stood as bare frozen tundra for almost 3000 years before the first vegetation took root. The mountain shed the ice to exist, yet again, amidst a wild desolate land devoid of any vegetation and limited in colour to the surrounding rocks, grey to green and brown with occasional red from iron-bearing outcrops. A sombre scene, which to the lover of wilderness is beautiful, while to others a place to be avoided. Today, there are many places among the Alps of Switzerland, Austria and Italy where glaciers are receding rapidly leaving behind scenes which provide us with a perfect example of what the landscape around Gable would have been like at that time.

For the past 10,000 years only minor modifications have taken place on the mountain with weathering by wind, rain, frost action, and rather more drastically by earthquakes causing periodic falls of rock. During the past 10,000 years Gable has basked in the Holocene age of warm summers and, in the mountain's experience, winters that are not too cold and indeed getting warmer. Winifred Pennington's research among Lake District Mountains and collection of pollen records show juniper was one of the first to colonise the area. Eventually a forest of birch and pine grew in the valleys and spread upwards to reach just over 2,000 feet. By 6,000 years before the present there would be primary forest surrounding Gable before elm decline and clearance by Neolithic people reduced the number of trees and created secondary forest cover.[18] During this time, whether approached from Wasdale, Ennerdale, Buttermere or Borrowdale, any attempt to reach Gable would be like walking through secondary jungle. The tree cover would be thinner around the higher crags but still a feature like the Napes Needle would not be easy to find. Beyond the tree line, open ground leading to the summit would be reached and from there the scene would be not unlike standing above the tree line in many far-east countries at present. Bare rock tops over two or three thousand feet rearing above a green canopy, stretching as far as the eye can see. Over time there was a greater variety of tree cover with growth of alder, elm and oak. From what is known of climate patterns over the past two million years this scene would not be unknown to Gable, in fact the mountain had become quite used to being clothed in this way before being stripped again by a combination of ice, water in torrents and fierce winds.

When the last glacier ice melted away we can imagine the mountain settling down in peace for at least 20,000 years of leafy protection and much warmer weather, with only a few cold spells from time to time. From this period onwards Gable could look forward to a quiet, undisturbed life for many thousands of years. This was not to be because, within 5,000 years some strange two-legged animals arrived to make axes from nearby stone, and with these they cut down much of the tree cover. Not satisfied with this method of thinning forests, they began burning trees and other vegetation. All this activity, together with a natural decline of elm trees, almost stripped Gable bare, just as ice had done so many times earlier.

Gable cannot be described as a botanists' paradise. Compared with the Highlands of Scotland or Upper Teasdale in the Pennines, plant cover on and around Gable is very sparse.[19] Gable, like most of the Borrowdale Volcanic Group is not rich in lime, being non-calcareous. From Scafell to the coast, the mountains, tarns, waters and meres in the valleys all become progressively nutrient-poor. On Gable dwarf shrub and mainly acidic grass is largely confined to cliff faces and to block scree. Between 1,500 feet and the summit of Gable only three species of mountain plant can normally be found: Dwarf Willow (*Salix Herbacea*), a form of Hawksweed (*Hieracium Holosericeum*) and Thrift (*Armeria Maritima*). Where vegetation can grow beyond the range of sheep, as on the top of large boulders, heather and bilberry can thrive; this can be described as a 'natural experiment'.[20] Within Lakeland, only mountains to the east can compare with the Highlands or Teasdale. Helvellyn has around twenty six species above 1,500 feet. On Gable, only Honister crag can offer anything worthwhile for the botanist, where calcicole mountain plants can be found. Only Borrowdale, of Gable's valleys, is rewarding for the botanist where there is rich and varied vegetation. The valley also has the greatest extent of native woodland. Other valleys around Gable have been largely stripped bare but add to the wonderful variety of western Lakeland, as when passing from stark Wasdale to lush Borrowdale. Buttermere valley takes up a position somewhere in between. The current plight of Ennerdale is discussed in Chapter XII.

References

[1] Wordsworth, W. 1906. *Wordsworth's Guide to the Lakes*, 5th Edition. Oxford: Oxford University Press.

[2] Marr, J.E.1916. *The Geology of the Lake District and the Scenery as influenced by Geological Structure.* Cambridge: Cambridge University Press.

[3] Clark, R. 1988. *Pattern and order in the Lake District landscape.* Proceedings of the Cumberland Geological Society, vol. 5(1), pp.17-34.

[4] Sparks, B.W. and West, R.G. 1972. *The Ice Age in Britain.* London: Methuen.

[5] Boardman, J. 1991. *Quaternary Landscape Evolution in the Lake District – A Discussion.* Proceedings of the Cumberland Geological Society, vol. 5 (3) pp.285-315.

[6] Clark, R. and Smith, R.A. 1998. *The recent investigation into the Quaternary geology of west Cumbria.* Proceedings of the Cumberland Geological Society, vol. 6 (2) pp.203-225.

[7] Heathcote, J.A. and McL.Michie, U. 2004. *Estimating hydrological conditions over the last 120 ka: an example from the Sellafield area, UK.* Journal of the Geological Society, London. vol. 161, pp.999-1008.

[8] Embleton, C and King, C.A.M. 1975. *Glacial and Periglacial Geomorphology.* London: Edward Arnold.

[9] Lamb, A.L. and Ballantyne, C.K. 1998. *Palaeonunataks and the altitude of the last ice sheets in the south west Lake District, England.* Proceedings of the Geologists' Association. vol. 109, pp.305-316.

[10] Ward, C. 1873. *The glaciation of the northern part of the Lake District.* Geological Magazine. v.108, pp.324-325.

[11] Wordsworth, W. 1888. *Independence and Resolution IX. Complete Poetical Works.* London: Macmillan.

[12] Lefebure, M. 1964. *The English Lake District.* London: Batsford Ltd.

[13] Walker, M.J.C. 2004. *A late-glacial pollen record from Hallsenner Moor, near Seascale, Cumbria, north west England with evidence for arid conditions during the Loch Lomond (Younger Dryas) Stadial and early Holocene.* Proceedings of the Yorkshire Geological Society, vol.55 (1), pp.33-42.

[14] Pennington, W. 1977. *The late-glacial flora and vegetation of Britain.* Royal Society B280, pp.247-271.

[15] Sissons, J.B. 1980. *The Loch Lomond Advance in the Lake District of Northern England.* Transactions of the Royal Society of Edinburgh, Earth Sciences, 71, pp.13-27.

[16] White, W.A. 1972. *Deposition by continental ice sheets.* Bulletin of the Geological Society of America, vol. 83, pp.1037-1056.

[17] Bryce, J. 1855. *Report to the British association,* p.80.

[18] Pennington, W. 1970. *Vegetation History in the North West of England: Regional Synthesis. In, Studies in the Vegetational History of the British Isles.* Walker, D. and West, R.G. (Eds) Cambridge: Cambridge University Press.

[19] Ratcliffe, D.A. 1960. *The mountain flora of Lakeland.* Proceedings of the Botanical Society of the British Isles. vol.4, pp.1-25.

[20] Halliday, G. 1997. *A Flora of Cumbria.* Lancaster: Centre for North-West Regional Studies.

IV. Early Life and First Settlers

First life
While Gable had millions of years without human interference life still existed on its slopes as shown by discoveries reported in the mid-1990s.[1] Evidence comes from rocks on the eastern edge of Gillercomb, where there can be seen some of the earliest traces of life to be found on land anywhere in the world. The discovery of these footprint traces is particularly strange because there are no fossils on or near Gable.

One route up Gable is to pass through an archway at Seathwaite Farm and climb steeply by the frothing waterfall of Sourmilk Gill or up the water-covered rocks if you prefer; some people, masochists possibly, think a waterfall is best viewed from the inside. When near the top, on rock, almost at the eastern edge of the combe, prints left by arthropods are to be seen close to the gill. These prints near the top of the waterfall are around 30 million years older than similar prints previously discovered in Australia. The print markings are of a kind left by a millipede-like creature and the earliest record of millipedes and centipedes is around 438 million years ago at the beginning of the Silurian period. When these animals first crept over the rocks there would be no other living creatures and no plants for food; these animals lived before the arrival of terrestrial plants. Cuticle and tube plants did not appear until almost 20 million years later, it can only be imagined that they lived on green algae.[2] Arthropods crawled across rocks where earlier there had been very violent hydro-volcanic eruptions and where surface water reacted with hot magma. Yet still these creatures were tempted somehow into this bare, forbidding landscape. Life in this form can survive and flourish in hostile surroundings today, which could be witnessed by various species of spider living on Mount St Helens just two months after the eruptions in 1980, and before plant life could be re-established. Arthropods today, like their ancestors on Gable, can colonise areas where plant life does not exist, and they may be among the last as well as the first to walk the land.

Earliest human settlers around Gable
We have no means of knowing when Great Gable first came into contact with human beings. People could have lived in Gable's upper valleys and even roamed around its sides, 200,000 years ago or even earlier. One of the earliest finds of fossil human material in England

has been found at Swanscombe, estimated at 400,000 years old.[3] Flint tools found in Suffolk have been dated to 700,000 years ago. In other parts of the world, particularly in Turkey and East Africa, where human remains or artefacts have been found dating back millennia, the evidence simply means that conditions for preservation have been more favourable than elsewhere; not necessarily that the earliest humans originated from that place. In Cumbria the last ice age and earlier ice ages, described in the previous chapter, removed all evidence of any human life previously. The ending of the last Ice Age overlapped what we know of human pre-history in Lakeland. Movement by early Palaeolithic people from the southern lowlands while hunting could have taken them up the west coast to Cumbria and into the valleys of Wasdale and Ennerdale, but no evidence remains. In southern Britain, especially south of the Thames, it is possible to follow linking events from earliest human occupation, but not around Gable; there are major missing links. Although absence of evidence is not evidence of absence, we may only speculate that people from periods before the last ice age moved sufficiently north to reach wild uninhabited valleys surrounding the mountain. Despite advances in pre-historic research methods, our attempts to explain pre-historic human life in Cumbria is largely one of imagination.

For Gable's contact with humans we can go back little more than 6,000 years to early late-Mesolithic or early-Neolithic, otherwise known as New Stone Age. To suggest an earlier time around 8,000 years ago is to imagine people from the Mesolithic or Middle Stone Age venturing inland from the coast into the upper valleys, which is a possibility but unlike the early Neolithic settlers there is no evidence of contact with Gable at this time. The date of a chert found on the slopes of Gable has been put at Upper Palaeolthic or early Mesolithic age, but could be later; this one piece of evidence that people of this time were on the mountain is not strong.

Where did the first people who did roam around Gable come from? Evidence from artefacts found at prehistoric settlements near the mountain points to influences from Eastern Europe. People crossed overland around 9,000 years ago and settled in East Yorkshire. Britain was not an island but part of a continental land-mass, including large areas of what is now the North Sea, and English Channel; access could be on foot from many points south and east. An outstanding early settlement to be discovered is at Star Carr near Scarborough. Here a group of around thirty settled near a lake. Eventually the need to hunt took these people further west, especially during summer months, into the Pennines where nearly 1,000 sites have been located. A route through the Stainmore Gap would have tempted them to continue their westward trek until a way was found through southern Lakeland, well south of the mountains. The flat plains, to the west of high ground, were fertile, with rivers for fishing and the nearby mountain-valleys for hunting. Flint tools from East Yorkshire have been found on the coast at St Bees and Eskmeals. In time they developed cereal growing and began the process of becoming the first farmers. Other settlers arrived from the west across what was then a land bridge with the Isle of Man and possibly Ireland; one of the oldest prehistoric settlements has been discovered at Ballynagilly in Northern Ireland which has been radio-carbon dated to approximately 6,500 years ago.

Humans arrived when there were plants to eat and animals to hunt, becoming the first to colonise, or re-colonise, what had been a very bleak inhospitable landscape for thousands of years. These overland migrations took place from the time that vegetation re-appeared, until the land-bridges disappeared under water around 8,000 years ago, for it was then that Britain became an island. The first settlers in Cumbria at this time found that the only sensible place to live was on the coast, or in lower valleys well to the west or south of the mountains. Gable's upper valleys of Wasdale, Ennerdale, Buttermere and Borrowdale would be desolate and entered, if at all, only for hunting. There is no evidence of human habitation immediately around Gable either to the north, east, south or west during the Mesolithic or Middle Stone Age period. To the north of the mountain people were very slow to develop upper Borrowdale as a place to live. The discovery of Neolithic axe working on the north side of Glaramara above the Borrowdale valley, and of axe heads in Langstrath leading into Borrowdale suggests strongly that the valley was visited regularly around 5,000 years ago, even if there were no established settlements. The valley, which tourists know so well, would be very different from today. Borrowdale, in its upper part, was one of the last of Gable's valleys to be cleared of thick forest and was covered in boulders of various sizes left by receding ice. Only the arrival of Norse settlers in the tenth century made this part of the valley habitable. They made clearings; their word for this is 'thwaite' and along the valley we have Rosthwaite, Stonethwaite, Thorneythwaite and Seathwaite. The Norse arrived in upper Borrowdale to find a place very close to the true meaning of wilderness. The lower reaches of the valley near Keswick do show signs of habitation long before the Norse settlements; one indication of this is the name 'Derwent' for both the river and water, which comes from Celtic meaning of 'abounding in oaks' and there were a number of farms in the lower Derwent valley long before any influence from Scandinavia.

The only evidence that Palaeolithic people lived within a days walking distance of Gable comes from Upper-Palaeolithic flint tools found at Kirkhead cave near Cartmell to the south and in settlements to the west of the mountain at Drigg and Eskmeals, but no trace exists of these people making settlements within Central Lakeland.

Then, as now, a special kind of individual was needed to subsist successfully in the upper valleys among the boulders and poor pasture. Many more years were to pass during the prehistoric age before this type of individual belonging to what we call the New Stone Age, or Neolithic, arrived to make a home below the mountain. Immediately south and west of Gable and Kirk Fell exists one of the greatest concentrations of pre-historic settlements in the country; there are stone circles, around fourteen burial cairns, mounds and building of early stone walls. West of Gable too, near the coast, there are signs of human occupation at this time, belonging to earlier Mesolithic people. The area of greatest concentration is bounded on the north by the River Liza, which runs from beneath Gable through Ennerdale, and to the south by the River Irt and Wasdale, and to the west by the coastal plains. Here among the lower foothills of Gable runs a track-way of unknown age but almost certainly used while these settlements were occupied and well before the Romans followed the route around 3,000 years later. From the banks of the Irt the way rises to Hollow Moor, over Sergeant Ford and along below Stockdale Moor where many prehistoric sites are to be found.

There are five stone circles near Burnmoor Tarn where you can look across Wasdale Head, each one found to contain remains of human cremation. Indications are that this settlement was developed later than those around Stockdale Moor. Results from pollen analysis at Burnmoor Tarn show that forest clearance took place around 4,000 years ago. The site was occupied for around 1,000 years into the Bronze Age, when the warm climate changed to colder damp conditions driving even these hardy people into the valleys.

The concentration of people on the coastal plains and in the lower foot-hills was understandable because routes from one place to another were very difficult to find. Going from surrounding valleys into central Lakeland is now a pleasant Sunday walk; but for these people any journey of this kind would be a major expedition through dense tangled forests, seemingly impassable mountains where hunting became more and more difficult with every step. That they did make huge efforts to settle inland should make us think again about the nature of these people.

The Ennerdale valley offered the only reasonable passage from west to east, using the line of a geological fault from that valley through to Langdale, but there were no effective means of forest clearance either by axe or controlled fire at this time. This fault line would be used many years later in an east to west direction as a regular route for carrying stone axes to the coast. An alternative line of travel would be through the Eskdale valley, over what is now Hardknott and Wrynose passes, but before any track-way could be established the journey would have been a major undertaking. When the more adventurous early settlers decided to live further inland they chose high ground rather than in the over-grown and boggy upper valleys, if only temporarily. The tree cover was light or none-existent and the land drained well. In most cases they chose sites with splendid views. Gable is surrounded by early settlements and stone circles where surrounding mountains can be seen clearly from many of them; the views can make you want to spend a long time there. The main reasons for Neolithics choosing sites on high ground appear to be clearly functional, but questions can be asked about more subjective attitudes towards these dwellings. Frances Lynch has written about a premise that, 'early man had a very real and sensitive appreciation of the landscape around him, that his relationship to his environment was not simply one of economic exploitation and struggle but was also one in which the beauty and grandeur of the rocks and mountains and the broad views over valleys and plains had an importance in their own right'.[4] Lynch was writing primarily about prehistoric sites in Wales but the premise is equally applicable to other highland areas of Britain. Most sites around Gable have wonderful views. One explanation offered is that these dwellings provided excellent look-outs, but experienced walkers know that despite being high and exposed, a sheltered place can normally be found which would be ideal for any longer-term dwellings, while at the same time being near more exposed positions for a look-out point when needed. The idea of mountain-appreciation in prehistoric times, however subjective, helps reinforce a feeling, developed in the next chapter, that as humans we have changed very little over the intervening years. As now, there appears to have been people who appreciated high places and others who preferred the flat-lands.

Their dwellings were of timber wattle-build with thatched roofs and normally an earth floor. This type of dwelling does not survive well and only available evidence is the remains of a timber structure and hearths at Drigg.[5] The stone circles we see at many prehistoric sites have raised numerous theories about their origin and purpose; it has been said that one early antiquarian was driven close to insanity in trying to find a realistic explanation for their existence. One explanation seems sensible and that is they were simply part of dwellings in which the wooden structures have rotted away. There is evidence that some people lived in a fortress-like way surrounded by earth mounds, mainly to keep away wolves which roamed freely and existed in Lakeland until the sixteenth century. There are sites which still show mounds of this kind and which could be of Mesolithic age.

Evidence from archaeological finds suggests that early settlers lived well from nuts, berries, plants, river and sea fish, ample shell fish and wild animals to hunt; the good life.

Major changes were made by early Neolithic people, living to the west of Gable around 5,000 years ago when land was used for the earliest forms of farming, and large areas of trees felled with axes or burned to make more land available to keep domestic animals. Pollen analysis suggests that early farming near the coast took place nearly 1,000 years before later Neolithic people began farming in valleys immediately to the north of Gable. Suddenly communities became more settled and spent their time growing vegetables and looking after animals. At each stage of human development we can ask the question, 'why change an ideal way of life for one of questionable benefit?' Interesting questions have been asked by David Lambert, writer on Prehistoric Man.[6] 'Why did New Stone Age people take up sedentary food production. Many hunter-gatherers already had enough to eat and leisure time in plenty?' Also, 'early farmers worked longer hours for a less varied diet at the risk of famine if the crops should fail'. The weather too made their hunting and gathering an even more enjoyable life, the passing years grew steadily warmer and they enjoyed an almost tropical climate throughout Neolithic time. One possible answer to Lambert's questions, in central and western Lakeland at least, is that arable farming would free the strong fit hunters to spend more time in stone axe making. The change from roaming for food to a more settled life of farming is very difficult to reverse and it can be imagined that many hunters had regrets.

Skilled axe makers

To be sure of identifying the people who first made physical contact with Gable we need to look among the skilled stone-axe makers who came to the area from the east and west. The first attempts to knap stone and flint into the shape of an axe ought to be recognised as one of the most important events in human history, if not the most important; it has been suggested that the Stone Age should be known as the 'Axe Age'. The making of axes was the very first industry in Britain and was the first demonstration of a highly-skilled act by humans. It is a sobering thought that stone-axe making was carried out in the mountains of Cumbria for at least 2,000 years, or as long as what we call our 'history'.

For almost ninety years it has been known that people of the New Stone Age moved around and on Gable 5,000 years ago. When R.G. Collingwood wrote about the pre-history of Cumberland,[7] he knew nothing of the extensive axe-working activity in the central mountains during Neolithic time. There was a general belief up to the 1920s, when Collingwood was writing, that the high central area of Lakeland was a largely deserted wilderness during pre-history. Despite finding numerous axe heads in Cumberland and Westmorland no link was made with the source of stone being in central Lakeland. Up to 1921 the only known stone-axe making site in Britain was at Craig Lwyd in North Wales.[8] Then in that year Professor D.M.S. Watson, reported the discovery of a working site on Mart Crag Moor near the Stake Pass between Borrowdale and Langdale.[9] This find was the first sign that prehistoric people had lived and worked among the mountains of Lakeland; this site was at 1,760 feet. Little more was heard of this discovery until 1949 when there were reports, from archaeologists Clare Fell and Brian Bunch, of significant stone-axe discoveries on Pike of Stickle not far from Professor Watson's first find.[10] Further major discoveries have followed over the years and many journal papers published, leading to the sites becoming protected areas.

In the 1950s while rock climbing on crags, alongside these sites above the Langdale valley, we must have clambered across chippings and axe heads without noticing them; our only interest was in the rock climb(s) of that day. We did hear talk of Stone Age people making axes high up among the screes near one of our climbing grounds, Gimmer Crag. These discussions normally took place over a pint or two in the climbers' bar of the Old Dungeon Ghyll Hotel, or when bedding down in the barn at Wall End Farm. Since these discoveries in Langdale it is interesting that evidence of axe-workings, or axes which have been dropped while carrying, have been found on our present-day paths around Gable, on Scafell and on routes from Great Langdale. Despite the tree cover our ancestors chose lines of least resistance when roaming the valleys and the high tops, as we do today. Climbers and walkers, in the steps of our ancestors, have passed over these artefacts since mid-Victorian times, without being aware of their significance.

The working sites became known as stone-axe factories because there was an identifiable production process in place. Some workers selected suitable stone from the scree or prized away fresh stone from the cliffs; the fresh stone worked better than weathered stone, which led to the need for some quarrying. Stone-axe workers would begin the task of roughing out axe heads, shown by larger chippings left on the ground. The stone was then passed to more skilled colleagues for final roughing-out, leaving behind on the ground finer chippings as they worked closer to the actual shape. These final rough-outs were ready to be ground and polished. The finishing work took place at various valley-sites around the Lake District, no polished axes have been found at the factory sites of Langdale or Scafell Pike. A main place for the finishing work was at Ehenside Tarn, to the west of Ennerdale. Axe rough-outs were carried from Langdale and Scafell Pike to Ehenside by going past Sty Head and over Windy Gap on Gable. Other possible finishing-sites near the coast were at Kell Bank near Gosforth and Stone Close at Stainton-in-Furness.

Axes from Great Langdale, Scafell and Glaramara are classified as Group VI, to distinguish them from axes made from other types of rock. Group VI axes made at these sites have been found throughout the British Isles. Axes are classified by the type of rock rather than by where they were found because one type of rock can come from more than one local site. Axes from Craig Lwyd, mentioned earlier, belong to Group VII. Recently, there have been finds of axe working on the summit of Fairfield, near Helvellyn, but no axe heads. This site appears to be another 'test' working of Group XI fine-grained rhyolitic tuff rock lying at around 2,800 feet close to a well-worn path. This find adds strength to the idea that at least some of the workers at the Langdale axe factory came by a high-level route from the east and the find on Fairfield may have been only one of their trial workings as they travelled further westward; eventually, reaching the 'gold mine' of ideal rock in Langdale.

Stone axe heads have been found within some Cumbrian stone circles suggesting that the circles were used as 'trading' posts for axes, or had ritual significance. On the other hand these circles could have been a place where trade and ritual went hand in hand. Or, as suggested earlier they are all that remains of human settlements. An important discovery for our understanding of this period is that stone-axe working took place in the Langdale valley before the building of stone circles in the Lake District. Earliest evidence of axe making in Lakeland is around 6,000 years ago while the beginning of circle building is estimated to be just over 5,000 years ago. The age of Castlerigg stone circle near Keswick, one of the earliest circles in Cumbria, is put at 5,200 years. That most of the major circles are on or near axe-carrying routes suggests some link between the movement of these implements and the beginning of stone-circle building. This link has been well illustrated by R.G. 'Dick' Plint, who first found axe-worked flakes on Gable, by mapping the circles to trade routes.[11] The route west from Langdale and Scafell Pike axe factories, includes the circle of Grey Croft, where during excavation in 1949 part of a polished axe of Langdale stone was found. A 'trade' route north-west from Langdale passes close to the circles of Castlerigg and Elva Plain. The axe route north includes the henges at Penrith and the circle of Long Meg. Going east the carriers would pass the circle at Gunnerkeld. One route south passed the circle at Swinside. In other words, all ways for the movement of stone axes include at least one stone circle and account for all the major stone circles in the Lake District. The one anomaly is the transport of axes down Windermere where the route includes no stone circles when they would be expected either near the north shore or south of the mere.

The concept of 'trade' is commonly used when discussing the movement of axes but this term can be problematic when speculating about the activity of prehistoric people living in the Lake District. At this time Neolithic people had all they could possibly want: ample food from fishing: molluscs, salmon, perch and pike. Hunting included wild horse, red deer, giant Irish deer, northern lynx, brown bear and aurock. Barley growing too was well established. They had a ready means of making shelter from an abundant range of hardwood; water, soil and air were all clean; nothing had been defiled by industry. We may need to look beyond trade to find an explanation for carrying heavy loads of stone great distances.

The main function of stone axes was for the clearance of trees, where, as explained earlier, they grew up to a height of almost 2,000 feet. Archaeologists have carried out experiments in knapping and polishing stone axes, as well as in felling different types of trees.[12] An experiment in Czechoslovakia was reported in 1970; a tree 6 inches (15cm) diameter was felled with a polished stone axe in seven minutes, and near Leningrad, a stone axe from a Neolithic site was used to fell a pine 10 inches (25cm) diameter in twenty minutes.

Some Langdale axes show signs of use in felling trees, but others are highly polished and flawless, suggesting that they could have been ornamental. The standard polishing of an axe can be done in around four hours, but some axes of particular sheen and beauty take many more hours, which strongly suggest some symbolic significance. Evidence for some kind of symbolic use of axe heads is provided by the finding of axes made from chalk at Stonehenge and Woodhenge.[13] There are beautiful jadeite axe heads, found buried in chambered tombs in Brittany, also axe miniatures with perforations suggesting that they were worn as pendants.[14] Fragments of a jade axe from the continent have also been found at a Neolithic settlement near Sidmouth in Devon, carbon-dated as 4,860 years ago. Another jade axe has been found further north in Kirkby Lonsdale.[15] Polished axes were taken north from Lakeland to be found centuries later in Scotland, south around the Thames valley and by sea to the Isle of Man; even into East Anglia where abundant axe heads were being made from flint; an early example of coals to Newcastle. W.A. Cummins reported in 1980,[16] that a distribution Centre for stone axes existed in Humberside; 60% of axes found there came from Langdale. The output from stone axe factories in Cumberland vastly exceeded local demand. There is no evidence of flint axes going in the reverse direction. Flint does not exist naturally in central Lake District, but there was a supply along the shoreline, washed up from a vein under the Irish Sea. Although of inferior quality to flints of East Anglia it appeared to serve their purpose quite well. It is difficult to imagine what could have been worth carrying back to their Lakeland valleys. There may have been items worth carrying, which could not easily be made at their own sites.

Carrying stone axes as gifts rather than trade may be a more appropriate explanation when thinking of people living in non-mercenary times.

Evidence comes from North America of people making gifts as a means of gaining prestige or as display of their skills around 5,500 years ago, roughly at the beginning of axe-making in Great Langdale,

Scafell and at Ehenside Tarn. Anthropologists have given the name of 'potlatch' to this practice. Archaeologists do not appear to take potlatch into account when discussing stone-age trade; there is a saying, adapted from a saying of Oscar Wilde, that archaeologists and anthropologists are separated by a common interest. From research by anthropologists, it appears that feasting was associated with the arrival of such gifts and we may imagine our workers from Cumbria being warmly welcomed, and having a good time before either returning to the working site or settling down permanently with new-found friends. We will never know whether the Central Lakeland dwellers carried their axes many miles north, east and south or whether they passed them to others they met at staging posts. The idea of potlatch suggests that they would wish to display the results of their skill personally and do so far and wide. Intuitively, the idea of potlatch is a credible explanation for the carrying of heavy axes great distances, long before the concept of 'trade' was understood.

One of the most remarkable finds on the Langdale Pikes was made in 1988, when what can best be described as a hoard of five perfectly good rough-outs of axe heads were uncovered close to the summit of Pike of Stickle at around 2,100 feet. The axes lay there for around 4,000 years instead of being carried to a valley-site for final polishing.[17]

Axe workers overlooking Gable
One of the most amazing axe-working discoveries took place on Scafell Pike in September 1954 when a walker picked up flakes to the east of the Mickledore track. The rock samples were confirmed by the British Museum as man-worked and, like samples on the Great Langdale sites, were of the Group VI category. There have been numerous discoveries on both sides of Scafell Pike since this earlier find. An axe head had been found in April 1931, close to the main track in a hollow between Broad Crag and the summit of the Pike.[18] After this find, Lake District historian W.G Collingwood did suggest that there could be workings among the mountains, but nobody appears to have made a direct link with axe working on the Scafell range at that time and there appeared to be no follow-up to discover whether more samples could be found there. This is not surprising because the idea of prehistoric people, around 5,000 years ago, doing factory-type work close to a summit on England's highest mountain is difficult to accept.

From parts of this site, workers sitting cross-legged chipping away at chosen pieces of stone could look westwards across the valley at Gable, and eastward to the Langdale Pikes where they most likely learned their skills. Among the later finds in the area was a chipping site on Great End. The rock, Esk Pike Hornstone, is similar to the fine-grained Seathwaite Tuff used in axe making but when knapped breaks with an angular fracture rather than the 'ideal' conchoidal shell-like form; it appears that this site was quickly abandoned. The chippings found on Gable between Tophet Bastion and Napes Needle also appear to have been trial workings. In both cases the signs are that the rock was not suitable. The first finds on Gable reported in 1962[19] were checked during a field survey reported in 1989 and confirmed signs of axe-working activity. The main problem on that part of Gable is disturbance of the rock cover by thousands of boots over the past 100 years. Scree-running by climbers and walkers has made the finding of evidence very difficult; it may well be buried near the foot of the scree slopes. The shattered nature of the area, and major rock falls around the Napes also makes it difficult to find further evidence of axe working.

The finds reported in 1962 were by the Treasurer of the Fell and Rock Club, R. G. Plint, who collected thirty two flakes of black fine-grained tuff on Gable. Of this sample the survey report of 1989 found that nine had been possibly worked on site but there was insufficient evidence of an axe-working factory.[20] The area was not included in the surveys' controlled field walking and they felt such a search in the future would be worthwhile. The survey was undertaken in 1984 and 1985; the team of researchers located 566 distinct axe-working sites on the Langdale Pikes, Scafell Pike, Glaramara and on high land between these tops. The sites were placed into thirty five working groups. This was production on a massive scale and throws a different light on people who were industrially active and skilled long before the Romans arrived.

Some of the rock flakes on Gable, found below the Napes ridges, are likely to be from axe working but are of silicified tuff, classified as Group XI and as on Great End would not satisfy the quality standards set by workers at the time. Our Neolithic ancestors first found the ideal rock around the Langdale Pikes, then extended their search further to the north and westward; the Scafell Pike area, though not as large in production of axes as the on the Langdale Pikes, did become a factory-type site and axe-workers had further success when the rock of Glaramara was discovered. Flakes from axe working have also been found in upper Eskdale near Yeastyrigg crag.

Geologists can now explain what makes the epidonised tuff so suitable for axes. Prehistoric axe makers did not have this knowledge but they knew what they were looking for because they expended great effort in quarrying into rock faces, often on dangerous ledges above Langdale and dug into the huge block field on the Scafell Pikes to reach un-weathered rock below. They may have made a link between what they knew of suitable rock and the lighter band of Seatwaite Fell Tuff; a rock to be seen running across Pavey Ark roughly level with Jack's Rake to the Langdale Pikes and beyond to Scafell and around to Glaramara.

First fell walkers

These prehistoric people were effectively the first fell-walkers as they wandered widely across Lakeland's central mountains trying various outcrops of rock in search of the ideal material. This exploring would take place in summer months when at this time the climate was on average warmer than today and it can be imagined that they slept on or near the tops, finding shelter among the crags. At each place where they thought suitable rock could be found, the group of workers would sit chipping away at different specimens until deciding that they needed to move on to try another place. Reading the many reports on these finds leads to numerous questions: Why would they walk miles over difficult country? There was more than enough rock to be worked above Langdale. Possibly they were looking for sites within shorter carrying distances of coastal settlements to the west, and perhaps this is the reason why they chipped at rock further west as on the Corridor Route below Spout Head and on the screes of Gable. One explanation given for them working on dangerous exposed ledges, suitable only for sure-footed rock climbers, has been territorial; would the choice of a dangerous site confine access to only a few select people? Could the high-level wandering far and wide looking for new sites have been in the form of staking a claim? Like oil supplies today there may have been a worry that suitable rock would suddenly be used up, and then where would they be?

These and other questions should be asked if we are to begin understanding the lives of early settlers. W.G. Collingwood said that re-enactment is not re-living events but re-thinking the thoughts of the actors at the time. Today, we can see what our axe-making ancestors did from evidence at the sites, but to know something of their thinking we need to pose questions of this kind.

We can imagine when thinking of skilled working in pre-history that, as now, there would be a reluctance to lose one skill in favour of another. At some point they closed down the stone axe workings with loss of the knapping and stone finishing skills, to be replaced by the new bronze metal working. The skills being used in Langdale had been developed over many generations. Tests by argon-argon dating show that stone-tool making began in Africa by what we know as Old Stone Age or Palaeolithic time. Around 40,000 years ago the skills and techniques of axe-making would be fully developed.

There is evidence that stone axe production continued after the introduction of bronze; no doubt there were claims that stone made very much better axes than use of metal. Especially in Cumbria, the use of metal was slow in being adopted when compared with other areas of Britain.

However, the emergence of the Bronze Age coincided with a severe deterioration in weather around 3,000 years ago. There were higher rainfalls and lower mean annual temperature, which would make stone knapping at around 2,000 feet extremely difficult. The metal working could be done in more sheltered valley locations, so we can imagine that a change from stone working would be made without too many protests. Almost all bronze-age sites in Cumbria are on the north, east and south edges of the Lake District; apart from a bronze armlet find near Aspatria and a flanged axe and spear head in Eskdale there is no real evidence of settlements on the west of the district and none in the central area.[21] Gable was no longer visited by men struggling over Windy Gap with stone axe heads and appears to have been almost totally deserted for the next 900 years.

This chapter has served as a rather lengthy background to my own speculation about who could have been the first person to climb Great Gable, which is discussed in the next chapter.

References

[1] Johnson, E.W. et al. 1996. *Lake District Pioneers: the earliest footprints on land.* Geology Today, vol12 (4) pp.147-151.

[2] Gray, J. and Shear, W. 1992. *Early Life on Land. American Scientist,* vol. 80, pp.444-456.

[3] Stringer, C.B. 2001. *Dating the Origin of Modern Humans.* In: Lewis, C.L.E. and Knell, S.J. (eds). *The Age of the Earth from 4004 BC to AD 2002.* London: Geological Society Special Publication, 190, pp.265-274.

[4] Lynch, F. 1975. *The Impact of Landscape on Prehistoric Man.* In, Evans, J.G. et al. (eds). *Effects of Man on the Landscape: The Highland Zone.* London: Council for British Archaeology, Research Report 11.

[5] Cherry, J. 1982. *Flint Chipping Sites at Drigg.* Transactions of the Cumberland and Westmorland Antiquarian and Archaeological Society, vol. 82, pp.1-6.

[6] Lambert, D. 1987. *Cambridge Guide to Prehistoric Man.* Cambridge: Cambridge University Press.

[7] Collingwood, R.G. 1933. *An Introduction to the Prehistory of Cumberland, Westmorland and Lancashire North of the Sands.* Transactions of the Cumberland and Westmorland Antiquarian and Archaeological Society, vol. 33, pp.163-200.

[8] Warren, S.H. 1919. *A Stone Axe Factory at Craig Lwyd Penmaenmawr.* Journal of the Royal Archaeology Institute, vol. 44, pp.324-365.

[9] Warren, S.H. 1921. *Excavation of the Stone Axe Factory of Craig Lwyd Penmaenmawr.* Proceedings of the Royal Anthropological Institute of Great Britain and Ireland, vol. 51, pp.165-199.

[10] Bunch, B and Fell, C.I. 1949. *A Stone-axe Factory at Pike of Stickle, Great Langdale, Westmorland.* Proceedings of the Prehistoric Society, vol. 15, pp.1-20.

[11] Waterhouse, J. 1985. *The Stone Circles of Cumbria.* p.28. Chichester: Phillimore.

[12] Coles, J. 1973. *Archaeology by Experiment.* London: Hutchinson.

[13] Cunnington, M. 1929. *Woodhenge.* Devises: George Simpson.

[14] Burl, A. 1973. *Dating the British Stone Circles.* American Scientist, vol. 61, pp.167-174.

[15] *Transactions of the Cumberland and Westmorland Antiquarian and Archaeological Society,* vol. 79, p.143.

[16] Cummins, W.A. 1980. *Stone Axes as a Guide to Neolithic Communication and Boundaries in England and Wales.* Proceedings of the Prehistoric Society, vol. 46, pp.45-60.

[17] Boyd, M.J. 1990. *A Hoard of Unpolished Stone Axes from Pike of Stickle.* Transactions of the Cumberland and Westmorland Antiquarian and Archaeological Society, vol. 90, pp.99-103.

[18] *Cumberland and Westmorland Antiquarian and Archaeological Society General Meeting, June 1932.* Transactions of the Cumberland and Westmorland Antiquarian and Archaeological Society, vol. 33, p.287.

[19] Plint, R.G. 1962. *Stone Axe Factory Sites in the Cumbrian Fells.* Transactions of the Cumberland and Westmorland Antiquarian and Archaeological Society, vol. 62, pp.1-26.

[20] Claris, P. and Quartermaine, J. 1989. *The Neolithic Quarries and Axe Factory Sites of Great Langdale and Scafell Pike: A New Field Survey.* Proceedings of the Prehistoric Society, vol. 55, pp.1-55.

[21] McK Clough, T.H. 1969. *Bronze Age metalwork from Cumbria.* Transactions of the Cumberland and Westmorland Antiquarian and Archaeological Society, vol. 69, pp.1-39.

V. Possible First Ascent

First person to climb Gable?
The only sounds around Gable to disturb the quiet of the mountain would be from wind, animals and rushing water in the becks. No human voices, shouts or mechanical sounds of any kind. This was the mountain's life for millions of years.

We will never know who made the first ascent of Great Gable; who disturbed the natural sounds and the silence, or when the climb took place. There appears to be a general feeling that mountain tops in Britain have no history, unlike those in the Alps, where details of first ascents are recorded even of lesser tops, but someone did stand on the summit of Gable for the first time. Who could it have been, and when? We can speculate and arrive at a number of possibilities, then reduce these to fewer, more likely possibilities. If asked for the earliest date that the first ascent could have taken place, a likely answer would be some time within our historical period, the earliest possible ascent being around the time of Roman occupation by native tribal members or even Romans themselves. The first human footsteps into high places of Lakeland, it was thought, could have been made by people of the Brigante tribe, singular 'Brigan', around the first or second century AD. The main reason for venturing into high places would be to avoid Roman soldiers, who were moving around in the lower surrounding valleys. The very name 'Brigante' suggests familiarity with life above the valleys. One interpretation of the name 'Brigante' is from 'beg', a summit, hence Brigantwys the people of the summits. Another is that the name derives from a Celtic root meaning, 'the high ones or hill dwellers'. Rough, remote, mountainous country held little fear for them so visits to the top of Gable and surrounding summits does remain a possibility. That a Roman could have made the first ascent can be discounted, there is no evidence of them being nearer Gable than Grange in the Borrowdale valley to the north and along the valley of Eskdale to the south. The first ascent could have been made much later by a Norse farmer. A farmer who was one of the early pastoral-settlers in Wasdale could have reached the top while gathering sheep. From Scandinavian tales it is just possible that the first titled people to stand on the summit of Gable were Viking King Olaf and his wife Gydia: on a top the centre of all things, like Olympus.[1] Almost certainly the first ascent would have been made some time before the monks of Furness Abbey took control of the area around Gable in the twelfth century. Both Brigante tribe's people and Norse farmers, if they did climb Gable, could still have been at the summit much later than the actual first ascent.

When a similar question, about a first ascent, has been asked of neighbouring Scafell it asks who the first amateur, rather than a shepherd, could have been to climb the mountain with a sole aim of reaching the top. The answer normally given is the poet Samuel Taylor Coleridge while on a circuitous tour of the district in 1802. He spent the night at Wasdale Head and followed easy slopes from Burnmoor Tarn to the summit of Scafell, rather than the more difficult northerly approach using Lord's Rake. The Burnmoor Tarn route is the most likely way that any first-ascent shepherd would approach Scafell. Gable, unlike Scafell and most mountains in Lakeland, does not have at least one relatively easy grass slope to its summit, where someone out hunting or rounding up sheep could suddenly find themselves on top with no further upward walking to do. On Gable, a climb to the top has to be a deliberate act, a 'route' avoiding the crags has to be found, rather than the result of casual wandering upwards. Today, the existence of well-worn paths can make this difficult for walkers to accept; to appreciate the task of someone making the first ascent they need to imagine the mountain in a virgin state without paths of any kind.

Finding a possible answer to Gable's first ascent can lead us back in time even into pre-history. There is now an alternative view about a possible first ascent, that it could have been made in prehistoric times and most likely during what is called the Neolithic or New Stone Age period. From what we now know about the movement of prehistoric people in Lakeland, there is a possibility that the first ascent took place as early as 5,000 years before the present. Few people would readily imagine the ascent to be made hundreds or thousands of years before this time. To understand how the first ascent could be been made in pre-history, it is helpful to know something of the circumstances surrounding the people who could come into contact with Gable at this time. Hopefully the previous chapter sets the scene and helps to demonstrate that the study of any prehistoric period calls for a good deal of speculation, imagination and visualizing of events. In this chapter I ask the reader to imagine themselves as a skilled stone-axe worker around 5,000 years ago. During warmer months of the year, life would often be spent working and sleeping in the open, regularly around the 2,000 foot contour and sometimes above this level. Winter months were spent in timber dwellings at lower levels. With a little imagination it is possible to put ourselves in the place of these people because we are essentially no different; in Freud's words 'the man of prehistoric times survives unchanged in our unconscious'.[2] We may have surrounded ourselves with various artefacts over the intervening years: vehicles, machines and sundry items made mostly from metal, plastic or composites, but all are merely incidental; as one climber remarked in current idiom 'the bum-fluff of life'. As individual humans with ideas, hopes and fears, independent of our various incidental possessions, it is difficult to see how we have changed over the past 5000 years. A Neolithic axe-worker returning today would be greatly surprised by our modern artefacts, but if crossing Gable with a group of walkers chatting about everyday personal matters, would feel comfortably at home.

Being an axe worker
There is little doubt that early Neolithic workers crossed Windy Gap between Great Gable and Green Gable, carrying roughed-out stone axe heads from the factory sites above Great Langdale or from Scafell Pike, described in the previous chapter, to a finishing site at Ehenside tarn near the coast and close to the foot of the Ennerdale valley. Radiocarbon dating from axe working at Ehenside, shows that this movement between sites began 5,700 years before the present, plus or minus 300 years.[3] Flakes from axe-working have also been found on the route between Windy Gap and Langdale. The roughed-out axe-heads would have been carried over Gable's north ridge and down the Ennerdale valley.

Imagine being one of these axe workers spending many days during summer months working around Broad Crag and Mickledore near the Pike of Scafell and occasionally going to a valley settlement in Langdale or Ennerdale for food supplies. To quote A.W.R. Whittle, 'what was it like, being there? Sometimes a remote past can seem tantalisingly close with a little imagination it is possible to picture oneself there'.[4] In the coldest days of winter your home would be a wood and thatch hut in one of these valleys, where you would cover many miles into forests while hunting. Some of your time, on fine days, would be spent looking for suitable rock for axe making, or knapping rock, that had been collected in summer, roughly into the shape of an axe head. Searching for suitable rock would take you to mountain tops of Great End, Glaramara and around Gable above the tree line.

The best rock for axe making was first found above the Langdale valley, but another major discovery of this rock was to be made higher than the Langdale site, across mountains in the direction of the setting sun. After a long day of walking and climbing over large rocks you and your companions could go no higher; so high in fact that you all felt the clouds could be touched, and there on the ground was some very good rock for working into axes. This place, one day would become recognised as the highest place in England, Scafell Pike. While the weather remained warm this rocky summit and hollows immediately below would be your workplace and your home, with only occasional visits to a valley.

Visualize the scene; you are one of six axe workers waking up in a sheltered hollow down below Broad Crag, near the summit of Scafell Pike. The morning is fine and warm, even before the sun appears above mountains beyond the Langdale site, where other axe-workers will be preparing for another day's work. A blue sky with only wisps of cloud makes you feel it will be like this until darkness comes. You take a drink of water from a nearby spring; cold deer meat, hazel nuts and berries are eaten before you prepare to leave your rock cranny which has been home for you and five other workers. There on the ground lie six large piles, each pile with around eight roughed-out heads in sling-like bags made of skin. Today these loads must be carried to a settlement near the coast. Heavy loads; by today's measure each rough-out axe is between 10 to 15 inches (25 to 38cm) long and half this dimension in width; weighing around 5 lbs (2kg). Your group worked extremely hard making those heads, now it is your turn to spend the day carrying them to a place where they will be ground more finely to shape and polished. On the following day you will bring food back to this remote site.

That morning, looking around from the highest ground in sight, you can see mainly tree-covered valleys for a great distance. Immediately in front of you, while standing with the rising sun at your back, is another mountain none of your people had visited, to become known as Mickel Gavel and much later, Great Gable. The tops of most mountains around have not been visited; you are living in an area of unclimbed mountains.

The day is to be one of hard toil, carrying a heavy load over rough country, but not as hard as the work done in making axe heads. The work done for some time now has been back-breaking toil, moving rock on the overlying boulder field to reach the lower un-weathered rock below. Quality is important and below-standard rough-outs are left lying on the ground. These 'failed' objects will be found around 5000 years from now, by a few curious and attentive walkers in what will be called the 1950s. In time, people will find more roughly-shaped axes and chippings which your group has left behind and would call your working site 'a stone axe factory'. Some of these people would look at your efforts and say, 'this is not very good knapping of stone,' forgetting or not knowing that the quality axe heads were carried away from the site to be finely finished and polished at settlements some distance from the mountains. On this day that is where you and your colleagues are going; to a place where your rough-outs will be turned into fine polished axes, some to be fitted with sturdy beech-wood shafts. As you lifted the load to begin a long descent at the beginning of your journey, other workers, scattered around in early-morning sunlight, are already working the rock.

Much of the early walking that morning is downhill to a stretch of water surrounded by trees; later to be known as Hederlangtern and later, Sty Head Tarn. Before reaching this place of fresh water a way has to be found through the forest. A track has been made by cutting through the trees using stone axes. You walk around the tarn where animal bladders can be filled with water, because in front lies a hot steep climb beside a stream bed which at this time of year is dry. Soon you come out of the trees into bright sunshine and immediately above can be seen a familiar gap between two mountain tops. This is the most difficult part of the route where the pack of axes swings around as you struggle over rocks. Eventually you reach the gap, a narrow but level stony place. Packs are thrown down and you all find comfortable spaces among the rocks to lie down. The gap is a regular stopping-place, the first rest to be taken during the journey. From what was to become known as Windy Gap, you could look far down a long valley and out to the sea. You have been here many times and like your colleagues, you welcome the chance to put down your load, drink water, eat a little food and then have a short sleep. Today you drink and eat but feel restless. On earlier visits to Windy Gap you were curious about what lay above your head, beyond a broken pile of rocks and wondered whether a way could be found to go higher. Looking up above there is a great rock wall stretching across to your right and quite un-climbable, to your left just the boulders and you begin to think about going that way. Pointing upwards to the others you hear only the sound of sleep; nobody will go with you.

First ascent?
The scramble over loose rock is done alone, a strange feeling because you have always been with other workers when above the tree-line. Suddenly, in front is a large flat area, you can go no higher. From here can be seen mountains and valleys far away in a great sweep round until only the sea is on the horizon. Your workplace can be seen across the valley, rising above the tree cover. Your route of that morning can be followed by sight, the track down from the highest point, where other axe workers will be busy but now too far away to be seen, then into the trees around the tarn and up to where your colleagues by now will be fully asleep.

The scene at this time is of no buildings, no roads, in fact no sign of anyone living in the valleys below. Looking closer at the ground around you it is not unlike the place where you worked yesterday, which makes you search for any sign of axe-working, but nothing is to be found. No chipping flakes or rough axe heads, only a large area of many small rocks lying undisturbed. Beyond your place of work can be seen the site, where you first learned the skill of stone-axe making, below the Langdale Pikes. The days spent carrying axes from there to Windy gap and beyond are remembered as being done by only the fittest and strongest workers among you. Now axe heads are being taken south down a valley below the site where the carrying is easier, or north over a ridge and along another valley.

You wander further around this high place and realise there is no trace of any other person being there, but suddenly a great find is made. Among a jumble of rocks you see a small pool of crystal-clear water. You take a long drink and think how the others wish they had made the climb; to see so much and to drink water that did not need to be carried was bliss indeed.

Unknown to you, today has been one of great significance, not any normal day of axe-head carrying, but marking the first ascent of a mountain to become known eventually as Gable. Your feet are the very first to walk across that summit. Thousands upon thousands of feet would follow, but yours are the first. Your eyes are the first to see a view that would become famous and be seen by people from all over the world. This would be a day to treasure, if only you could know at this time. Just as significant was the idea that you would be one of very few people to see the view as one of true wilderness, long before any human-inspired changes took place.

You take another drink, then a problem, which way to go down? Walking around the edge of the summit a few places looked like the way you had come up, but which one? You walk around again, this time shouting and suddenly you can hear sounds from below and you recognise the broken rock passage where you had clambered up earlier. Voices become clearer as you see the gap below and soon the others are reached, as they prepare to move on. When you join them there is no talk of first ascents, only that a drink of water could be found and next time at the gap they should go there too. With the load of axes straining your shoulder you follow the others down a rocky ravine and eventually into the welcome shade of trees. Again, earlier colleagues had been at work with axes to thin out branches to make a track. You walk alongside a gurgling, rushing stream which flows into a lake further down the valley. For some distance there are large mounds of earth, not seen on any of the other axe-carrying routes, so your party has to wind in and out to avoid having to climb over each one. Then the track goes straight between the trees where shafts of sunlight come into clearings and where small waterfalls can be heard as you pass along the track.

Eventually, very tired, your group arrive at a small settlement on the left side of what now looks like a river, to be called the River Liza, large stones have been put in the water to help the crossing. Leaving your packs on the ground you cross safely to the other side. Men, women and children greet you warmly and all go to the nearest hut that provides a thatch cover where you can sit shaded from the sun to eat and drink. Inside, an imposing woman always meets you; the head person in charge of the settlement. In the centre of the hut there is a dull glow from the embers of a fire used earlier for cooking.

Through the open door can be seen a group of people busy using stone, found lying around, to build stronger shelters. Evidence of this work would be seen thousands of years later (until some thoughtless people covered the area by planting foreign trees). At this settlement they still spend most of their time hunting wild animals and fishing. The tools they use are made from pieces of flint picked up on the coast. At each visit there is interest in what you carry and what you have been doing, but little desire to make axe heads themselves. You tell them about going by yourself as high as possible to a rounded top they see regularly when on hunting trips up the valley. None of them thought it worth going there because animals are unlikely to live in such a place; hunting was best done in the valleys. For men and women at this settlement, the making of axes is seen as hard work and less pleasurable than hunting and fishing. The long tedious work of knapping stone and polishing is done nearer the coast and the head woman said she was happy for them to keep that work for themselves.

After food and drink has been taken with old friends, you move back across the river to join your track westward. Another settlement, close to the lake, is passed but you must keep moving to reach shelter before dark. The sound of stone working and voices could be heard as you approach a settlement, the final destination that day. Again, there are warm greetings as you are all shown a hut for the night. This was the end of the journey from Scafell Pike; a perfect place to recover before returning the next day. Everyone is very busy around the site. Some people cooking on two open hearths while children helped or simply played. Some adults were sitting cross-legged knapping axe heads into a final shape while others used large blocks of course red sandstone and gritstone with water to grind and polish the finished axes.

Ehenside Tarn workshop

Forward to the present: this site as a hive of activity with sounds of grinding, cooking and children's voices, was later to become known as Ehenside or Gibb Tarn. To-date, Ehenside remains the one site, in Lakeland, where we can be sure that roughed-out stone axes were ground and polished to the finished tool. In 1869 a local tenant farmer Mr Quayle, from the farm of Middle Ehenside, drained the tarn for use as farmland covering around six acres. When the water had flowed away the first of many pre-historic implements were found by the vicar of Beckerment, Rev. Stanley Pinhorn and reported in the *Whitehaven Herald* of November 19, 1870. Rev. Pinkhorn died shortly afterwards and further work was done in 1871 by members of the Society of Antiquities and a paper was presented by Robert Durkin Darbishier, a Manchester solicitor, in 1872.[5] Eventually it became clear that here was a Neolithic settlement, or possibly earlier as Mesolithic.

The stone axes found on the site have been petrologically identified as Great-Langdale origin. The movement of axes from Langdale and Scafell to this site would be unknown for approximately 80 years. When polished axes were uncovered from the bed of the tarn no link could be made with central Lakeland. A particularly valuable find was a polished axe complete with beech-wood haft which was donated to the British Museum and is illustrated below. Mr Darbishire, in his paper, described the implement with some feeling. 'The whole is a beautiful specimen of the skill and finish of the ancient workman. The chipped dressing of the surface is so neat that one cannot avoid detecting in it a certain idea of ornamentation'. Looking at the illustration, particularly the rounded top which has been carved with a pattern it is apparent that some sensitive feeling had gone into finishing the haft.

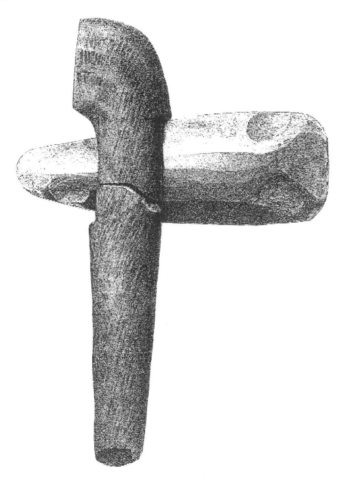

Langdale Stone Axe found at Ehenside Tarn axe polishing site
R.D. Darbishire, 1874

At the site could be seen clearly the remains of six hearths, earthenware vessels and a large corn-muller, indicating that cereals were being grown by this time. One fine polished axe head uncovered from the drained tarn was used as a door stop in Low Mill Farm until 1960. It is of interest that no flint implements were found, all smaller tools made for fine cutting were of feltstone. Other finds suggest that the site was occupied well into the Bronze Age and during the Roman 'interlude'. Work by Lakeland archaeologist Mary Fair, in collaboration with the British Museum, established that a shard of pottery found at the site was indeed Roman.

Returning to the Neolithic: you and your colleagues spent a pleasant evening seated beside a fire with around thirty men, women and children. Little did you realise that the combined skill and effort of your work on Scafell and of workers at Ehenside was to be fully appreciated more than 5,000 years later. Such a pity because it would have been a good thought to have before wrapping yourself in fur for a well earned sleep.

Early morning and loaded with food: meat, fish, nuts and berries, you walk out of the settlement and back into the Ennerdale valley. Two member of the group do not carry food because they have a load of harder rock picked up near Ehenside to be used as hammer stones; tools for working stone into axe heads. This harder rock, now known as Ennerdale Granophyre, was invaluable for stone-knapping at the Scafell site and used also in Langdale. Other types of rock, like one piece to become known as hornblend diorite, found some distance north, has been found useful for this purpose, but what your group carries makes the most effective tool.

On the return journey, only a short rest is taken with the friendly group busy building their stone shelters by the river. A fast pace was set along the valley until the steep climb up to Windy Gap was reached. There is time for only a short stop at the gap because you are all eager to reach the other workers before dark comes. No sleeping this time as you move down the rocky stream bed to the lake. By now very weak legs are struggling to reach the factory site. The other workers are pleased to see the six returning travellers but more especially, to see the fresh food spread on the ground before them.

When reaching Windy Gap on later outward journeys to Ehenside you take some of the other workers for a drink of water and look around from the highest point. The more industrious among you sit down on Gable's summit to have a session of knapping. Soon the busy 'knappers' realise that this mountain has the wrong kind of rock, and the pieces are not sufficiently large; this place was not to become another axe factory. There would be no point in coming back to these rocks, a disappointment because it was so much closer to the Ehenside axe-finishing site. You and a couple of other workers felt this was a good place to be, to look around and thought it a fine place to build, one day, some kind of dwelling or symbol from all the stone lying around.

In this way the second third and fourth ascents of Gable would take place. You go on searching for the ideal rock around the high tops surrounding the Pike and Gable. During a later trip to Ehenside a small group on the return journey go from Windy Gap, quickly over the summit of Gable, to see whether rock on the far side of the mountain would be more suitable. You lead the way down from the top at the far end of the summit, carefully between steep rocks until you reach the edge of the forest. Far below and looking out to sea lay another valley and being very flat looked a good place to make a track through the trees. This valley was to become known as Wasdale. Gradually, with the others, you moved around the mountain keeping just above the forest. High rocks reared up on your left and finding a place to put your feet was difficult. The rock was well broken and a large pinnacle nearby looked as though it could fall upon the party. This looked a promising place to find axe-making stone. Half your group begin taking rocks away from the scree to reach the un-weathered rock below while you and the others prize loose rock away from the face beside you. After much knapping, heads began to shake in the group and all that could be done was to leave the site. On the ground lay chippings to be found thousands of years later. After more difficult scrambling you could see the clearing made around the tarn and soon your feet were on the track back to 'home' on the highest top to be seen.

This journey of imagination into the Neolithic can seem fanciful, though it may not be too far from what could have happened. Various possibilities for a first ascent have been considered and not unreasonably we can imagine that it could have taken place much earlier than commonly thought. A Brigante is still a possible candidate, so too an early Norse farmer settled at Wasdale Head, certainly not a Roman. On balance, I favour a Neolithic axe worker, someone strong, adventurous and highly skilled who spent many hours living and working at around 2,000 feet above Langdale or even higher near the summit of the Pike. Someone who roamed the high tops looking for the ideal rock; who could survive on little food and was at one with nature. English people ought to be proud to have such early ancestors.

The first known settlers around Gable lived in what we call pre-history, but Gable's development from earliest days in the Southern Ocean to now add up to the mountain's history. The arrival of human beings can be seen simply as part of this development; a rather minor interlude in an evolving process. The idea of pre-history was not discussed until the mid-nineteenth century when the three-age system of Stone Age, Bronze Age and Iron Age was developed.

Internationally pre-history was taken to be before the First Dynasty of Egypt 5,000 years ago. In Britain it has come to mean before any written records; taken to be before the occupation of Britain by the Romans and their writings, almost 2,000 years ago. In this way we set artificial boundaries around events which add little to our understanding of what actually happened. The same is true for terms such as Mesolithic, Neolithic and Bronze Age, to describe people who have lived around Gable in pre-history after the last ice age. There was a good deal of overlap between these stages amounting to hundreds of years in each case. We can be excused for thinking it better to imagine human beings living through one continuous period of change and to make reference to any one stage, simply state the date. There was no clear distinction or cut-off point between the Neolithic settlers in the district and the later Bronze Age people; both pre-history and history can be seen as a series of overlapping stages, merging into one. The first ascent of gable, if taking place around the time suggested here, was done by one or more ancestors many generations ago.

References

[1] Size, N. 1930. *The Secret Valley: The Real Romance of Unconquered Lakeland.* London: Frederick Warne.
[2] *Pelican Freud Library,* vol. 12, pp.85-86
[3] Evens, E. D. et al. 1962. *Fourth report of the sub-committee of the south-western group of museums and art galleries on the petrological identification of stone axes.* Proceedings of the Prehistoric Society, 1962, vol. 28, pp.209-266.
[4] Whittle, A.W.R. 2003. *Archaeology of People: Dimensions of Neolithic Life.* London: Routledge.
[5] Darbishire, R. D. 1874. *Notes on Discoveries in Ehenside Tarn, Cumberland.* Archaeologia, vol. 44, pp.273-292.

VI. Roman Interlude to the Middle-Ages

Roman interlude

There is evidence of a Roman settlement in only one of Gable's upper valleys. Possibly the nearest they came to Gable was at Castle Crag in Borrowdale, where Samian and other Roman pottery have been found, suggesting that they made a 'home' there but without having any real influence upon the upper Borrowdale valley. Elsewhere in Borrowdale, Roman coins of 64-66 AD and 110 AD have been found.

Soldiers may have moved further up the valley at some time, even possibly to the valley head at Seathwaite, closer to Gable, but going further over to Wasdale is highly unlikely; there is no evidence of Romans trying to link the southern and northern parts of the central mountainous area by using Sty Head Pass or any other high-level route. Possibly the most reliable reference we have comes from William Hutchinson's *History of Cumberland*, where he writes that the Romans would probably have linked their road in Borrowdale with their road at Hardknott in Eskdale.[1] Shortly before Hutchinson's history, Thomas West speculated that a route could have existed between Borrowdale and an important Roman camp at Ambleside. He writes, 'whoever chooses an Alpine journey of a very extraordinary nature may return through Borrowdale to Ambleside or Hawkshead. A guide will be necessary from Rosthwaite over the Stake of Borrowdale to Langdale chapel';[2] this would have been the most likely route for Romans making a direct north-south link over the central area, but there is no evidence of this being done.

The one exception of Romans forcing a way from south to north over high ground is by High Street, from a camp near Ambleside to Carlisle. Modern guide-book writers like to credit the way over High Street, on the east of the district, to the visiting army as a 'Roman Road' when some of the earliest records in the thirteenth century refer to the way as a road made by the Britons, or Brettestreet. Given that prehistoric people forced a way over Gable's north ridge to and from Scafell Pike and Great Langdale, described in the previous chapter, it is to be expected that they were also able to move over what is comparatively easier ground going to or from the coast through the Eskdale valley, and along the smooth plateau we now call High Street. Both routes were to be followed by the Romans much later.

Although the Romans were in Britain from 43 AD, it was not until around 80 AD that they ventured towards the Lake District, then only to circumvent the central area. They did not come close to the Lakeland mountains until 110 AD when soldiers moved west across higher ground to the coast. Romans passed over existing tracks whether along the coast, over High Street to the east or through the Eskdale valley. The Romans seem to have had a gift for using what was already there and claiming it as their own.

The only suggestion that Romans came near to Gable from Eskdale is evidence of Roman occupation at Muncaster; coins of Theodosius were found there in 1800. The armies treated central Lakeland as 'blank on the map' and concentrated their attention on the coast at Ravenglass and Maryport and in the north at Carlisle. There were two main reasons for crossing high ground through Eskdale; to reach ports on the coast, and to have some control over rebellious tribes occupying the upper valleys.

During their stay it can be said with some certainty that any influence from the Romans was felt only in the lower valleys. A claim is made that the Romans introduced improved farming techniques, in particular a new approach to ploughing. This would be especially welcomed by local people because more intensive farming became necessary when the Romans insisted upon levies being paid usually as food for their garrison forces. That Roman soldiers could be fed from the time of their arrival suggests the local people had already established reasonably sound agricultural practices.

Where possible, 'natives' occupied more remote valleys or higher ground as a way of avoiding the intruders; they settled in the valleys of Langdale, Wasdale and Ennerdale, as well as ground above these valleys up to around 1,500 feet. These early Cumbrians had developed through the New Stone Age, Bronze Age and Iron Age to a point where they recognised the need for leaders, one of the most prominent was Cartimandua and it is likely that she led groups opposed to the Romans. William Hutchinson in his *History of Cumberland* said that 'it was no disgrace to the bravest people to be governed by a woman, disgustful effeminacies had not then contaminated the sex'. One reason for this early tribal leader coming to our attention is that Cartimandua, Queen-Regnant of the Brigante, eventually negotiated with Roman leaders, but that is another story not relevant here. By this time there were very small settlements immediately below Great Gable where trees had been felled or burned and where people could find room to build crude timber and clay huts, keep animals, grow barley and find shelter beneath the crags.

The time Romans spent in Cumbria has been well named by historian W.G. Collingwood as an 'interlude'; he commented that in Cumberland, 'we are almost at vanishing point in the scale of Romanisation'. Although called an 'interlude' it is worth reflecting that they were settled in Cumbria for around 300 years. Today, this would be like having Roman soldiers living here in 2010, getting ready to leave after being in occupation since before the last battle on British soil at Culloden, between Scots and English; a long interlude. In using this term I feel Collingwood meant a period of time when events were different from what happened previously, and what happened afterwards.

Collingwood commented that, 'during the centuries of Roman rule, the people of our district, if they learned little, certainly did not forget much'. The old practices of agriculture and type of dwelling places in use continued largely unchanged. There appears to be a strong case for saying that the Brigante did not benefit from Roman occupation, they found them a hindrance and would have made more progress if left to develop in their own way. People of the upper valleys around Gable were fortunate that the Romans were not drawn to the wild higher ground unless forced to by needing to go from one base to another. Industrial archaeologist Arthur Raistrick described the invasion of Roman armies to Lakeland as 'arrogant' and that, 'they remained foreigners and were never assimilated'.[3] To the early people of Cumberland, mainly the Brigante, Romans were simply a nuisance and they would be pleased to see them leave.

The fort built by Romans at the top of the Hardknott pass is one example in central Cumbria where they did not adopt existing features, the fort was called by them 'Mediobogdum'. The name Hardknott came much later from Old Norse, *hardrknut*. The fort is the one place where soldiers of Rome lived on high ground in central Lakeland. From inscriptions found at Hardknott, in 1964, it was discovered that the fort was erected for Emperor Caesar Trajan Hadrian Augustus. The construction was carried out by Dalmatian soldiers from what is now Yugoslavia. Occupation was from 120 to the year 138 AD when it was used only by some hardy locals, then again by soldiers between the years, 160 to 197. During the third and fourth centuries, Romans as well as locals would pass the deserted fort.

Most of the Roman settlements and forts, in central Cumbria, were completed during the second century and little more was done until they left the area, almost 200 years later. Strangely the ruin of Hardknott lay unnoticed for around 1,500 years until someone on horseback from Kendal re-discovered the site and raised the interest of historians and of the general public. To stand in the fort on a wet, cold misty day with wind whistling between the rock walls, the sound of ravens overhead and distant bleating of sheep is to re-live, almost, a central-Lakeland experience of native Celts or visiting soldiers. Apart from this fort, there is strong evidence that Romans built not on land that had to be cleared, but which was cleared in prehistoric time. Prehistoric settlements were used by the Romans, as at Ehenside Tarn, and continued in use when the Romans had gone.

After the Roman interlude

When the Romans had gone late in the fourth century the Celtic people were quick to adopt a more traditional way of life. Clare Fell, archaeologist and pre-historian, makes the point that they reverted more easily to the leadership of their traditional chiefs than did the more Romanised communities further south.[4]

It is difficult to discover what life was like around Gable between the Romans leaving and the twelfth century, when records from Furness Abbey were being written. Ian Whyte writing about this period points out that, 'careful detective work is needed to put together scattered fragments and clues'.[5] Events during the years following the Roman withdrawal are an enigma and we must rely upon the naming of places and folklore to piece together a picture of life at this time. A lack of 'history' refers to the North West of England and Cumbria as a whole but applies even more to the remoter upper valleys around Gable. We know that Brigante leaders had survived through the Roman interlude and when Roman soldiers finally left the area, various tribal chiefdoms were re-established, eventually to group together and set up a kingdom named Rheged. The power and influence however within Rheged was felt only around Carlisle and down the eastern side of Cumbria. Of the leaders during the sixth century, Urien is possibly the most well-known, who strongly resisted the arrival of Angles.

Around 200 years after the Romans left the district, yet another group of strangers arrived, who made changes to the landscape that would make people say in future that it was 'man-made'. Angles under King Aethelfrith moved slowly into Cumberland, no doubt like others before him seeing this land and its people as wild and strange. The upper valleys were as they had been for hundreds of years; still thickly wooded, with only isolated clearings, where travel was still difficult. Each of the scattered populations could be counted in tens rather than hundreds. Dwellings were still made of timber, wattle and mud and the only changes would be a more effective control of animals, in particular sheep and deer, use of improved farming implements and the beginning of a form of crop rotation. Otherwise life had changed little over the years.

Although Aethelfrith has a reputation for repeatedly beating the Britons in battle, the Angles did eventually settle in Cumbria to co-exist with the native population. A number of small villages existing today around the foothills of Gable were first established by the Angles. From what is known of these people it is imagined that they also had little effect upon Gable and its immediate surroundings. Angles colonised good arable land, while native populations, and later the Norse, were mainly pastoralists who seemed to be happier among the upper valleys. Angles preferred large areas of flat land where crops could be grown and where animals could be tended with least effort. The upper parts of Gable's valleys with their very small communities, little larger than those in prehistoric times, managed to keep their independence. Some people kept animals which previously roamed in a wild state; others used bloomeries to smelt small amounts of iron, the remains of such smelters can be seen today in Wasdale and Ennerdale. As with later Norse settlers, there was little sign of hostility from various incomers towards native people.

The assumption must be that over the next two to three hundred years the Angle influence, being not far away, would be wholly adopted throughout the valleys of Gable with an increase in arable and dairy farming. On the other hand, thinking about how fiercely independent the earliest settlers had to be it is still possible that their way of life endured among small communities in the upper valleys.

We can be reasonably certain that during the Roman interlude, and afterwards until around 950 AD, Gable's valleys were still largely forested with no major disturbance from outside influences. A short distance beyond the mountain's valleys at this time life was very different. Various people came and, for reasons better known to them, laid waste to Carlisle and large areas around the city. According to the Anglo-Saxon Chronicles, a Danish leader Healfdan or Halfdan destroyed what he could before retiring to Yorkshire, and an area that was at the time part of the Kingdom of Northumbria became of little use to anyone. It is believed that the destruction of Carlisle was the nearest the Danes came to central Lakeland.

After almost 100 years, when it is assumed local inhabitants on the periphery of Lakeland were making a recovery, Eadmund King of Wessex copied Healfdan as an agent of destruction and in his fighting defeated Dunmail, the last king of Cumbria, in 945 AD. The area was then granted to Malcolm II, King of the Scots, who ruled until 1032. Reflecting upon this time there is a feeling that the farming communities made up of people from axe-making ancestors, Angles and recently arrived Norse could have lived peacefully and happily with a minimum of threat. They would have peopled the upper valleys and lowlands by tilling the land, looking after animals and mining a number of minerals found around them, and been happy. Threats came largely from power-hungry earls and kings, backed by people who were misguided enough to follow them: Ecgfrid, Edward the Elder, Edmund, Malcolm, Gospatrick, Rufus and Aethelred; these men fought and plundered in quite futile exercises. Gable and its neighbours stood aloof while below, quiet industrious people busied themselves in feeding and developing harmonious communities. There are only two places near Gable which stand witness to these on-going troubled times: In Ennerdale's How or Castlehow, seat of the Patricksons, and not far away Muncaster Castle, now the seat of the Penningtons.

The Norse arrive

The Norse colonisation during the tenth and eleventh centuries was one of the most important developments ever to happen in the upper valleys. The Norse way of life had a very strong influence upon the scattered people already living in the valleys around Gable. It appears that total peaceful integration was achieved over the next 200 years and that the Norse legacy was the most influential force in Central Lakeland during the closing stages of the historical first millennium and well into the second millennium. Three events brought major changes to Gable's upper valleys, first the effective colonisation of the area by Norse settlers, second the establishment of a large powerful monastery at Furness and third, the dissolution of monasteries.

The Scandinavians came from Ireland, although they were of Norse origin. In Irish annals they were described as Finn-Gaill or 'Fair Strangers'. When the Vikings first sailed around the west coast they eventually settled in Ireland, after being repelled by the Welsh. Those who chose to make the sea crossing to Cumbria can be described as Norse-Irish, but it is believed that some settlers came more directly from Norway. These people were much more like some earlier Neolithic settlers in Lakeland. They preferred the upper valleys and even the higher tops where they could carry out their sheep farming. What can be called the Norse colonisation brought sheep farming to high ground on a much greater scale; from that time to the present day there can be no re-generation of forests up to 1,500 feet as existed before the Norse arrived, sheep and young trees do not live well together.

There is evidence that Cumbria was independent of England and Scotland, even if not officially. Cumbria, particularly the higher central part was largely in the hands of the Norse settlers at this time. During the year 1000, further attacks were made upon the settlers in Cumbria from an army led by King Aethelred to make sure the people were under English control. Still, very few families lived in the valleys around Gable, only a small mixed native and Norse population. The blending of Neolithic and Bronze Age people in the upper valleys around 3800 years ago can be seen as building the original native stock which endured throughout the period of interference from Romans. The arrival of Norse people complemented the individual ruggedness of this native population, and established personal characteristics which endure to this day. These Norse people share with earliest settlers, and today's native Cumbrian farmers a way of life that made them as one with their surrounding mountains. In appearance they were tall, sinewy, silent and above all honest and independent, relying totally upon their own skills and judgement throughout all weathers, not unlike farmers in the upper Alpine valleys of Austria, Switzerland and Italy. Norman barons who arrived later described the upper-valley people, some descendants of the first Norse settlers, as 'distant' and 'proud'. Eventually, the combination of late New Stone Age, Bronze Age, Brigante and Norse settlers provided worthy human neighbours for Gable.

Early travellers in the eighteenth century described the inhabitants of Wasdale Head used words: blunt, simple, and honest; one adding that, 'neither science nor fraud have yet got much footing here'. William Gilpin commented that when moving quietly around the mountains their clothing blended with their surroundings; in what has been described as 'the simple livery of nature'. Sheep and shepherds were clothed alike. We can be forgiven for contrasting them with some people today, especially hordes of charity walkers, who fill the mountains as noisy, brightly-coloured rabble.

When the first Norse settlers arrived in Wasdale they would recognise close similarities with their homeland and be happy to live upon higher rugged terrain. The valley has a particular grandeur, not to the scale of a Norwegian fjord but no less impressive especially when, as often happens, dark clouds and mist swirl around the tops. Just as Fen People, or lowlanders, have a feeling of belonging to their landscape of wide horizons, and can become claustrophobic among mountains, so highlanders only feel at one with their surroundings when steep slopes of scree and crags tower above them. There seems little doubt that had the early Norse visitors found an East-Anglian type landscape in Cumbria they would have moved further inland to settle in the Pennines.

The arrival of the Norse should have been a welcome relief, bringing with them skills in farming upland pastures and able to integrate with the few existing valley dwellers. A common perception is that Norse settlers made life very difficult for people on their arrival, but a good point is made by Sedgefield using archaeological evidence.[6] The evidence he says: 'bears witness to a degree of artistic achievement only possible in a settled population'. He also points out that some of the finest Scandinavian literature had its origin in Norwegian colonies in Britain and Ireland. Further evidence for the coexistence of Anglian and Norse peoples comes from place names around Gable's upper valleys; Anglian and Scandinavian names are to be found grouped together throughout lower ground below 250 feet.

During the early years of their settlement a large number of the Norse population lost their lives at the hands of Aethelred's soldiers. This was a time when the country was divided into Kingdoms which changed hands from time to time, and it seems that Cumbria was destined to belong to what was known as the English Kingdom. Yet compared with other parts of the Kingdom, Cumbria was independent with a significant part of the population being Norse rather than Danish found elsewhere. During this period various people who settled mainly in the lowlands of the district were Anglo-Saxon, then Norman.

Some Normans could be described as positively evil. If the Angles and Norse settled in a relatively peaceful way and contributed to the area in their own particular manner, the Normans were described as a non-productive ruling class. The Normans were said to give nothing and to take a good deal. Fortunately unlike the Norse settlers they had little influence upon Central Lakeland. Carlisle became effectively a Norman town while Central Cumbria not far away remained free from their savagery. The Normans did not include Cumbria and its people in their Doomsday survey of the late eleventh century. Even today Cumbria, especially the western part around Gable has an air of isolation from the rest of England and it is easy to feel you are getting away from it all in more than a physical sense. A remark often made about dales people was that they do not live in England, but in Westmorland or Cumberland.

Unfortunately during the Norman 'incursion' people of the western valleys were not entirely free of their influence; Normans, who for inhumanity would put Nazis in the shade, were claiming to protect the locals from Border Raiders. Earthworks of a castle at Beckermet to the west of Gable remind us of this time when such structures were built as protection from the Scots. The castle site is close to Ehenside tarn where peaceful axe-finishing people used to live; they were fortunate to have occupied the site much earlier and avoided the Norman way of life. Almost equal savagery came from Scots on the border and was felt most by people in the north of Cumbria, down the west coast and the Eden valley to the east. Medieval fortified buildings and pele towers, built to protect the locals were actively used in these areas. Nearest to Gable on the west side were Crummock Water Pele, Lamplugh Hall, Haile Hall and Irton Hall, but none existed in the central high land or immediately around Gable.

Language of the upper valleys
The complete opening up of the central mountainous area was done by the Norse settlers and they used Celtic names as well as their own which has become known as Old Norse. The Old Norse language lives on in the names of features throughout Central Lakeland, in contrast to the Celts where few of their names survive. One exception exists on Gable where Base Brown is considered to be a rare use of a Celtic name, imported by the Norse from the Isle of Man. Norse and Norse-Irish place names cover the whole of Cumbria with a greater concentration in the central and southern parts. There are no names in the high central tops of Lakeland influenced by either Romans or Angles. The Celts gave names to many rivers and some places but, like the Angles, mainly on the fringe of the district. Celts could be more imaginative than either the Angles or the Norse in naming

settlements or natural features. The Norse settlers in particular named landscape features by the way they looked using shape, colour or location; their names for Sty Head, Gable and Windy Gap are good examples. Otherwise they used their own personal names; W.G. Collinwood, in a letter, described this as an epidemic of eponymitis. In Alice de Rumelli's deed of 1209 and 1210, Styhead has the Old Norse name of *Hederlaghals* which translates to the long pass of the heath or fell, in Norse, *fjäll* or *fjëld*. In Icelandic this is *heidar-vegr* or path over the moors. *Hederlangtern* was the name given to Sty Head Tarn, though tarn also comes from *tjörn*. The name of 'Sty' for the pass comes most likely from the Old Norse *Stigi* for ladder or ascent. In the sixteenth century there is reference to Stime or Stye for this well-known pass. From the thirteenth century Great Gable had the name of 'Mickle Gavel' from Old Norse of *mikill* or great and *gafl* taken to be gable-shaped or in Norway *gavl* being a wall connecting two parallel mountain ridges; which is to be expected because this gable-like form would be the first sight Norse people had of Gable. The full name given in the 1338 bounders was *Le Heye del Mikelgavel*, being the 'the height of Mikelgavel'. 'Gavel' still exists elsewhere in the Lake District: Gavel Fell north of Ennerdale is a gentle top, not remotely Gavel-like; Gavel Pike on St Sunday Crags above Brothers Water is, like Gable, more worthy of this name; though its shape, from its most impressive side, is a pyramid. The name for Gable of Great Gavel persisted into the nineteenth century. The Norse would see the gavel shape, gable end, of the mountain as they first entered the Wasdale valley; *Vasdal* is still found in Norway and the name 'Wasdale' most likely derives from Old Norse of *vatr* for water and *dalr* for dale or valley.

Nearest neighbour to Gable on the west side, Kirk Fell most likely comes from the Old Norse of *Kirkja Fiall*, suggesting connections with a church, though in some early documents the name is given as Kingefell. Windy Gap between Great and Green Gable was known as *Windeg*. Going north from Green Gable, the next top is named Brandreth which was the name given to a three-legged cooking pot and this top on Gable's north ridge does have three minor ridges and can be seen as standing on three legs. There is another way of seeing this top; this is where the lands of three owners used to meet, the lands of Lord Lowther, Lord Egremont and Sir Wilfred Lawson. Below Windy Gap in the Ennerdale valley the beck named Liza is called after the Norse name *Lyse*, meaning bright water, which describes it beautifully. There is a Lyse Fjord in Norway and a river Lysa in Iceland. The common term for a stream in Cumbria is beck; in Norway it is *bekkr* and force for waterfall comes from *foss*. Many place names in Cumbria can be identified on maps of Norway or Iceland.

The origin of place names, of both man-made and natural features, is strongly debated to the present day, but the starting point is somewhere around the end of the tenth century. This was a time that politics and fighting between various factions fully emerged and even Gable and its valleys could not remain totally aloof from such nonsense.

Ownership
Unlike the south of England, records of land-dealing between the departure of Romans, around 409 AD, and into the early Middle Ages, around 1,200 AD, are poorly recorded in the north and particularly weak in the north west. By the beginning of the Middle Ages there should have been reasonably strong accounts of at least general commerce but as N.J. Higham writes, 'despite the best efforts of several generations of historians, Northern England retains an opacity during the early Middle Ages which is barely penetrable: the lives, group identities, cultural perspectives, economic activities and world-pictures of the vast majority of its inhabitants are all but a closed book to us'.[7]

We can only begin tracing any dealing in land around Gable during the thirteenth to sixteenth centuries. This was a time when ideas and records of land ownership, of buying and selling, became well entrenched in society; what now can be called the fetish of property. Gable would have been fully justified in saying, 'stop, nobody has a right to own me, I'm not a slave to be bought and sold I should be as free as the wind that blows around my head'. Such an outcry, if it could be made, would be in vain because Gable was to be bought and sold a number of times. With ownership comes the danger of people with no feelings for wildness having as an objective the desecrating of mountains with roads, pylons and other man-made objects; these threats to the mountain are discussed in Chapter XII.

A clear sign of 'ownership' was the dividing up of land: plains, valleys and mountains were parcelled up within boundaries and given the name of forests; not necessarily tree-covered areas but 'forest' meaning hunting territory. Gable found itself somewhere in the middle of a bounded area called the Copeland Forest which lay between Ennerdale and the river Esk. 'Copeland' has the meaning of to buy, Old Norse 'Kaupaland', as opposed to inherited. Nearby were the 'forests' of Allerdale, Inglewood, Ennerdale and Skiddaw. There were royal and private forests. Gable became part of what was described as 'free chase' for the Lords of Copeland; free from Royal interference and classed as a private forest.[8] The Ennerdale valley escaped the attention of the crown for some years after dissolution, until young King Edward VI granted the area of St Bees, including Ennerdale, to Sir Thomas Chalmer.

Farming and iron-making bloomeries around Gable seemed to have low priority between the thirteenth and fifteenth centuries. Where people walk and climb today there were often groups of hunters looking for deer, wild boar, sow and hawk; by 1510 wolves had finally become extinct in England. Eventually Wasdale Head was to become effectively a 'park' for the keeping of deer. This was not hunting as practised for food, by earliest settlers in the district, but more for amusement and a somewhat elite activity, to continue until banned 1,000 years later.

There are mixed views about whether mountains like Gable, Scafell or Helvellyn should be owned in a way that plots of land in and around towns or cities are bought and sold. Gable had existed for millions of years free from the concept of ownership, but the day finally arrived when the mountain was parcelled up and became someone's property. It is believed that Norman control, roughly between 1090 and 1130, over the area led to Copeland being private forest when many others were Royal; this topic is for debate among historians. The barony of Copeland was 'given' to William De Meschin who married the well-known and respected heiress of Skipton, Cecilia De Rumelli. It was their daughter Alice De Rumelli who became heiress of Copeland when her brother William was drowned in the river Strid, and became possibly the first recognised 'owner' of Great Gable, even though she spent most of her life in Yorkshire. Alice held the barony of Allerdale and granted 'to the monks of Furness Abbey the whole of Borrowdale with all its liberties'. Alice was to be paid the sum of £156-13s-4d plus two stirks, the name for yearling heifer or bullock. The Abbot paid her £50 in September of that year and a further £100 in December plus 10 marks, roughly an extra £7, in place of the stirks. When King John finally confirmed the grant of the whole of Borrowdale to the monks, Great Gable had acquired new owners, after being 'traded' as some kind of commodity. The monks of Furness could include Gable among their possessions through much of the Middle-Ages until 1537, and the Dissolution of the Monasteries.

As pointed out earlier, Norse 'colonisation' brought the biggest change to Gable's upper valleys since humans settled during the new Stone Age and the second major change was brought about by the establishment of Furness Abbey in 1127. The monks controlled thousands of acres around the abbey; the Abbot was virtually King of Cumbria. The first monks were of the Benedictine order from Savigny in Normandy and later became Cistercian. Being of Norman stock it is unlikely that they showed much interest in the valleys around Gable beyond collecting money for doing very little. Generations of monks occupied the abbey for around 400 years, living a highly privileged existence. Collectively, the monks owned farms, woodland, salt pans in Borrowdale, small iron-ore mines, mills, hunting and fishing rights and wool trade. The Abbot was reported as being involved in smuggling based at Piel Harbour, activity discussed in Chapter VIII on smuggling. Brownbill's *Coucher Book of*

Furness Abbey volume III,[9] shows accounts listing all the tenants paying rents to the Abbot. At the time of dissolution the monk's total income was around £900 per year, estimated to be around half a million pounds today, using the retail price index. The Abbey was said to be the second richest Cistercian house in England. The Abbot and monks also received a considerable number of gifts to secure burial places in the Abbey cemetery. In 1516 the Abbot and monks were accused of having buildings pulled down to make pasture in a place called Sellergarth, where fifty two people lived.

Shortly before the monks were driven from the Abbey, the Abbot became associated with the Pilgrimage of Grace, a mainly northern rebellion against the king, centred in east Yorkshire but also drew support in 1536 from some farmers at Wasdale Head as well as other parts of Lakeland. Although the Abbot and monks made every effort to give the appearance of supporting both the rebels and the king, the end of their power in the area was only one year away.

Two major events happened quickly: the border raids ceased and eventually the strangle-hold of the monks was removed by King Henry VIII taking control of the Abbey on April 19, 1537. A story is told that the king's troops were unable to find Furness Abbey and while leaving the area heard, in the distance, a tolling of bells that was from the monks' celebrations. They turned around and dealt with the monks as planned.

The years immediately following this event was a period of dire hardship for the monks as they attempted to find work and settle into the community while some were accused of treachery. They would travel on foot far and wide, often beyond the area but others walked into the wild valleys north of the Abbey, being dependent even more than before upon the small hill farms for their food and drink. There was little enough food for those living in the upper valleys because there had been two years, 1535 and 1536, when harvests were ruined.

It can be argued that the dissolution of the monasteries created one of the most significant changes of all time to take place in the valleys around Gable. The change created by Henry VIII triggered a series of buying and selling of land which at times included Gable and, most often, at least one of the upper valleys. Henry needed some control over that wild area in the north-west and appointed two Borrowdale men, John Fyssher and his son Lancelot as bailiffs. Much of the land previously owned by Furness Abbey monks was held by Henry and the crown until James I became King. Then a part of upper Borrowdale was granted to two men William Whitmore and Jonas Verdon; two men who could be called entrepreneurs or asset strippers, depending upon your point-of-view. They kept ownership of the graphite mine at Seathwaite and sold off the remainder around upper Borrowdale in thirty-eight parcels of land. Most buyers were farmers who lived in upper Borrowdale. One exception was Sir Wilfred Lawson who had already bought land from the Graham family who, in turn, had been 'granted' the land from Henry which had belonged to Fountains Abbey in Yorkshire before the dissolution of monasteries. This was land around Stonethwaite in Borrowdale. Most of this business took place in 1614 and was contained in what became known as *The Great Deed of Borrowdale*. Among the names to the deed can be recognised Lakeland families to this day: Braithwaite, Fisher, Birkhead, (Birkett) Lawson and Jopson; a number signed themselves as 'Yeomen of Borrowdale' but from 1632 many people of Borrowdale were customary tenants of Lord Lawson in what was called Lawson's Manor.[10] They were among the first to become more generally recognised as 'statesmen'. The buying and selling of land including mountains was made common practice by this deed. Even now when Gable has been bought by a local climbing club and 'handed over' to be held in trust for the nation, there is still the concept of being owned or 'held' by some named organisation.

By this time the various changes over the years had begun to influence practices in the upper valleys. Stone structures used in higher pastures were being adapted for permanent living. What had been shielings or saetr, described in Chapter VIII, became homesteads and even today places with 'scale' or 'saetr' in the name are likely to date back to this time; both words are Scandinavian in origin, roughly meaning 'summer pasture'. Names used for shieling settlements vary with height levels: 'Erg' is used in low-lying land around Lakeland, Saetr on lower lying fells and 'Skali' in higher central Lakeland.[11] Stone was slowly replacing timber in the construction of dwellings and some still stand today.

Many pages of this chapter could so easily have remained blank or have no chapter at all. There is however something to be gained by having a chronological thread through Gable's story, and events leading up to the mountain becoming owned seem to be worth recording.

References

1   Hutchinson, W. 1797. *The History of Cumberland, vol. 2.* Carlisle: F Jollie.

2   West, T. 1784. *A Guide to the Lakes.* London: B. Law.

3   Raistrick, A. and Forder, J. 1987 *Faces of Lakeland.* Kendal: Peters.

4   Fell, C. 1972. *Early Settlement in the Lake Counties.* Clapham: Dalesman Books, p.68.

5   Whyte, I. 1989. *The dark Age Landscape*, in Rollinson, W. (Ed.) *The Lake District: Landscape Heritage.* London: David and Charles.

6   Sedgefield, W.J. 1915. *Place names of Cumberland and Westmorland.* Manchester University Press.

[7] Higham, N.J. 2001. *Britons in Northern England in the Middle-Ages: through a thick glass darkly.* Northern History, vol. 38 (1) pp.5–25.

[8] Liddell, W.H. 1966. *The Private Forests of South West Cumberland.* Transactions of the Cumberland and Westmorland Antiquarian and Archaeology Society. pp.106-130.

[9] Brownbill, J. (Ed.) 1919. *The Coucher Book of Furness Abbey: Three Volumes.* Manchester: Chetham Society.

[10] Johnson, S. 1981. *Borrowdale, its Land Tenure and the Records of the Lawson Manor.* Transactions of the Cumberland and Westmorland Antiquarian and Archaeological Society. pp.63–71.

[11] Whyte, I.D. 1985. *Shielings and the upland pastoral economy of the Lake District in medieval and early modern times,* pp.103-117, in Baldwin, J.R. and Whyte, I.D. (eds.) *The Scandinavians in Cumbria.* Edinburgh: Scottish Society for Northern Studies.

VII. Workplace

Farming the upper valleys

Dissolution of the monasteries brought with it a frenetic buying and selling of land in and immediately around the upper valleys, and major changes took place during the early seventeenth century. With the buying of land, previously owned by monasteries, new farming communities appeared and some farmers became known as Statesmen who were either landowners, or farmed a small acreage in the upper valleys. Some referred to themselves as Yeoman and in the years following, some writers classed them as 'Lakeland Yeoman'. The independent upper-valley farmer did not necessarily have to be an owner-occupier to be called Statesman or Yeoman by name, but would normally own and/or farm land of between 50 and 150 acres. This kind of farmer's very existence seemed to come from a need to fill a gap between a very thinly spread gentry in Cumberland and a greater number of farm workers. William Wordsworth, in his *Guide*, recognised this new relationship when he wrote, 'perfect Republic of Shepherds and Agriculturalists'.

Immediately below Gable there were communities of tenant farmers at Wasdale Head where life could be difficult because the valley floor offered little opportunity for cultivation; the only crop was oats. Most fields were small, enclosed by dry-stone walls and used mainly for meadow or pasture. Poorer farmers were helped only by having extensive common rights over the mountain sides. Around the sixteenth and seventeenth centuries Wasdale Head supported little more than eight families with only two or three being owners of land. Around fifty people lived without shop, public house, mill or a tradesman of any kind. The local population has fluctuated over the years but has never reached what can be called an overcrowded upper valley. Ennerdale and Buttermere followed a similar pattern of development, while Borrowdale became part of what can be called a mini-industrial revolution.

The period when Statesmen were thriving was between 1610 and 1780 and had apparently declined by the early nineteenth century. The terms Statesmen or Yeomen are not used now and much controversy surrounds the question of when they no longer existed. What seems the most sensible view comes from J.K. Walton[1] who claims that the decline of Statesman or Yeoman was 'largely illusory'. Despite many journal papers about when and how Statesmen ceased to exist, it seems upon reflection that only the name went out of use.

Many farmers became involved in more commercially orientated enterprises. Providing accommodation for the early tourists or woodland management are two 'business' activities which come to mind.

One important change, the enclosure of land including commons had been done during the late eighteenth century but was formalised with the 1801 Enclosure or Inclosure Act. In valleys where stone walls were used to create these enclosures there is a regular rectangular pattern of walling, whether in the valley bottoms or on the higher fell sides. Wasdale Head enclosures are highly irregular, strongly indicating that their forming was earlier than late eighteenth century. In Wasdale and other valleys around Gable farmers with small acreage lost pasturage on common land and became poorer. At this time there began a move by some people to towns and the new factories which was said to be a capitalising of rural life.

Methods of farming in the upper valleys have changed since Statesmen or Yeomen first became active, from subsistence farming to a more commercial activity which includes anything legal which can be done to earn a living. People visiting a farm today, often as paying guests, can see a family unit working the land and tending livestock which in purely human terms is close to the independence of Yeomen; only types of transport, equipment and commercial activity has changed the scene. The major changes were almost revolutionary by replacing cart tracks with roads. Timber dwellings and crude single-room stone structures were replaced by more substantial stone houses roofed with slate. The Norse influence in type of dwelling place is very difficult to find in Cumbria because the sites have been built-over or lost. Small, scattered communities in the upper valleys were increased as people, expert in mining techniques, joined them to exploit the heavy industry of processing iron, lead, copper and graphite. The intense industrial activity created conditions very unlike the scene around Gable today.

Some people in the upper valleys were slow to change, mainly because the sheep and cattle farming had become already well established and though offering a hard life, it can be said that they enjoyed a good quality of life. There was enormous satisfaction to be drawn from tending sheep and cattle; producing much needed and worthwhile products and enjoying the close-knit co-operative companionship of those around them. There was no hint of capitalism where profit takes priority over the needs of people in the community.

Farming of cattle, as opposed to sheep, brought the development of what was called *demesne vaccaries*, where cattle were kept on managed stock farms. The first was at Gatesgarth, Buttermere in 1267, followed at Stonethwaite in Borrowdale in 1302 and finally Wasdale Head and Ennerdale in 1322. The upper valleys of Gable could be called 'cattle country' at this time, though for Wasdale Head, despite the vaccaries, the term could be seen as an exaggeration.[2] These changes also brought a population increase to the upper valleys where people were able to exploit the valley floors, cleared earlier of trees and boulders by Norse farmers and their descendants. As greater areas of the fells were converted to pasture the hunting activity became more restricted. Tracks were becoming more like roads, though not exactly highways, as Gable's valleys were being made ready to enter an industrial age.

Gable's sheep

The first people to work on Gable were the earliest shepherds who were following on from late prehistoric settlers by tending and controlling animals as an alternative to hunting daily for food; deer and sheep were among the first to be kept in this way.

The first documentation of domesticated sheep comes to us from Iran, Turkey and Greece around 8000 years before the present. The practice of keeping domestic sheep in Cumbria is probably between 4,000 and 5,000 years old.

Gable and the native Herdwick sheep are looked upon as inseparable; their collective image is one of the strongest symbols of Lakeland. There is good reason to suppose that Herdwick sheep

Sheep at Seathwaite Farm
Kenneth Sherpherd (Permission of Westmoreland Gazette , 1989)

roamed the valleys and tops many years earlier than previously thought; they may well be older in genealogical terms than the farming families which have reared them over the years. There have been various stories about these animals being brought over by Norse settlers in the tenth century, but there are no breeds to match the Herdwick on the Isle of Man or Ireland, where the Norse had lived before crossing to Lakeland. The Norse farmers would be farming with sheep found on their arrival in the upper valleys of Wasdale, Eskdale and Ennerdale. Sheep flock numbers had begun to increase almost 2,000 years before the Norse arrived when a decrease in woodland provided pasture, and sheep-wool clothing has been found at a bronze-age burial site in Yorkshire.

Herdwicks come most likely from the tan or white-faced horned sheep closely related to one of the earliest known breeds, the Soay. Probable lines of evolution show there is a direct link from this earliest breed to Herdwick, Shetland and Cheviot.[3] Early sheep were small-boned, similar to the Herdwicks. One word-of-mouth account describes the first Herdwick sheep in the district swimming ashore from a wrecked Spanish galleon near the port of Ravenglass, and people farming around Wasdale quickly added them to their flocks. There is no conclusive evidence to show where the Herdwick came from or when. There are no known written accounts of Herdwick sheep before Clarke's *Survey of the Lakes* in 1787[4] and a number of his observations have been described as 'not too accurate', possibly based on hearsay. Clarke believed the Herdwicks came from a Danish ship. Later in the mid-nineteenth century another writer stated that the vessel of origin was most likely Norwegian.[5] More accurate descriptions of Herdwick sheep behaviour comes from H.D. Rawnsley in his book *By Fell and Dale* in 1911.

There were sheep in Neolithic times; skeletal remains have been found at sites around the south of England and from lake dwellings in Switzerland. Sheep came into Europe from the Near East with migrating Neolithic people;[6] the most likely explanation for the arrival of Herdwicks is that the animal is an indigenous species from sheep which roamed around Central Lakeland before the Romans arrived which had entered the area along with domesticated and wild sheep after the last ice age. Even now it is difficult to think of Herdwicks as domesticated animals; their whole aura is one of independence and belonging only to high places.

The origin of Herdwick sheep may be uncertain but there is near certainty about the origins of the name 'Herdwick' which comes from a type of sheep farm developed by the monks of Furness Abbey in the twelfth century. The farms were known as Hardwick or Hardwicke, and the breed adopted that name.

Questioning the origin of Herdwick sheep is of little importance to Lakeland farmers; they are only too pleased to have such wonderfully robust animals ideally suited to the rugged mountain tops. A Lakeland sheep farmer, B Armstrong, recovering in hospital after a fall on the fells wrote:

> *Sheep are sticking to their honest creed,*
> *And helping us in our most urgent need'*
> *King of the Lakeland fells and dales,*
> *Pride of the shepherd, hard as nails.*

There are around forty breeds of sheep in Britain, all well adapted to their particular area. While Herdwick is the main breed around Gable because they are particularly well suited to the harsh environment, there are other mountain sheep to be found on the Pennines: Swaledale, Rough Fell and Cheviot are most common. Why do Herdwick sheep from Wasdale Head, Seathwaite Farm in Borrowdale and Gatesgarth at Warnscale Bottom, wander high up on Gable's stony barren waste? Food is scarce, only lichen, moss, fern, heather or furze, if they are lucky. There seems to be a hunting instinct that if they keep moving something will be found, even if all they can see around Gable's summit is mainly rock. All upper valleys of Gable have been home to the Herdwick. Ennerdale had over 2,000 before the planting of forestry while other valleys have maintained flocks. A recent estimate gives a number of 50,000 Herdwicks on National Trust fell farms in Cumbria.

One of the finest descriptions of the Herdwick sheep comes from a shepherds' guide written at Gatesgarth Farm in Buttermere; a farm famed for the breeding of Herdwicks.[7]

'The ears should be white and sharp, and stand well up, as any tendency to droop betokens a want of spirit to grapple with hill life. In colour the head should be light grey, with a hoar frost-nose, rustiness about the poll, as well as a lion-like mane. These are all solid requirements. The body should be shaped like a barrel, the legs well to the outside; a broad breast placed forward as the forequarters are chiefly relied on both for constitution and the scales. The knees should be strong, and the bone thin to fetlock; and then a big white foot to follow. The hind legs to spring from a well-muttoned thigh, thin shaped, with plenty of bristles, looking rather upwards. The tail to reach no farther down than the camerals, and thick at the root. A sheep should be well ribbed up, the greater their power to endure hunger; the back broad, and well filled in behind the shoulders; when turned up to have a deep and broad breast, with soft, kindly wool upon it.'

A further comment about facial expressions could be added, if it was not so difficult to define because of their varied nature. Expressions of curiosity, aloofness and resignation are descriptions I would offer.

The farming of Herdwick sheep was, and still could be, a major industry for wool, milk and meat. Farmers have been known to keep Herdwicks for up to seventeen years. A modern trend is to breed animals which will provide fine wools and sturdy mountain sheep are cross-bred with fine-wool breeds to 'improve' their coats. The outcome of Cheviot-Herdwick or Swaledale-Herdwick is a finer wool, larger animal and better meat but not with the adaptability of Herdwicks to live through the harshest weather on higher rough ground. Herdwick wool makes hard-wearing carpets and is superior for the making of quality clothing, which is especially long-lasting. One farmer described having a suit made from around 10 lb (22 kg) of Herdwick wool which lasted a lifetime and shed water wonderfully. The wool can be woven into imaginative blends of colour which reflect pure nature: light to mid-grey, dark brown to black and white to grey. The durability and natural colouring of carpets and clothing is of no concern to most people in the fashion industry; but fashion is no indicator of value or worth so once again the product of these sheep could, in time, become fully appreciated. There is too, valuable use of Herdwick wool in the manufacture of fire-retarding insulation material which also combats condensation and is ideal for use in the insulation of buildings; a recent product for building-insulation is thermafleece which contains around 85% sheep wool. Fire-retarding sheep wool is also ideal for curtains which have to be used in public places, such as theatres. One problem in the use of wool is the monopoly held by the British Wool Marketing Board, anyone holding more than four adult sheep must register for the sale of products from the sheep, there are some exempt breeds of sheep but Herdwicks are registered. It appears that this marketing arrangement stifles innovation by preventing farmers from working independently. In an attempt to be more independent, some cooperatives have been established, among farmers, to the south of Lakeland in the Duddon Valley and in the north at Caldbeck.

There are many stories about Herdwicks and their typical behaviour. There was the incident when Lord Cockburn, an eminent Scottish judge, was with a local farmer as guide above Wasdale Head in winter, who remarked about sheep being out on the open weather-side of the mountain instead of sheltering on the lee-side. The farmer's reply implied that if the sheep had the Judge's intelligence they would. As with humans, who have multiple types of intelligence, sheep are capable of behaviour which is intelligent for particular circumstances, and in this case would be avoiding the danger of becoming buried under drifts in sheltered areas. Some doubt has been cast recently on this particular behaviour of Herdwicks, because they do become caught in drifts. I have observed them weathering out snow storms rather than seek more sheltered areas in Central Lakeland, but many years ago now; it is possible that a lack of severe winters in recent years has affected this behaviour, to make them more vulnerable when heavy snow falls do arrive. Another possibility is that they are casting doubt on the behaviour of sheep which may not be pure Herdwick.

The Herdwick is closely tuned to its immediate surroundings, through a number of generations, and will keep to the mountain where born, to wander within an invisible boundary of their pasture or heaf. So strong is this sheep's sense of 'home' that when taken to a farm, some miles away, they have been known to escape and walk back for many days or in some recorded cases, for weeks. A ewe walked back to Ennerdale after being sold to a farm at Torver near Coniston Water; readers who know Lakeland will appreciate this amazing and difficult feat.

Contrary to common belief sheep do have strong individualism. Sheep herding together is often used as a metaphor for people following mindlessly; this is unfortunate because sheep only flock together when being herded. Release them without interference on a mountain side and they will go off and spend all their time in ones, twos or very small groups. Camping alone high in the mountains, I sometimes have a visit from one sheep alone or with a lamb not far behind; coming closer and closer towards the tent in an inquisitive way, head on one side and eventually becoming quite used to my presence. Some sheep, in contrast, keep a wide margin between themselves and humans. Sheep are highly individualistic and would laugh if they could know of the view we hold of them, especially if they could watch crowds of humans crossing Waterloo Bridge every work-day of the week or together in any city centre on a Saturday night. Herdwicks have been described by the Rev. H.H Symonds, a great defender of Lakeland as, 'having powers of resistance and ready wit unlike any other breed, with a better supply of obstinacy and common sense; in other words more difficult to domesticate. In both wits and strength the Herdwick outdoes all other breeds of sheep'.

There have been sightings of larger, older sheep standing close to a dry-stone wall so that other younger sheep could clamber over her body and over the wall; of sheep stories this needs to be seen to be believed, perhaps someone has a photograph?

The pure Herdwick is as much a part of Gable as Napes Needle or Kern Knotts but it is quite possible that in a few years this small sturdy animal could be gone. As pointed out earlier in this chapter, Herdwick sheep have an enormous contribution to make when, as expected, the need to manufacture more durable cloth independent of oil-based synthetic products will in time become necessary. I feel sure it was the Herdwick breed Coleridge had in mind when tramping the Lakeland tops; he saw sheep in an affectionate way, 'bless their dear hearts, what darlings mountain sheep are'.

Mining interests

Gable has been spared the mining of minerals, so common in other parts of Lakeland. Copper, lead, zinc and barites have been mined around Keswick and copper mined to the east and south of the district. If any of these minerals had been found alongside iron, graphite and slate, the mountain would indeed have become a centre of major and intense mining activity. If the geology of the north ridge had been repeated to the south, Gable would have been virtually surrounded by mining and quarrying from the late eighteenth century to the late twentieth century.

Most industry was concentrated to the north around Honister for slate, east at Seathwaite for graphite and west in Ennerdale for iron. Wasdale Head to the south did become, for a time, a centre of mining interest. In 1774 a fourteen-year lease was granted to search for slate at the foot of Gable and around the head of the valley. A further application was made in 1809 to search also for slate; a licence was given for twelve months. On reflection, if prospectors had known more about the geology of Gable, they would not have begun the search.

Iron became the focus of industrial activity in Wasdale but only through the working of small-scale smelting hearths called bloomeries. In comparison with the industry that may have existed south of Gable, the mountain now overlooks a quiet, tranquil scene; not yet back to near-natural surroundings because cars and heavy vehicles still defile the area by coming far too close. One local artist, William Green wished for a 'softer' Wasdale, 'if divested of its stone walls and more profusely planted would truly be a pastoral paradise'. We may see the walls now blending into the upper valley because the surrounding grandeur is what gives Wasdale Head its overwhelming presence. The valley has been fortunate to escape the various mining interests virtually unscathed.

Graphite or Wad

On almost every day of the year cars will be seen parked by the road leading into Seathwaite Farm; walkers don their boots to climb up to Sty Head or Esk Hause bound for Gable or Scafell. A lesser-used route to Gable goes up beside Sourmilk Gill, around Base Brown and on to Windy Gap. At around 500 feet above Seathwaite across to the right is Newhouse Gill, at times known as Wad Hole Gill, and nearby can be seen mine spoil tips. Mining for graphite began here in the early sixteenth century and was the next industry to follow the farming of sheep on the flanks of Gable. The earliest recorded account of commercial mining at Seathwaite is from August 26, 1555 but graphite was being taken from the ground before this date and was known to farmers around the mid-fifteenth century. Graphite has been found on the Pennines around Rochdale and Halifax which must

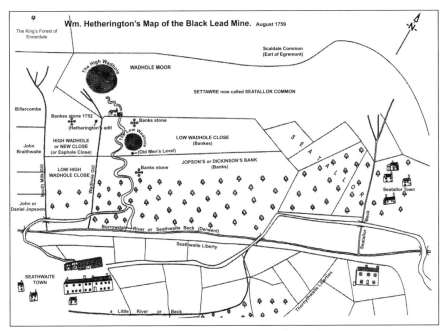

Seathwaite Graphite Mine Surface Plan
William Hetherington, 1759

have come from Cumbria[8] and the position of these finds in layers of peat points to them being there in Neolithic time, associated with stone axes also from Cumbria found in the area. On this evidence, Seathwaite graphite was known to New Stone Age people.

The industry began by accident, someone picked up a piece of graphite which had come to the surface; probably disturbed by the roots of a fallen tree. Graphite, known also by a range of names such as wad, black cawke, plumbago or black lead, occurs underground, up to a depth of 300 feet, in what are known as sops or pipes and could only be used by farmers if discovered initially on the surface. The material was used in the late fifteenth century by locals to mark sheep, blacken stoves to avoid rusting and when a small morsel 'to cover a sixpence' was added to beer or wine it became a cure for a range of medical ills.[9] The use as a marker has been known for centuries which gave the name graphite from the Greek 'to write'.

One of the clearest indicators of the date when graphite was being used in Cumbria comes from a find of a graphite mould for the making of counterfeit coins. The mould was found by a Daniel Tyson of How End in Wasdale in 1865, lying among a pile of stones near Starholme, a short distance from the village of Netherwasdale. The graphite mould in two parts had been engraved to produce five coins of silver groat and silver half-groat for the time of either Edward IV or Richard III and three silver pennies of Henry VII. In a paper read at

Hexham in 1876, R.S Ferguson cleverly developed what today would be described as a profile of the forger.[10] Ferguson describes the person responsible as: highly skilled and educated to engrave the Latin inscription backwards; he lived in the reign of Henry VII, such a person would be attached to a monastery, like Furness Abbey where the monks once owned Borrowdale. The graphite must have been brought over Sty Head pass from Seathwaite and made into moulds sometime in the sixteenth century. It is likely that the forger had travelled abroad, because at the time the heat-resistant power of graphite was unknown in Cumbria. Most counterfeit money came from Luxemberg, imported in bales of cloth so it is likely that he had gathered skills and knowledge from that country. To quote Fergusson, 'his name we cannot hope to know; he never returned to reclaim the tool he had secreted in the place where it was found in 1865'. Exactly 100 years after Ferguson's paper, another explanation for the coin mould was given by George Boon.[11] According to this later assessment the coins would have been of poor quality and could be passed off only in a busy marketplace. Boon did not share Fergusson's high impression of the forger as an intellectual. From experiment he showed that good graphite takes an impression of a coin hammered into its surface, and some crude engraving was done where the impression had not fully taken. There is a strong possibility

View of the Black Lead Mine, at Borrowdale.

Sketch of Graphite Mine showing Overseers House and Guardhouse
Saturday Magazine, 1832

that this graphite was traded illicitly because records show transport from the mine to be north to Keswick before going on to Newcastle and then by sea to London or directly to the continent, or from Keswick directly to London; all under the control of Newcastle or London Merchants. The stock of graphite, awaiting sale in the city, was kept in a Unitarian chapel in Essex Street. The sale took place on the first Monday of each month at a nearby public house. Even the pencil makers of Keswick had to buy their graphite from the London dealers. This method of controlling the market in graphite directly and only from London made the selling of any illicit, and readily available, material even more lucrative.

Discovery that graphite had value beyond a Lakeland valley coincided with the early development of copper and lead mining in the district, and the farm at Seathwaite, below Gable, became the site of the first commercial graphite mine in the world. The value came firstly from graphite being greasy to the touch making it ideal for the lubrication of pulleys, wheel bearings and wood screws. Further uses were soon discovered, most importantly in the making of crucibles used in forging, glazing and the manufacture of round shot and canon balls. Ownership of the mine changed many times; the first owners could have been the monks of Furness Abbey if they had remained in business long enough. When Henry VIII decided that their business should come to an end the area of the mine, including Gable, became the property of the Crown. The next change of ownership came in 1614, when sold to William Whitmore and Jonas Verdon. From that time to the day of final closure, around 1890, the mine passed through many hands.

To appreciate the development of graphite mining on the flanks of Gable, it is useful to have some understanding about the growth of mining in valleys immediately north of the mountain. In July 1561, Queen Elizabeth was asked to grant permission for 300 or 400 foreign miners to work the copper ore containing silver in Cumberland. The Queen granted permission and also agreed to the felling of trees to provide timber for the construction of ore-smelting buildings. Lord Burghley then arranged for German miners from Augsburg to bring their expertise to mines near Keswick and especially the Newlands valley to work the Goldscope mine, which had been known as a source of minerals since the thirteenth century. The mine in Newlands was the site of the first 'railways' around the mid-sixteenth century to carry wagons out of the mine. Mining techniques were well advanced in Germany, for example they were using gunpowder for blasting 75 years before its use in Britain. The use of German mining expertise was not the first venture of this kind; there are records of German miners on Alston Moor as early as 1359. The minerals looked for at this time around Borrowdale were lead, copper, silver and possibly gold.

Graphite mining was not looked upon as a major underground

activity; the Mines Royal Charter, set up by the Queen, made no reference to black lead, wad, graphite or any other name to identify the mine at Seathwaite. In the charter, Elizabeth was to receive 10% of any precious metals found in addition to agreed royalties. Also included were freshwater pearls which had been taken from local rivers to the west of the district since Roman times. The river Irt, near Drigg, was most productive and the queen was keen to hold these rights. Just over 100 years ago, pearls were still being taken from the River Ehern which comes out of Ennerdale Water.

The mining expert responsible for the miners and the development of mines was Daniel Hechstetter, there are various versions of this name but he signed using this spelling, a man with enormous influence upon the development of mining and indeed upon the economic well-being of the district. He had to overcome considerable opposition from local folk in Keswick, including the murder of one of his men, Leonard Stoulz by a Keswick man named Fisher. The murderer was eventually released on probation at the request of influential Lady Radcliffe. The reason for her action could well have been linked to the Radcliffe family supporting the Earl of Northumberland who claimed rights to the mines and who made life difficult for the German miners. Daniel Hechstetter and his wife Radagunda and five children were, in time, fully integrated into the English community. Two sons, Emanuel and Daniel, followed him into the Lakeland mining industry. Later, Daniel junior like his Father had an eye for business opportunities and took a personal share in the graphite mine. Together with a London Armourer John Masefield, and Emanuel Hechstetter, Daniel entered this business venture independent of the Mines Royal Company in 1607.[12] The mining of graphite would be known to the Hechstetters when in Germany because it was carried out at Passau near the Austrian border in the fifteenth century, and had been known of in the thirteenth century, long before the Borrowdale mine opened. Accounts for the graphite mine in 1632, held by the Duke of Northumberland, show entries where Daniel and his nephew Joseph Hechstetter are paid their share of income from the 'wad'.

A measure of how far German integration had taken place was that the second Daniel retired to Soham in Cambridgeshire where a Roger Hechstetter was clergyman. One of Daniel's grandsons took an MA at Oxford and became Master of Carlisle Grammar School.

That German miners moved around mines in the Lake District and that some married local girls is well documented, as in the case of Thomas Kalker, one of the initial twelve miners to come with Hechstetter. Kalker worked at the Newlands mine and married Janet Dickinson of Newlands in 1602. The couple moved to the copper mine in Coniston, where they had three children before returning north to the graphite mine and lived in Borrowdale where another child was born. In 1565, quite early in the settlement of miners, births of children to German fathers were recorded in the Crosthwaite parish register, and around 170 births were recorded over the next twenty years.

More than two generations of Hechstetters from 1564 to 1634 dominated mining in Cumbria and the remains of their work can be visited today, but the real value was in the contribution made to the nation's development; their skills were passed on where previously there had been none.

The Mines Royal Company suffered badly in the mid-seventeenth century, during the Civil War, when parliamentary troops destroyed most of the workings. Cumberland, seen largely as royalist, at least among the holders of power, also suffered with greater deprivation and poverty at this time. The graphite mine lacking any obvious association with 'Royal' was not seriously affected. Ian Tyler has done extensive surveying of the graphite or 'wad' mine and has written what can be seen as a definitive book about mining in Borrowdale and in particular the graphite mine, this book should be referred to for both technical details and human interest.[13] Before publication of Tyler's work the main source was John Postlethwaite's book on mines and mining in the Lake Distict.[14] but his writing on the graphite mine was based upon the work of geologist J.C. Ward in 1876.[15] Possibly the finest descriptive prose about the mine comes from George Smith of Wigton writing in the *Gentleman's Magazine* in 1751. Smith wrote around 100 articles for the magazine, normally signing himself 'GS', he can be said to have been well ahead of his time, both in his love of Lakeland mountains, which comes out clearly in his writing, and his interest in geology. A term he used for the area was, 'romantic beyond expression'.

When the mine was open, a great deal of activity was to be seen in getting the 'wad' from high on the mountain side to the valley track, then to horse-drawn carts complete with armed guard. The wad was contained in casks weighing about 140 lb (63 kg). A visitor reported that when close to the mine workings: 'the depths of the earth often resound with sweet singing, whereby they lighten a toil which is of the severest kind and full of the greatest dangers'.[16] Graphite below ground and in waste tips lay like black gold and a great temptation to impoverished people of the upper Borrowdale valley. Some visiting writers thought that finds of graphite on the waste tips were honest gain; not a view shared by mine management, or the law. After so many robberies an act of Parliament was passed in 1752 which made both the robber and receiver guilty of felony.

The black stuff also became a temptation for a not-so-impoverished young man tried in court at Carlisle for stealing from the mine. The charge could not be upheld because there was no precedent for the act he committed. He did not steal from the waste tips, from the carts or as an employee; the three known methods for this crime. The young man, William Hetherington had leased land close to the mine from the surface owner Daniel Jopson, and opened an adit in search of copper. Although successful as a copper miner he tunnelled from the main gallery, within his leased area, into a sop of graphite which was part of the nearby mine. Whether this was his plan from the beginning or simply 'stumbled' upon the find is not known. After the trial, and unsuccessful prosecution, John Bankes owner of the mine bought the nearby ground and gave Hetherington the job of Mine Steward at the grand salary of £20 per year, equivalent today of £30,000 using average earnings. He worked there until his death in 1766. For William, enterprise eventually had its reward.

When walking and climbing in Borrowdale, I heard a story from many years back about a smart young man who moved into the valley and occasionally went off to London on business. He courted the daughter of a local farmer, believed to be at Thornythwaite near the mine, who could not discover the source of the young man's apparent wealth, until it was discovered that he was charged with trading stolen graphite. The outcome being that in law he could not be found guilty. The local telling me the story made no mention of copper mining only that the young man lived near the mine and leased rights there to tunnel for minerals while secretly looking for graphite. Further research has uncovered an account which comes very close to what I was told.[17] The year was 1780, the local farmer was Randal Fleming, the girl in question was his daughter Alice and the young man living in a cottage just above the Borrowdale yew trees used the name Gawain Everstett. Randal was impressed by Gawain's apparent wealth and saw him as a suitable husband for his daughter. As a demonstration of his wealth the young man deposited £5 each week with Alice's father. Gawain tunnelled from a floor of his cottage into the mine and his sudden trips away were mainly to Penrith where he disposed of around £2,000 worth of graphite. Gawain planned to flee the country with Alice after they were married. Shortly before the wedding, two police officers arrived at the cottage with the clerk of the mine. The mine was closed from time to time as a means of maintaining the value of the graphite and had been closed during the time of Gawain's activity, yet graphite was still being traded outside the strict controls between Keswick and London; this is what alerted the company to problems at the mine. Gawain was tried at Carlisle but could not be found guilty because there was no precedent to work from; the theft was not within common law. With this case in mind, a special Act of Parliament was passed to make such surreptitious 'mining' a criminal offence. He was confined for a few months then released. Alice Fleming never married. The year of this account being 1788, fourteen years after Hetherington's death means that either there were two robberies of this kind or the second date is incorrect.

Graphite, like diamond, consists solely of crytallised carbon.[18] Heat diamond in a vacuum at around 1,800°C and you will have a pile of graphite powder. Although makers of synthetic diamonds use graphite there is no known reverse conversion of graphite to true diamond.

Writers have speculated that with greater heat during volcanic activity in Borrowdale the graphite mine could instead have been a diamond mine. Possibly the first person to make public this idea was John Postlethwaite during a lecture in Keswick in 1914, who in speaking was said to fly a few geological kites. He imagined Seathwaite as a world-famous diamond mine. This would only have taken place if the volcano of Borrowdale had been like that of Kimberly in Africa, but it was not. The true source of diamonds comes from tapping magma more than 93 miles (150 km) in depth. The ideal condition for diamond creation is to have temperatures around 1000°C and pressure of 50 kilobars.[19] Seathwaite graphite in comparison was formed at temperatures between 120 and 600°C and pressure of 1 kilobar.[20] Diamonds found in Africa come from a rare type of volcanic rock called kimberlite, but no kimberlite volcano existed near Gable. The comparison with diamond however adds to the interest of graphite as a material; graphite is a good conductor of electricity but diamond is not. Diamond is a major conductor of heat, around four times that of copper, while graphite is not so effective. Diamonds are often called 'ice' because they conduct heat away from the lips and so feel very cold, yet many women are 'warmed' by their contact in a way not possible with graphite. The differences between these two materials is said to be the most remarkable contrast in all mineralogy.

We are extremely fortunate that only graphite was intruded within the Borrowdale Volcanic Group of rocks at this site; by potassium-argon dating given as 376 million years ago.[21] Scenes above and around Seathwaite Farm of diamond mining can only be imagined with horror. By now a company like Rio Tinto would have gouged away most of Base Brown and possibly Gable itself in their normally destructive way.

That graphite has not been discovered in any other place in England, Scotland or Wales led to people thinking it was a unique find. The actual, high quality, deposit as found at Seathwaite is unique in Britain because as Ian Tyler points out, 'no universally accepted theory of its origin has been produced'. The standard-quality material, while not common throughout the world is far from unique and can be found in the United States of America, Rhine valley, Ceylon, Mexico, Siberia and most productively of all, Korea. There are records in the diary of Isaac Fletcher of Underwood Cumberland [22] to show that plumbago was imported from America in 1770, despite having supplies of the finest kind virtually on his doorstep. Possibly the American delivery at Whitehaven was more reliable and convenient than having to buy from merchants based in London.

Graphite had great value during the time it was mined between the early years of the sixteenth century and the close of the nineteenth century which made security a major problem for mine owners. One of the most valuable strikes, produced graphite to a total market price of £105,000 in 1803; equivalent to around £5 million at present-day value. Despite the building of a guard house in 1800 and rigorous searching of miners at the end of each day, graphite did find its way to a black market. Jewish traders in particular appeared from London to carry out deals in selected public houses in Keswick.

Iron bloomeries

Iron ore mining and smelting has a long history in the Lake District and the sounds of this industry came to the feet of Gable in the Wasdale and Ennerdale valleys. The technique had changed little since late pre-historic times. Charcoal was burned in bloomeries, domes of clay to smelt the haematite. However, before the seventeenth century it was common practice for iron ore to be sent to Ireland for smelting.

Field research has shown that at least six iron bloomeries were worked at some time in the Wasdale valley. Some names are redolent of an ancient smelting practice such as Smithy Beck and Cinderdale Bridge. One bloomery was at the foot of Wastwater, at a place called Broad Span, where a stone landing stage took boats which ferried the red oxide or 'smit' across the water to Smithy Beck. Much of the smit was taken from Hall Gill above the Broad Span site. The smelting was carried out where wood was plentiful and near good natural draught, or where forced draught could be created. Whenever bloomeries were built to process iron ore there was an inevitable stripping of trees, not just normal coppicing but mass felling to provide charcoal for the smelting of ore. There are numerous becks flowing into Wastwater on the northerly side some with little-visited impressive waterfalls, especially in Over Beck near Bowderdale Farm and the force of these becks together with a nearby supply of wood made the valley an ideal site for small-scale iron smelting. Given the choice of locating bloomeries near the ore, or near a supply of timber, the site chosen would be as close as possible to trees. Charcoal was needed in great quantities and is particularly bulky to transport. Also at the time, ore sold for £1 per ton while charcoal could be as much as £10 a ton. Eventually the small-scale smelting of iron ore was no longer viable in the Wasdale valley and the work moved to the coast; leading to large-scale iron works. Most bloomeries were suppressed or closed by Elizabeth I because large amounts of woodland were being cut down to provide fuel and the cropping was needed as food for cattle. This ruling probably more than any other event brought an end to small-scale iron workings in Wasdale. In contrast there are numerous iron mining sites and smelting locations on both sides of Ennerdale Water. These are discussed more fully under the subject of shielings in the next chapter.

Slate

The north ridge of Gable ends in a huge crag dropping to Honister Hause and the Honister slate mines; wrongly called quarries because slate was removed by mining into the mountainsides and not by quarrying. An alternative view is, 'underground quarries'. On Honister Crag the green-slate lies in beds, created by fine-grained ashes being altered by compression between rocks of the Borrowdale Volcanic Group.

From records at Cockermouth Castle, commercial mining at Honister began in 1753, though records of slate being moved from here go back some years before this date. There is evidence of Romans making use of slate but not of any active mining or quarrying for the material. A twenty one year lease was granted to a John Walker in 1728, for the taking of slate from Fleetwith or Fleetworth as it was called then and he was possibly the first person to develop the mine.

To appreciate fully the impact of slate mines on both sides of the Hause we need to visualise the area in its natural state before mining began. There would be no road leading west out of the Borrowdale valley at Seatoller, only open fellside rising steeply in splendid wildness from Gable to Dale Head and on to dear-old Cat Bells above Derwent Water. Only a faint path would link the Borrowdale and Buttermere valleys. The Hause or pass, below Fleetwith Pike would not mark so distinctly an end to Gable's north ridge, but the eye would follow the ridge further northwards. From this pass, looking west, the path would lead steeply down a rock-strewn mountainside to the valley bottom where a rough cart track could be joined alongside Buttermere. If you stand at Honister Hause in future, visualize the scene around you without the road and without the mines; sense what could be much greater isolation from the valleys below with much wilder landscape all around you.

The slate mines can be justified but very few people would claim that the landscape has been enhanced by the road and mine workings. Even Wainwright had developed a 'soft spot' for Honister in its present state, implying that the workings have become part of the mountains. Standing in the then abandoned mine he said, 'it is a scar on the landscape, but is such an integral part of Lakeland life nobody really objects, I certainly don't'. I feel this is being kind to what can still be seen as an ugly scar upon grandeur and overlooks what the mine was like during post-war years of full production. From the corrugated-roofed dressing sheds came the noise of sawing and grinding; the sound and smell from heavy vehicles and pollution of nearby streams. Earlier, another major change brought to Honister mining the sound of explosions. Gunpowder which was being produced locally in Langdale allowed miners to drive the underground levels very much further and faster.

The past practice of tunnelling into bands of slate until it could be removed from vast underground caverns has spared Fleetwith Pike and Yew Crag the dreadful fate of open quarrying. As the years passed, the inclines and tunnel entrances are beginning to mould themselves into the mountainside in a natural, almost organic way, as Wainwright suggested. The mine has been partly reopened to provide work for a small number of people and a slate-mining experience for tourists. The mine working, when in full production, described by Harriett Martineau, Mrs Elizabeth Lynn Linton and depicted in Hugh Walpole's writing provide scenes of almost unbelievable human effort.

If at any time you are finding a climb up Gable or Scafell a struggle physically, pause and think of slate workers who lived in the cottages at Seatoller and walked steeply up to their place of work. They reached the mine after covering over 800 feet in one and a half miles.

Slate Barrow descent, Honister Mine
Abraham Bros. Permission of Alastair Cameron Honister Mine

Some slept in rough stone dwellings on the site but some did come each morning from the valley. When work began one job was to haul a wood sledge, which they called a barrow, almost half a mile up a steep track through piles of waste slate to reach a platform where around 500 lb (227 kg) of dressed slate was handled onto the barrow. Before 1890 the rough blocks of slate were split and dressed either in stone huts within the mine or near the entrances. Later this work was done in sheds at the Hause which are to be seen today. Each workman, who had brought up an empty barrow weighing around 80 lb (36 kg) on his back, 'walked' the load down the mountainside his back against the front of the sledge and one foot braced against the ground as each forward step was made; see the illustration. The strain upon that person was immense. One local writer who described the scene was Mrs Linton who later lived at Brantwood by Coniston Water with her husband; eventually they sold the house to John Ruskin. Few writers have captured like Linton the working lives of people in Cumbria so well,[23] standing at the summit of Honister pass she wrote about watching the slate miners at work:

'The long swift steps seem almost to fly; the noise of the crashing slate comes nearer; now we see the man's eager face; and now we hear his panting breath; and now he draws up by the road-side, every muscle strained, every nerve alive, and every pulse throbbing with frightful force.'

The empty barrow was again taken up and the whole process repeated; the work was relentless and punishing. Moving around on the mine tracks which snake up the cliff face could be dangerous, as well as having to live with the obvious dangers below ground. From the coroner's records for 1848 in Egremont, a John Rigg and his two sons had to crouch low against a fierce whirlwind known to pass periodically over the Hause; the father was lifted bodily over the edge to his death while his sons survived.[24] Generally lifespan was short with many cases of lung disease, heart disease or consumption.

Many years later, local miners still recalled the achievement of Joseph Clark, who came up to the mine from Stonethwaite. In one day Clark made seventeen journeys carrying his barrow up to the top of the steep incline and bringing it down, each time loaded with 640 lb (290 kg) of slate. In total he climbed and descended 17 miles and moved 10.880 lb (4945 kg) in one day and that is assuming he slept at the mine, possibly he walked to Stonethwaite three miles away to return the next morning. An average workload in one day was to make seven or eight journeys of half hour climb with barrow and a few minutes down with each 500 pound load. Joseph Clark far exceeded a day's work and Lynton described him as, 'a giant of the elder time'. It is doubtful whether anyone could repeat the feat today.

For some Stonethwaite men there was another successful slate working at Rigghead across the valley from the village; though nearer there was still around 1,200 feet to climb before work began.

The end of Gable's north ridge continued as a site of major industry for almost 250 years; a fraction of a second in the mountain's life but nine generations of miners spent their entire working lives knowing only the sounds of blasting and hammering of slate. At the end of each day it would be difficult to summon sufficient energy to eat before going to sleep. The living conditions on-site were rough beyond present-day imagining. The dry-stone huts, or hovels, had one or at the most two rooms with a raised wood platform for sleeping and open fire, usually of peat, for cooking, and surrounded by rough dry-stone walling, plugged with turf to keep out draughts. In the words of William Gilpin, 'stealing their whole dominion from the waste; repelling winter-blasts with mud and straw'. Groups of miners lived in these conditions all week before going to the valley for respite. Eventually a more spacious building was constructed at around 2,000 feet but living conditions would have been little better. It is highly unlikely that any miner would suggest on a free day that, 'a walk along the ridge to Gable would be nice'.

When the Honister mines closed in 1985, only one slate working site remained in Lakeland. The high-quality slate, mined or quarried, in Lakeland is still valued for its use as architectural material, domestic applications, ornaments and for the more common use of roofing. Like the use of Herdwick wool there can be a feeling that slate is a resource not fully exploited. In the interest of employment for people in the valley we should be prepared to sacrifice the quiet of areas like Honister Hause and it is encouraging to see the mine being worked once again.

References

[1] Walton, J.K. 1986. *The Strange Decline of the Lakeland Yeoman.* Transactions of the Cumberland and Westmorland Antiquarian and Archaeological Society. pp.221-233.

[2] Miller, E. 1976. *Farming in Northern England during the Twelfth and Thirteenth Centuries.* Northern History, 11, pp.1–16.

[3] Ryder, M.L. 1964. *The history of sheep breeds in Britain.* Agricultural History Review, 12, pp.1-12

[4] Clarke, J. 1787. *Survey of the Lakes of Cumberland Westmorland and Lancashire.* London: Printed for the Author.

[5] Dickinson, W. 1859. *Glossary of Words and Phrases of Cumberland.* London: John Russell Smith.

[6] Mitchell, W.R. 1966. Men of Lakeland. London: Phoenix House.

[7] Ryder, M.L. 1959. *The domestication of sheep.* Wood Knowledge, 4, p.19.

8 Davies, J. 1963. *Prehistoric Finds of Lake District Origin in the Yorkshire Pennines.* Transactions of the Cumberland and Westmorland Antiquarian and Archaeological Society. vol. 63. pp.53-60.

9 Nicolson, J. and Burn, R. 1777. *The History and Antiquities of the Counties of Westmorland and Cumberland.* London: W. Stahan.

10 Ferguson, R.S 1876. *On certain plumbago moulds found in Netherwasdale Cumberland.* Transactions of the Cumberlandand and Westmorland Antiquarian and Archaeological Society. Old Series, vol. 3, pp.27-30.

11 Boon, G.C. 1976. *An early Tudor coiners mould and the working of Borrowdale graphite.* Transactions of the Cumberland and Westmorland Antiquarian and Archaeological Society. vol. 76, pp.97-132.

12 Hammersley, G. 1988. *Daniel Hechstetter the Younger: Memorabilia and Letters, 1600-1639.* Stuttgart: Franz Steiner.

13 Tyler, I. 1995. *Seathwaite Wad and The Mines of the Borrowdale Valley.* Carlisle: Blue Rock Publications.

14 Postlethwaite, J. 1877. *Mines and Mining in the English Lake District.* Beckermet: Michael Moon.

15 Ward, J.C. 1876. *Geology of the northern part of the English Lake District.* Memoir of the Geological Survey, Great Britain.

16 Agricola, G. 1912. *De Re Metallica,* translated from 1556 edition by H.C. Hoover London: The Mining Magazine, p118.

17 Payn, J. 1858. *Leaves from Lakeland.* London: Hamilton Adams & Co.

18 Pearl, R. 1955. *How to Know Rocks.* London: McGraw-Hill.

19 Harlow, G.E. 1998. *The Nature of Diamonds.* Cambridge: Cambridge University Press.

20 Strens, R.G.J. 1965. *The graphite deposit of Seathwaite in Borrowdale Cumberland.* Geological Magazine, v.102 (5), 393-406.

21 Mitchell, J.G. and Ineson, P.R. 1975. *Potassium-argon ages from the Graphite deposits and related rocks of Seathwaite Cumbria.* Proceedings of the Yorkshire Geological Society. v. 40 (3) pp.413-418.

22 Winchester, A.J.L. 1994. *The Diary of Isaac Flectcher of Underwood Cumberland,* 1756 to 1781. Cumberland and Westmorland Antiquarian and Archaeologica Society.

23 Linton, E.L. 1864. *The Lake Country.* London: Smith, Elder & Co.

24 Ward, E.M. 1929. *Days in Lakeland Past and Present.* London: Methuen.

VIII. Smuggling

Smuggling as a way of life

The west coast of Cumbria was a smuggling area, not of the scale practised in Kent or the West Country but significant in the eyes of Customs and Excise officials because a considerable amount of smuggling took place along the coast and within Cumbria. The Ordnance Survey in their *Guide to Smugglers' Britain* (1991) did not recognise the extent of illicit 'trade' in Cumbria; virtually ignoring the area.

The illicit business began in the thirteenth century with smuggling of wool. King Edward I introduced a tax on the export of wool. Before this time, wool was being exported free of duty and re-imported as cloth at a lower price than could be charged by local producers. One clever smuggler who appears to have escaped punishment was the Abbot of Furness Abbey who owned numerous flocks of sheep and shipped wool from the abbey's Port of Piel Island, without paying the necessary dues, in his ship the *Mari Cogge*. When his smuggling came to the notice of Edward III, in 1347, the Abbot was charged. Seventy years later another Abbot of the abbey was accused by merchants in Calais of landing cargoes of wool in Flanders. This Abbot was believed to smuggle wool out and wine in without paying taxes. The outcome in both cases did not lead the Abbots to be considered officially smugglers. People of the valleys around Gable who smuggled were not so fortunate and were regularly punished when caught.

In the seventeenth century, the smuggling of wool was a felony and the ultimate penalty could be hanging. It has been reported that, between 1670 and 1735, forty three smugglers were hung. Severe punishment did not deter some people, it has been estimated that two-thirds of tea drunk in Britain late in the eighteenth century was smuggled into the country. At this time tea in Holland was two shillings per pound and in Britain ten shillings (twenty shillings to the pound weight), the rewards could be great.

For many years smuggling was part of Lakeland life, mainly of wool, whiskey and salt. More specifically around Gable, stolen graphite was added to smuggling activity. Graphite could offer high rewards for smugglers, especially if they could reach a port on the coast with the booty of 'wad' because the material was in great demand abroad. Ravenglass was the port where for some years the main activity was to buy duty-free surplus salt from the Manx herring business in the Isle of Man when salt was heavily taxed in Britain.

There was a strong connection between the Isle of Man and smugglers operating through Gable's upper valleys. Before 1765 the Isle of Man had its own fiscal laws when people on the island could import many goods without paying taxes; the place was described as an Eldorado, especially when taxes became higher on the mainland. When, in 1765, the Lord of Man sold the rights they held to the Crown the advantages to be gained from smuggling contact with that island were lost, apart from salt. The Isle of Man herring industry could still import salt duty free and some found its way into smuggler's hands. Ravenglass remained important for Lakeland smugglers, for almost another hundred years.

Four smugglers around Gable

There were three prominent smugglers who passed through Gable's upper valleys: Moses Rigg, Lanty (Lancelot) Slee and Whiskey Walker, a lesser known smuggler was Black Sal or Sal Robson who has become renowned in folk law as the poacher turned smuggler who was hunted to death by wolf-hounds on Thorneythwaite Fell above Seathwaite. The three men and a woman worked at this 'trade' between 1780 and 1870, risking a heavy fine, imprisonment or even transported if caught.

In the eighteenth and nineteenth centuries it was common for women to use their voluminous clothing to conceal goods which could be flasks of spirits, wool or lengths of silk, and in Sal's case, illicit whiskey or graphite. Probably the most famous smuggler of this kind was Lovey Warne, the sister of two smugglers who lived in the fastness of the New Forest and smuggled well into her old age.

William Palmer, Lakeland writer and Editor of the *Fell and Rock Climbing Club Journal*, heard from a local game keeper how Sal Robson set snares and was expert at concealing her poached animals.[1] Sal, it was said, came from a family of poachers, drinkers and thieves. Her home was in Rosthwaite, Borrowdale and it was there that a store of graphite was found in a wall when part of the stonework collapsed. Palmer describes poacher lasses at the time as, 'blowsy, impudent, with shrieking invective for the slightest imagined occasion'. While most of these lasses kept to poaching Black Sal became involved in smuggling and would either conceal graphite to be taken to Keswick or glean from the spoil tips at the mine.

Whiskey Walker, like Moses and Lanty, worked in Borrowdale slate mines or quarries, but after becoming a smuggler he lived over the mountains in Langdale. Walker was known as a well-read man who befriended Robert Southey, Hartley Coleridge and knew 'Wudsworth' well enough to call him Rydal Waddy.[2] By necessity, he was a shadowy figure, appearing suddenly in northern valleys of the Lakes, then in the south; he has been associated in the memory of locals as the man with a white pony carrying side panniers. On reflection it seems strange that he should choose such a conspicuous animal, but on the other hand could easily plead innocence by saying, 'now would I have such an animal if I wished to conceal anything?' The normal way for smugglers to carry spirits at this time was in two containers either side of the animal, holding half an anker each; an anker was roughly seven and a half gallons. Over a few years Walker became part of the region folk law together with Lanty Slee. Later in their criminal career Walker and Slee had a violent confrontation with excise men, they escaped but soon afterwards Whiskey Walker went to America. The last heard of him was as a soldier fighting with troops in the American Civil War.

Lanty Slee was born in Borrowdale but spent most of his working life around Langdale. From time to time he was charged with smuggling illicit whiskey, evidence of the brew being made was difficult to find, so the local Magistrate would fine him an appropriate amount of money for simply selling illicit whiskey. The fine could be seen as lenient or made lenient later because a number of influential people were among Lanty's clients, including some Magistrates who were reluctant to see a reduction in the supply of particularly good liquor at a good price. There is little reason to suppose that Walker or Moses would be treated differently if they were caught.

Lanty farmed at Low Colworth in Little Langdale before moving to Arnside. He was said to have whiskey stills at Tilberthwaite and Hallgarth and possibly at Red Tarn above the Langdale valley. A windowless room at Fell Foot Farm, below the Wrynose Pass, was said to be a place for storage. This suggests that apart from smuggling routes through the mountains to the north, he went westward over Wrynose and Hardnott to the coast. Routes north were made either from Great Langdale or Wasdale Head. Slee and Walker with men from Borrowdale collected whiskey at Wasdale Head, which had been brought from Eskmeals on the coast. Walker, with his supply, went over Sty Head into Borrowdale while Slee left him at the top of the pass to go past Great End, Angle Tarn and down Rossett Gill to hide the liquor in a gill above Wall End Farm. Lanty Slee became quite prosperous and bought Greenbank Farm in Little Langdale, where he died in 1878.

Moses Rigg, like Slee, Walker and Black Sal have gone into Lakeland-smuggling folk lore but unlike Slee and Walker, Moses and Sal have remained elusive figures, as all good smugglers should be. What is known about Moses will be considered later.

Gable's smuggling routes

There is little doubt that smuggling was conducted within Gable's upper valleys. The obvious smugglers' routes were to and from ports on the coast, using quiet secluded tracks through the mountains. Small churches close to the coast were known as 'safe' places to store illicit goods, with local clergy getting their due reward. One reported example was of Whitbeck church below Black Combe where smugglers left spirits in the church over a Sunday when it should have been moved. The Vicar announced that he was indisposed and no service would take place that Sabbath. Ennerdale Bridge was also a hiding place for booty and it would be carried by a track south of the river Ehern past Ennerdale Water and up the valley to join Moses Trod either around Gable or along to Honister.

Beyond the central mountains, lower Borrowdale became an important centre for the handling of goods. The highly secluded way up to Watendlath with places to hide and recover on a route eastward was used for traffic going beyond the Lake District.

The more obvious routes from Gable's upper valleys to the coast could be patrolled by Excise men, looking for smugglers. From Seatoller, over Sty Head to Wasdale and particularly over Honister Hause to Buttermere were routes used by smugglers but they became increasingly difficult to travel without being caught and charged. Whiskey Walker used the Sty Head route but later adopted a wilder terrain by going across Greenup Edge or down Langstrath into Borrowdale and back again. Lanty continued to use Sty Head pass but he had to plan and time his journey with great care, in particular when weather could offer him adequate cover. Smugglers at this time were highly accomplished hill walkers. Around the higher tops they knew the outline of hills and mountains in detail, even on dark nights, and could often detect where they were from the sound made by bubbling water in different becks and waterfalls.

On each route, Slee and Walker had legitimate trade as a cover for their smuggling. During their journeys over high ground they picked up red haematite which farmers used, like graphite, to mark sheep. Among the tales told about Slee and Walker was that whenever they delivered sheep marker or as they called it, ruddle or rud, farmers were known to ask if there could be a drop of the 'other stuff' in the delivery; meaning the odd skin of liquor or 'mountain dew'.

A route allegedly used by Moses Rigg was much more difficult for Excise men to cover. From Honister Hause, a track going south to Wasdale makes such good use of contours it could be called a mountaineers' route, instead it has the name of Moses Trod or Sledgate. The track makes a very good link between Wasdale Head and Warnscale Bottom into Buttermere, as well as to Honister. The name 'Sledgate' suggests that sledges, used at Honister mine, were taken this way loaded with slate. One problem with this interpretation is that the common name at the time was trail barrow, not sledge. Sledges were mainly associated with bringing peat down to the valleys and this could well be the origin of the name for this track when it was first used, long before slate was mined commercially at Honister. Even with the aid of horses or ponies it would be virtually impossible to navigate a wooden sledge loaded with slate weighing around 700 pounds (318 kg) across very rough ground, especially when passing around Gable's rock-strewn sides.

A normal practice was to use packhorses and this is the most likely method for taking slate across to Drigg, St Bees or Ravenglass on the coast. An oil painting by James Pyne in the mid-nineteenth century shows people with packhorses on the Trod overlooking Buttermere and Ennerdale. The people could be Victorian travellers but equally could be slate-carriers. Fragments of mined slate have been found on this route over the years most of which have been traced to Ash Ghyll on Honister Crag. Climber R.B. Graham described these finds as clinching archaeological evidence.[3] Mr Johns, Manager of the Buttermere Green Slate Company told Graham that in conversation with old miners he discovered that slate was carried by pack-horse or donkey from the Ash Ghyll part of Honister mine to Drigg via Wasdale, and that this practice began around 1730 and continued until 1851 when the coach road across Honister pass was used to transport slate from the mine. On this evidence the making of the Trod pre-dates an adult Moses.

Although the track has been well-known to local people and to climbers there was no reference to it on early Ordnance Survey maps at the beginning of the nineteenth century, and even a guide-book, *The Thorough Guide to the Lake District* by M.J.B. Baddeley made no mention of the track. In the mid-nineteenth century, Edward (Ned) Nelson of Gatesgarth Farm would speak often about Moses Trod but it must be remembered that tracks and paths at high level were rare at this time, unlike the present day, and any which did exist became major features in the landscape and invariably were there for a specific purpose.

Apart from movement of slate to other parts of the country or abroad, there was early use for the material in the Wasdale valley where no slate exists naturally. Before the mining of slate at Honister, buildings in Wasdale were roofed with split stones. The slate at this time was taken by pony, said to be the sturdy Galloway breed, or pack-horse. Slate came also from a small working in Ennerdale below Scarth Gap; the obvious route from this mine would be down the Ennerdale valley but loads could be taken either over Black Sail Pass or eastward to join the Trod around Gable.

Any slate miners at Honister who had the energy after finishing their day of unremitting toil could cross south-east over Seatoller Fell to the graphite mine waste tips to join other nightly gleaners. Graphite became a major item for smugglers. Often at night on the mine tips above Seathwaite Farm could be seen flickering oil lamps as men and women scrabbled about looking for graphite among the waste. If successful, a nights' work could provide much greater reward than a full weeks work for these people elsewhere. Local people took a considerable risk when 'gleaning' wad from the mine tips which they saw as honest gain. The practice was thought of as stealing and so serious that an act of parliament was passed in 1752 to make the crime a felony; the punishment being imprisonment with hard labour.

The price of graphite at the end of the eighteenth century was thirty shillings a pound; today's value by retail price index is £78.[4] Average earnings for miners in 1800 was nineteen shillings per week; today's value £49. Local people were committing a serious offence by this practice but the mountainsides were difficult to police whether by day or by night. In addition, there were only around thirty policemen for the whole county.[5] Slate miners could take their finds of graphite to Honister to be hidden among the rocks in secret stashes. Miners then had to take the risk of being caught while carrying the 'wad' into Keswick to be sold illicitly over a jar of ale at The Bunch of Grapes public house, now the George Hotel. Alternatively they could ask womenfolk like Sal Robson to move the bounty down the valley, under petticoat-cover. People in Borrowdale have found small stashes of hidden graphite when either digging the ground or re-building dry stone walls. Small pieces of graphite have also been found in the Grisedale forest, some miles to the south of the mine. The most obvious way to dispose of stolen wad would be in a packhorse's side-panniers carrying slate supplies to the coast.

Moses Trod could be reached on the west side of Grey Knotts by going uphill from the graphite mine but the miners would have no time to complete the journey to Wasdale; the only option was to hide the material to be picked up by passing slate carriers. This is why speculation exists that the hut on Gable's north face, discussed in the next section, was used as a storage place. Workers at the Seathwaite mine could also dispose of any illicitly-gained graphite by going up by Sourmilk Gill around Base Brown and on to Green Gable to reach the Gable hut, or join the Trod where again slate carriers could take the wad. This route offered a much safer way for graphite to be delivered to coastal Ports than via Sty Head pass.

Thinking about the controversial Trod; it is curious how the name 'Moses', and 'Aaron' the name of a rock climb below Green Gable, feature on the west side of Gable's north ridge and the name 'Aaron' also exists on the east side. Two men, it is believed, who had their differences on another mountain, Sinai. There is however a theory that the name 'Aaron' applied to the Slack on Gable is really 'Iron' which lies around in the district rather than after some Hebrew character of the past. The name for the rock climb, which came much later, would be simply transferred from the east side.

Speculation about Moses and the Gable Hut

Moses Rigg, by hearsay reputation, can be recognised as Gable's most prominent smuggler and has been associated with the mysterious stone shelter known as the Smuggler's Hut or Smuggler's Retreat, which was to be found on a ledge of Gable's Ennerdale face, better known as Gable Crag, at a height of around 2,800 feet.

Climbers in particular who hear of Gable's hut being used for smugglers to either brew whiskey, keep illicit goods or simply as a look-out dismiss the idea because they claim that the sure-footedness of a climber would be needed to reach the place. The hut could be reached by a scramble up Central Gulley avoiding what non-climbers would call difficult sections, classed as moderate in climbing terms. The hut stood close to grass ledges which offer the easy right-hand exit to the gulley. From close to the ledge on which the hut stood there is a more difficult direct exit which would not have interested Moses, but moving right along the ledge lies a narrow gulley and a scramble can be made to the top of the crag. There is also a rock climb called Smuggler's Chimney but this would be too difficult and strenuous to offer a way to the hut given that an easier alternative lay a short distance to the east in Central Gulley. To reach the hut from the top of the crag a smuggler would need to know the exact starting point where a scree slope descends for around 80 feet, then rock scrambling leads to a wide ledge of loose rock and grass. Here the hut, in its useable state, stood with walls five feet high and a floor area of around nine feet by six feet. The hut's positioning was ideal as a hiding place; extremely difficult to be seen from above at the top of Gable, and could not be seen from below the crag because it was set back against the rock face. To get the correct angle of sight, a person had to move so far away from the crag that the rock of the hut simply merged with the background and could not be seen.

The highly respected Lake District historian William Gershom Collingwood wrote about the hut in an inventory of ancient monuments of Cumbria in 1923, 'on the Ennerdale face of Great Gable, down a scree gully in the centre of the crags from the summit, a ruined hut on a crag platform was the refuge of Moses the smuggler'.[6] Now the site is difficult to locate because there is no sign of a hut ever being there. The hut was discovered on the first day of June 1889 when three climbers: John Wilson Robinson, Walter Parry Hasket Smith and Geoffrey Hastings, climbed up the central gulley.[7] Near the top, on a ledge, there could be seen what remained of a dwelling place with semicircular dry-stone walls, remains of what had been a roof and the floor was roughly flagged. Close to the site stood a small cairn, which had been built as a landmark.

Before the central gulley climb and discovery, Robinson in discussion with Edward (Ned) Nelson, Flockmaster of Gatesgarth Farm, was told, 'that Nelson's Grandfather spoke often about Moses and his private still on Honister Crag and was known to have a secret hiding place for whiskey and no doubt for himself also near the top of Gable, but no one knew where it was'. That Robinson had been given this information before finding the hut on Gable gives some credibility to the claim that the building was used to store illicit whiskey. Also in years later than Moses there was talk of a whiskey still in upper Ennerdale; how far up the valley is not known, but far enough can bring you to Gable itself, where it was said brewing took place.

Moses Rigg who worked in Honister mine was said to use loads of slate as a cover for carrying his mine-brewed whiskey. Like Lanty Slee and Whiskey Walker it is imagined that Moses used pig's bladders to hold the spirit, supposed to be origin of the term 'to have a skin full'. Liquor and the odd bag of graphite could be hidden among the slates being carried around Gable. The most likely use for the hut was as a hidden store for whiskey and graphite.

The idea that whiskey was made in the hut is difficult to accept. Why would anyone haul supplies of water, peat for fuel and ingredients of potatoes or barley up to such a place to make whiskey, when nooks and crannies are to be found below Moses Trod around Brin Crag or Green Gable Crag, not to mention within Honister mine itself? The upper reaches of Honister near the start of Moses Trod offered a number of places where spirits could be made. Various items were needed to make whiskey: a paddle to stir the barley and boiling bog water, a critical process, then after passing through a cooler into a large drum the mix would be fermented with yeast, before being put over a peat fire to begin the distilling. At this stage the vapour would pass into a 'worm' which was coiled copper tubing inserted in a container filled with cold water; here the vapour was condensed. The distilling would be done at least twice. The fire had to be carefully controlled to avoid over-heating and cold water had to be added to the worm. This basic description of what Moses and his illicit whiskey-making colleagues did helps to demonstrate how difficult it would have been to produce whiskey in a hut high up on Gable Crag.

Naturally strict secrecy was an essential part of this illicit business so it is not surprising that very few people knew of any stashes held by Moses. So successful was Moses in this respect that finding information about him is extremely difficult, unlike Lanty Slee, across in Langdale, who was named in court records and who become notorious in his lifetime. Information about Moses is so scant that his very existence in the flesh has been questioned; was he a fictional character made up from an amalgam of lesser smugglers at the time? He features in the novel, *George Ashbury* by O.S. Macdonell, a novel set around Honister mine and Buttermere. Macdonell knew the area and its people very well and though writing in the early 1930s, some years after the events, he could have talked with locals who had parents living at the time of Moses Rigg. The oral tradition was still very strong among the valley dwellers throughout the nineteenth century and into the twentieth, allowing Macdonell to tap into stories about smuggling.

One of the most reliable sources of information about Moses Rigg was George Abraham, climber and pioneer mountain photographer based in Keswick. Abraham, born in 1872, was old enough to have met Dan Tyson who claimed to have worked with Moses Rigg and was convinced that the account of 'Gable Whiskey' was true; Abraham told Harry Griffin, climber and Guardian Country Diary writer, that at the end of the nineteenth century the hut had a roof, stone-flagged floor and showed signs of containing a still. Mrs Enid Wilson, daughter of George Abraham, also recalls her father saying that Moses making whiskey was common knowledge in the dale. Abraham was 93 when he died in 1965, so some friends he spoke to about seeing the Gable hut as a near-complete dwelling, and of links with Moses Rigg, could be alive today.

Another source of Rigg's activities was Auld Will Ritson, Landlord of the Wasdale Head Inn from 1856, when the first licence was granted, until 1879 when Dan Tyson took over as landlord. Ritson, born in 1808, was described as a man who has much natural cleverness and simple honesty such as no education can bestow. Ritson told Richard Jopson from Thorneythwaite Farm how he used to see Moses come around Gable with his pony and how he would hide his liquor in one of the many piles of stones at Wasdale Head. This was the position when Moses Rigg was at work; his interest lay in graphite and home-made whiskey: graphite because it was still very valuable and whiskey because it carried duty, in the making and the selling; Moses could avoid paying tax on both.

Before the Inn was established at Wasdale there was still the drinking of what was called malt liquor at a Wasdale Head farmhouse where visitors could stay but which did not hold a licence. Will Ritson himself was fined £20; a large sum in those days, when he gave liquor to a lady who had fainted. This was an act of deception on her part because she was the wife of an Excise Officer. Even a poem was written about the lack of alcohol at Wasdale Head:[8]

> 'There was a house in Wasdale,
> Where the only thing they wanted was ale;
> You could have milk and water,
> But not ale or porter,
> At that snug little house in Wasdale.

At this time there were five occupied houses at Wasdale Head with around thirty folk, including farmers and shepherds who welcomed a drink, as well as any passing walker. The poem refers to the lack of suitable drink at the valley head after Ritson suffered his fine. What liquor passed through lips came from smugglers; in from the coast; through Eskdale from Langdale, or over Moses Trod.

The boy Ritson who remembered seeing Moses Rigg, grew to be a well-known story teller who, it is said, could be quite a stranger to the truth, but that is not a reason for saying that his recollection of Moses Rigg was untrue. At around this time on the continent a well-known writer Alexander Dumas was writing about Marie Paradis, a working maid in Chamonix, the first woman to climb Mont Blanc and his account has been largely dismissed as unreliable because he was a story teller. There is no reason to assume that story tellers are incapable of telling the truth when recounting, first-hand, events of the day.

If Moses did distill whiskey at the Gable hut, or simply held supplies there, it would have been easy for him to descend from near Green Gable to the upper reaches of the graphite mine and exchange the liquor for a parcel of graphite. A named place where wad could be hidden is the Hanging Stone on the side of Base Brown, where a broken crag and large boulders can be seen after reaching the top of Sourmilk Gill. Moses could meet carriers of the stolen 'wad', or collect from hiding places near the stone high above the uppermost levels of the graphite mine; beyond the arm of the law and beyond the notice of guards posted at the mine guardhouse, which had been constructed in 1800. The wad could then be taken, along with more liquor, on his route to the coast or a deal done somewhere in Wasdale.

For fit, strong Moses the route to Windy Gap and up the central gully of Gable Crag to his secret hideaway would have been an easy task compared with his normal work at Honister mine. The original people to use the hut, and indeed build it in the first place, would be either shepherds who built shielings of similar construction or slate workers at Honister mines; in both cases men who were happy to move around crags and far stronger than most people are today, including climbers. Moses and slate workers like him used to hang from a rigging of chains to chisel shot-holes in vertical walls of slate, many feet above ground level; described by Harriett Martineau as, 'hanging like summer-spiders quivering from the eaves of a house'. Reaching the chosen site high on Gable Crag and building the hut would provide no major difficulties for such men.

In many remote places of the country whiskey was made illicitly, the general idea being that if porridge can be made from oats, then whiskey can be made from barley; what could be more innocent than that? Housing for the whiskey stills was normally in stone huts very similar to the building on Gable but with one very important addition, running water nearby. Water supply on the Ennerdale side of Gable is below Stone Cove in a stream that becomes the River Liza, a long haul from there to the hut, and water which is not as good for making whiskey as that to be found in the peat-bogs near Fleetwith Pike. One place for distilling whiskey on Gable, suggested to me by a local living in Seatoller many years ago was at the foot of Gable Crag near the start of a rock climb called 'Engineer's Chimney'; a water supply is not too far away, reasonably close to Moses Trod, and the hut, but on reflection still an unlikely site given the alternatives available.

The true reason for building the Gable hut will probably never be known. The use as a hideaway and look-out during the earlier Jacobite Rebellion of 1715 and as a bolt-hole for the Jacobite, James Radclyffe Third Earl of Derwentwater, while plausible is again unlikely because the rebels, some recruited from within Lakeland, passed down the east of the district from Penrith to Kendal, before going on finally to defeat at Preston.[9]

An important clue to the hut's possible age is the time it has taken to disappear. The walls of Gable hut were in reasonable condition when first discovered in 1889, but stood only around one foot high 40 years later and by 1995 had gone completely. Just over 100 years from being a clearly recognisable hut to obliteration. Around 100 years before it was discovered by climbers is a reasonable assumption for its date of construction, or late eighteenth century to early nineteenth. This places its usable existence at a time when Moses Rigg was a young man. A much earlier date for construction is unlikely given the almost complete building found in 1889.

The possible use of slate transport as a cover for the movement of illicit goods eventually came to an end when slate could be taken down the west side of Honister Hause, past Buttermere, to ports further north along the coast. This was a route far easier for Excise men to control than across Gable to Wasdale. From that year, Moses Trod would be used no more for transporting slate and the Gable hut would remain unvisited for around forty years.

The mystery of the Gable hut, when it existed, cannot be considered in isolation but needs to be seen as part of a hut-building practice around the district. Much has been written about the hut on Gable, but it is not alone as a structural mystery high up on a Lakeland crag. At a similar height to the Gable hut stands another stone dwelling, though smaller, again near the top of a major crag, on Bowfell at the head of the Langdale valley. Climbers on the Bowfell Buttress rock climb could visit the place but it is not wise for walkers to explore the area. So who built and used this hut? As a look-out it is unsurpassed, but looking for what? Could either smugglers Lanty Slee or Whiskey Walker who would pass the crag from time to time have built this eerie? The general feeling is that shepherds were responsible.

Across to the east of the district, above Thirlmere, were found two bronze armlets dated as late Celtic or early Iron Age, typically worn by a young female of the time. The find was made on the west side of the mere, close to the foot of a crag just south of Launchy Gill; there are all the signs of being dropped from above.[10] On further inspection of the crag a made path was traced to a small flat area on the crag with all the appearances of an old inhabited site. Anything dropped from the ledge would land close to where the armlets were found. At this point, imagination takes over to go beyond looking for reasons why these people built dwelling places half-way up crags; at the time it was suggested that there could have been romantic reasons for the armlets being there; a young couple making use of a secluded shelter, 'up there on the crag'.

Also in the Thirlmere valley on Castle Crag there is a rock buttress, where despite the danger of falling rock a small hut similar to the Gable hut has been built at around 800 feet, 200 feet below the summit. This is a substantial dwelling with walls 2 feet 6 inches thick. W.G. Collingwood pointed out that this hut and those like it cannot be dated without exploration and finds.[11]

The building of huts in especially remote places is an extension of shielings found mainly in Scotland but in Cumbria too. The name seems to come from the Scandinavian, *Skali* meaning hut or shelter. They were built as early as the twelfth century to help manage the farming of sheep and cattle on the fells and higher mountain sides.[12] Shielings were similar in shape, size and structure to the Gable hut. Most shielings have distinct characteristics: walls are between two and three feet thick, rectangular seventeen to forty feet by nine to twenty-five feet and side walls below six feet high with normally a turf-covered apex roof. There were no windows and even valley-level cottages around Gable would be without windows, well into the eighteenth century. Below Gable, in the Ennerdale Valley, remains of buildings have been found at around 1,600 feet in Great Cove at the head of Deep Gill; immediately above the remains is the summit of Haycock.[13] There is evidence here of a dwelling site which had been cleared to make grazing pasture. There is no sign of mining near the cove so the conclusion must be that shielings had been built here for summer use. Lower down in Ennerdale there are around fourteen ruins of huts which follow a shieling description, clustered above Smithy Beck to the north of Ennerdale Water. With veins of haematite in Ennerdale and signs of an iron bloomery at the foot of the beck and ironstone workings around 1,600 feet above make it most likely that these huts were miners' dwellings.

To be seen as shielings in the true meaning of the word, buildings need to be for pastoral use, where farmers looked after livestock on higher ground in summer. Another working to the north of Ennerdale Valley is Knockmurton mine near Cogra Moss; here were found clog-prints in the mud of the mine, fresh as the day they were made. There are two further remains which are more likely to be for pastoral use on the south side of Ennerdale above Revelin Crag near Ben Gill. Another shieling not far from Gable stands to the north of Blackbeck Tarn near Warnscale Beck; an upper pasture for Gatesgarth Farm in the Buttermere valley. Shielings were also known as convenient romantic trysts for young couples in the days when parental restrictions down in the valley were strong. Another use for shielings, apart from pastoral and romantic, was to hide smugglers and their goods. A woman was charged at Loweswater court on October 18, 1519 charged with harbouring thieves in such a place.[14] Evidence exists of a shieling above Rosthwaite in Borrowdale. The building lies below High Scawdel and close to Scaleclose coppice.

We do know that over the years many people will have had practice in building dry-stone huts, as living quarters for slate workers on Honister Crag and much earlier down in the Ennerdale valley for iron miners and farmers; the Gable hut can be seen as an extension of this work, simply higher and even more remote.

Thinking of Moses Rigg, who worked at Honister mine and found time to make and carry away illicit whiskey and trade in graphite it is difficult to see how he found time to sleep or conduct any form of social life. The slate, when taken by pack horse along the trod and around Gable must have provided a welcome diversion from a day in the mine, but still hard work and he needed to find time for his 'other business'.

Moses, if he could return today would find some activity at the mine, but not the extremely hard work he had experienced. He would find no need for smugglers with legitimate whiskey readily available on both sides of the Hause. Graphite is no longer prized and salt is no longer of interest to Excise Officers. All the excitement would seem to have gone out of life. Probably his biggest surprise would be to watch people arrive at the Hause in square metal boxes on wheels, to walk a route named after him. Then walk up Gable on a track not far from his hut. As a final note on this speculation, a writer of extensive works on the Lake District, William Palmer, had little doubt about Moses Rigg and his smuggling, or of his connection with the track around Gable.[15]

Moses, Lanty, Walker and Sal had a friend in high places; John Ruskin knew of smuggling activities in Lakeland and had his own views on the subject. He subscribed to a work by a Devon-based smuggler, William Rattenbury. In a note to the smuggler he pointed out that he was not a smuggler himself, but had great respect for smugglers and he held that 'frontier duties of any kind the foolishest and wickedest ways of raising money that can be practised by Governments'.

References

[1] Palmer, W.T. 1945. *Wanderings in Lakeland.* London: Skeffington & Sons, Ltd.

[2] Denwood, M and Thompson, T.W. 1950. *A Lafter O' Farleys in T Dialects O' Lakeland, 1760-1945.* Carlisle: The Lakeland Dialect Society.

[3] Graham, R.B. 1923. *Moses Trod.* The Journal of The Fell and Rock Climbing Club. Vol. 6 (2) pp.206-212.

4   Officer, L.H. 2008. *Purchasing Power of the British Pound from 1264 to 2007*. MeasuringWorth.com

5   Marshall, J.D. 1970. *Some aspects of the social history of 19th century Cumbria (11) Crime, police, morals of the countryman.* Transactions of the Cumberland and Westmorland Antiquarian and Archaeological Society. pp.221-245

6   Collingwood, W.G. 1923. *An inventory of the ancient monuments of Cumberland.* Transactions of the Cumberland and Westmorland Antiquarian and Archaeological Society. p.263.

7   Robinson, J.W. 1904. *Smuggler's Hold on Great Gable.* Transactions of the Cumberland and Westmorland Antiquarian and Archaeological Society. pp.351-352.

8   Payne, J. 1858. *Leaves from Lakeland.* London: Hamilton Adams & Co.

9   Oates, J. 2006. *Cumberland and Westmorland in the Jacobite Rebellion of 1715.* Transactions of the Cumberland and Westmorland Antiquarian Archaeological Society. pp. 89-101.

10 Collingwood, W.G. 1904. *Two Bronze Armlets from Thirlmere.* Transactions of the Cumberland and Westmorland Antiquarian and Archaeological Society. pp.80-84.

11 Collingwood, W.G. 1916. *The Castle Rock of St. John's Vale.* Transactions of the Cumberland and Westmorland Antiquarian Archaeological Society. pp.224-228.

12 Ramm, H.G. et al.1970. *Shielings and Bastles.* London: Her Majesty's Stationery Office.

13 Fletcher, W. 1986. *Deep Gill Ennerdale.* Transactions of the Cumberland and Westmorland Antiquarian Archaeological Society. p.248.

14 Carlisle Records Office (CRO). D\Lec /299/16m.15.

15 Palmer, W.T. 1937. *More Odd Corners in the English Lake District,* p.106. London: Skeffington & Sons Ltd.

IX. Romantic View

Why romantic?

Romantic views of mountains in the Lake District are generally expected to come from writers and artists during the eighteenth and nineteenth centuries. Over these years the flow of visitors seeking out landscape views steadily increased in what has been called the, 'romantic invasion of Lakeland'. Today, a romantic approach to mountains and valleys is seldom shown openly even though deep-down, some walkers and climbers are likely to have romantic feelings equally as strong as those expressed 200 years ago.

Standing below a Napes' ridge on Gable waiting to do a rock climb or walking the traverse path on a cold December day with sleet sweeping across in the wind, climbers or walkers may be heard to say, 'what am I doing here?' Romantic views could not be further from their minds. On days of the most severe weather people will be seen on Gable, sitting at the summit crouched beside rocks offering only meagre shelter, while eating lunch. Ascents and descents are made in thick mist when very little can be seen, yet even under these conditions people are drawn to its flanks, often with the hope that sun will shine through the cloud cover, but if this does not happen a day spent on Gable will almost invariably be felt worthwhile.

Memorial Sundays seem to collect the worst of weather, yet hundreds of people struggle to the top of Gable from many different directions. The main reason for making this journey is to attend the memorial service, but there are memorials in many remote places which do not attract people in such numbers in the harshest weather. The last time I witnessed this gathering was with my son; we followed the north ridge with wind and snow making it difficult to see ahead and there were walkers all around us with one aim, to be on the summit by 11am. On that day along the ridge from Honister Pass to the top we did not see anyone turn back.

For people returning to Gable the ascent can be for the second time, third time or many times. During a foot and mouth disease outbreak, when fells and mountains were closed to visitors, one walker wrote to a national newspaper that he went up Great Gable every Easter and for the first time in many years he could not be there. He was speaking for other street-bound walkers and climbers around the country.

Although the romantic age is seen to be well in the past, over 200 years ago, it is still possible to experience wild and extravagant images on Gable; even when distant views are not to be seen. There can be a magic around you when rocks suddenly appear and then are gone; fairy-like, rarefied moments among the crags with almost vertical drops at your feet, as clouds swirl below and familiar distant objects may be seen for only seconds before they too are gone. There are wonders to be seen close at hand and even in minute detail. Small clumps of moss and heather lying among glistening rocks, as mini-waterfalls trickle over them; a scene to be enjoyed, a rarefied almost fairy-unreal setting, wild beyond every-day life. Our experiences of this kind can be seen as romantic. Mountain writer Walt Unsworth described Gable as being, 'as much romance as reality like the Matterhorn symbolises the Alps so too Gable symbolises Lakeland'.[1]

One justified reason for the ascent of Gable is to enjoy probably the most outstanding view in Lakeland, in which case it becomes, arguably, the most outstanding view in England. Pilgrimages to witness this view have been made day after day, and since around 1945 have been made by a steadily increasing number of people. Between the wars, walkers and climbers would be seen but much less frequently and many hours could be spent there without seeing anyone.

Over the years road access to the mountain's valleys has become easier and people have more time to escape from their confining urban life. However, this does not explain why people make such an effort to visit the summit, only that they have the time and means to get there more easily than before. One strong reason for repeated visits to Gable is that the mountain can become close, like a friend, through its associations with people in the past. People known to us personally, known through word-of-mouth or through various readings. 'Oh my Great Uncle Fred came here by the light of a full moon after a party at Gatesgarth, sometime in the 1920s' is a comment heard on the summit of Gable and many more 'associations' of this kind will have been exchanged over the years. Association in this way is particularly common among climbers; they can feel closer to those who climbed on Gable and who have been read about in books and journals. The climbs on the Napes are so distinctive with holds unchanging since the first climbers took to these crags that it is easy to imagine Owen Glynne Jones, Abraham brothers or Godfrey Solly grasping those very holds and being in the very same position as yourself, only over 100 years earlier. There is here a direct link with the past in very human terms.

Artists' influence
There is a strong case for saying that familiarity with wild places came first to the general public through the work of artists, rather than writers or poets. To quote Paul Shepard from his book *Man in the Landscape*,[2] 'the conversion of our natural surroundings into

scenery was a milestone in the history of human perception which signified not only an enlargement of our aesthetic experience, but also a profound change in attitude toward the physical environment'. The conversion was a slow process, many years passed before artists began to represent wild nature for its own sake, rather than as simply a backdrop to some human activity. There is an assumption that all people before this time lacked such insight and instead viewed what was seen as wild and terrifying, to be avoided whenever possible. This assumption is based on limited evidence, is difficult to justify and refers only to certain people in the Western World. Chinese were sensitive to mountains and wilderness for many centuries before our romantic period. A major question is why nature was revered and indeed loved by early Chinese civilization while in the west it was either feared or ignored. There has been some suggestion that the Chinese had strong spiritual links with wild places, particularly mountains and desert wastes; being places where they would retreat for ritual worship.

Artists who sketched or painted visited Cumbria in the early eighteenth century. Based on the Royal Academy catalogues, some of the most productive artistic activity took place in the Lake District between 1770 and 1790, when fifty works were produced; there were fewer works of art during the nineteenth century than before 1800. The busy years for artists were at a time when people of means were planning what was called the Grand Tour, but political unrest in Europe brought the tours temporarily to an end; the reaction was to look for adventures at home. Journeys to remote Westmorland, Cumberland and Scotland became a form of mini-tour when compared with their journeys planned for Europe.

Works from early artists who visited the area were either commissioned as pictures or as sketches to be converted by an engraver for use as book or magazine illustrations, before the days of photography. The term 'picturesque' was used to describe the viewing of wild landscape as a series of pictures. This approach did much to make people more familiar with wild country, to lessen what previously had been a fear of the unknown. Strangely, early Neolithic settlers saw the mountain region as a source of livelihood which held little fear for them otherwise it is highly unlikely that they would have behaved so adventurously on the high ground of Lakeland. Later people thought of wild places as 'waste' and obstacles to progress. For this reason, mountains were avoided and being unknown became feared.

Few of the early artists identified with place when naming their work. Up to the beginning of the nineteenth century it was rare for landscape painters to use place names. Most works were produced in kit-form mainly from imagination and a need was felt to put the randomness of nature into a more orderly scene. It was William Gilpin who said that what is sublime or beautiful in nature did not always work as art, so gave the term picturesque beauty to the kind of beauty that can be captured well in a picture. Gilpin wrote a book purely about trees in forests and woodlands and how they relate chiefly to picturesque beauty.[3] Writer Coleridge, probably with tongue in cheek, called it 'pikteresk'.

Gable, together with close neighbouring mountains, was largely neglected by artists from the beginning of the picturesque period, and even after the arrival of the 'romantics' through to the early twentieth century. The early artists were attracted to Lakeland because picturesque views were to be found on almost every corner as they passed along tranquil valleys, and mountains for their own sake were largely ignored. Gable does not fully satisfy the requirements of the picturesque. Very little vegetation, steep, aloof and, in those days, was inspiring to very few hardy walkers. To be appreciated fully, Gable needs to be viewed as an individual mountain.

Various artists developed what could be considered picturesque landscape which included pastoral and rural scenes; Claude, Rosa and Poussin were early promoters of this form of painting. Another, lesser-known but important landscape artist was Gaspard Dughet. Landscape paintings by Dughet are in galleries throughout the world, rather unkindly he is best known as Nicholas Poussin's brother-in-law. Dughet and other landscape artists at the time took liberties in their work; composing pictures to resemble no particular object and would have had little interest in Great Gable or neighbour Scafell as mountains alone; they would be seen only as background. For some reason, probably better known to art historians, artists in Europe as early as the fifteenth century produced paintings purely of mountains without any extraneous 'props'. In Britain, mountains would only be included as backdrop together with woods, streams, smaller cliffs and the odd random rocks here and there. Somewhere in the scene would be farm animals, dogs, and people either tending their flock or simply as part of the 'picture' in the artist's mind. In Britain one of the first artists to adopt this approach was Richard Wilson; John Ruskin said that English landscape art began with Richard Wilson. A good example of Wilson's work is the painting of Cader Idris around 1774. What could be a scene of stark wildness has in the foreground carefully placed cattle and a human figure.

Art is not nature; a picture represents the idea of picturesque, normally someone's creation of what they would like to see. Wordsworth questioned the value of the picturesque whenever an artist introduced extraneous features into an otherwise relatively natural scene; probably what he meant when speaking of 'inferior wonders of an artist's hand'. Wordsworth encouraged people to see the simple and beautiful scenery as it is, rather than through pictorial conventions. Another writer who disliked buildings in Lakeland and development of artificial landscape was Sir Uvedale Price. In his *Essay on the Picturesque*, in 1794, he said we should appreciate how things grow slowly and naturally without 'improvement', and how this should be seen as a virtue in society as well. John Ruskin too did not favour picturesque set-piece views, but needed to know something of the topography, landscape and geology which allowed him a number of perspectives of a scene before him, which is reflected in his book *Modern Painters.*

For those who truly love wildness there can be no substitute for being there; it is then that a multitude of feelings crowd in, prompted by time of year, time of day, passing cloud shadows, changing colours, past memories of earlier visits together with sounds and smells around you. Above all a lack of orderliness is experienced, so different from the work of artists in the eighteenth century who tried to impose formal patterns and symmetry upon nature and who disliked what they called 'uncultivated waste'.

There is great art to be seen among the mountains, especially if we take time to view rock formations or even individual rocks; we can absorb their many subtle colours and shapes, depending upon the particular angle being viewed. Gordon Stainforth makes the point that if a man-made sculpture, a copy of a prominent rock pinnacle on one of our mountains, was displayed in Hyde Park it would be considered by many to be an impressive work of art, but standing as a natural feature among mountains we do not see it as a work of art. 'We see these rock shapes but when you stop and move closer to touch and explore the many faces, cracks and pinnacles you see in a completely different way, not as an artist but as a true lover of mountains.'[4] Artists of the picturesque would see a single rock as barren and featureless, possibly even ugly. There are groups of rocks among the Napes on Gable that in colour and form surpass anything I could hope to see as painting or sculpture in any gallery whether in London, Paris or Venice.

In the eighteenth and nineteenth centuries, travellers and followers of the picturesque would even turn their backs to the scene being admired so that they could view, over their shoulder, through what is now mistakenly known as a Claude Glass, The plano-convex mirror normally used was four to five inches across and known as a Landscape Glass, Landscape Mirror or otherwise as the Gray Glass.[5] The mirror could be backed with black foil for use on sunny days or with gold or silver foil for dull days. Sometimes a transparent tinted filter was used and this was known as the Claude Glass, named after Claude Lorrain. Some visitors on coming across a view could be heard to say with a flourish, 'give me my glass, I must throw a tint over these scenes of beauty'. Early travellers to Lakeland ready with their glass to frame a view is little different from our present practice of

LMS

SPEND YOUR HOLIDAYS IN THE LAKE DISTRICT

ILLUSTRATED GUIDE FREE FROM ANY LMS ENQUIRY OFFICE

MONTAGUE B BLACK

LMS "THE BEST WAY" SERIES No 25   McCORQUODALE & Co LIMITED

previous page: *Napes Needle Great Gable. LMS Poster*
M.B Black, 1923. Permission of Science and Society Library

Gable from Sprinkling Tarn
Permission of Ann Bowker

Herdwick Family overlooking Wasdale
Permission of Ann Bowker

Gable Crag from Green Gable showing site of hut
Permission of Ann Bowker

View down Great Hell Gate. Great Gable
Permission of Andrew Leaney

Gable from Kirk Fell showing Moses Trod
Permission of Ann Bowker

Ennerdale Valley from Gable
Permission of Ann Bowker

Gable Sphinx with ridge in profile
Permission of Andrew Leaney

right: *Kern Knotts after the rock fall*
Permission of Andrew Craig

Memorial plaque, Gable summit
Permission of Ann Bowker

looking through a viewfinder or at the small screen of a digital camera.

Using one or both glasses visitors could frame the view within what could be seen as a small, composed picture. The place to stand was also important; a series of viewing places around the district became known as 'stations' and travellers visited stations recommended by Thomas West. These stations were included on one of the early maps produced by local man Peter Crosthwaite who made the first attempt to produce a map of Lakeland to a scale of three inches to the mile.

I still have this idea of stations in mind when thinking about the best places to view Gable; not through a glass, but taking in the whole experience including the immediate surroundings. Early travellers sought out the 'Stations' prescribed by West but today some readers will have their own favourite viewing places. One that gives a spectacular view of Gable is at the top of Lingmell, but not popular despite being close to a busy route up Scafell Pike. On a clear day, standing beside the large summit cairn of Lingmell, Gable dominates the view and the traverse paths below the Napes and across Great and Little Hell Gates can be traced, and with field glasses individual rock climbs can be identified. From this station there is an added bonus of the airy view straight down into the recesses of Piers Gill.

Another impressive Gable-viewing station, to see the mountain rearing up before you, is from the highest point of Kirk Fell, or at a position around 100 feet down the path on the east side. A station at Great Round How near Blackbeck Tarn is high on the list for an imposing view of Gable Crag on the north side but is seen best in good early morning or late evening light. The reaction of some viewers at other times can be like that from my wife saying, 'what is that black thing over there?' pointing to Gable in an unfavourable light. A station at the west end of Innominate Tarn on Haystacks provides a close panorama with Gable at its centre. Pillar Mountain too provides a dramatic view, but unless the station is carefully chosen Gable can be elusive. Harry Griffin, in one of his *Guardian Country Diaries*, described Gable from Pillar as peeping over Kirk Fell like an atomic explosion. Stations do not have to be close to the mountain; a well-known distant-view and a favourite for Wainwright, is at Orrest Head above Windermere; there the prominent shape of Gable lies at the centre in a panorama of mountains. To one side can be seen Scafell Pikes, Crinkle Crags, Cold Pike, Wetherlam and on to the Coniston tops. To the other side of Gable lies Pike of Stickle, Harrison Stickle, Pavey Ark and on to High Raise. At times there can be surprising views of Gable when in the middle of a distant village, and not expected, such as near Loweswater village hall. Also nearby, the curved shore of Crummock Water below Mellbreak was a working station for the Grasmere-based painter William Heaton Cooper who wrote, 'this is the place I enjoy more than anywhere else in the world'.[6] In one of Cooper's works from this station, Gable is the farthest mountain to be seen seven miles away. The whole scene, with Rannerdale Knott prominent, surely cannot be surpassed for tranquillity and grandeur. Coleridge commented on a distant view he had from near Greta Hall, in a letter to scientist Humphrey Davey in 1800; describing Gable as 'distinct in deepest sablest blue'. When thinking of favourite stations to view Gable which are previously known to us or of those we still hope to find, dwell on the words of Wordsworth:

> 'Full many a spot
> Of hidden beauty have I chanced to espy,
> Among the mountains.'

Numerous paintings and engravings of scenes in Cumberland were produced throughout the eighteenth and nineteenth centuries, but rarely near Gable. One of the first etching and line engraving to be done in Lakeland was done by William Bellers in the mid-eighteenth century. His view up the valley of Borrowdale became the first to make the mountainous views of the area more accessible to the general public. Around 1800 Thomas Girtin, a well-known watercolour artist produced a picture of Borrowdale, it is believed without ever being in the valley, based on a sketch by George Beaumont.[7] In 1841, William Turner of Oxford captured Gable as seen from the flanks of Scafell, which means he spent time there in sketching and went there prepared for such work. The other Turner, Joseph Mallord William, spent time at Sty Head to paint a view of Lingmell, Scafell and Mickledore, but did not finish the work. When Constable stood on Esk Hause, Gable was either in cloud or he felt it not worth a mention, the mountain not having the necessary picturesque qualities. He did paint a scene set in more picturesque Borrowdale in 1806 and managed to include Great Gable. Constable made up to seventy sketches in the area, but did say that the solitude of mountains oppressed his spirits. Constable spent two months in the Lake District, but clearly he was a flatlander who needed the excitement of Suffolk. Ford Madox Brown an artist associated with the Pre-Raphaelite Brotherhood, though not a member, visited the Lake District in 1848 and crossed Sty Head into Wasdale. The artist was at the foot of Gable and known for painting landscapes; at one time had made a considerable effort to include sheep in a painting. Had he been sufficiently moved, we may have had a famous picture: '*Herdwicks on Great Gable* by Ford Madox Brown, a landscape painting in the Pre-Raphaelite style'. An opportunity missed by this magnificent artist, and a loss to all lovers of Gable and of the Pre-Raphaelites. Brown continued over Sty Head into Wasdale and eventually walked through Eskdale to Windermere where he painted a scene from the northern end of the mere, in stormy weather.

The view of Gable from Wasdale Head, a pen and wash drawing done in 1781 by Joseph Farington, probably better known as a diarist, is a wonderfully true creation of the mountain and its valley head at this time. Over the years this view has been drawn or painted numerous times; one of my favourites is the watercolour, used for the cover of this book, by Alfred Heaton Cooper, father of well-known Lakeland artist William Heaton Cooper and grandfather of equally well-known artist Julian Heaton Cooper.

In the nineteenth century, images of Lakeland's wilder parts came to the general public, mainly through the work of artists who 'exhibited' in railway carriages, best known being Charles Knight and Leonard Russell Squirrell. The poster of Napes Needle, reproduced in this book (see page 129), is by railway-artist Montague Birrell Black for the London, Midland and Scottish Railway (LMS). Railway-art could be seen framed, normally in a set of five or six on the walls of each train compartment, at a time when railway travel was a civilized experience.

One artist to work in Gable's upper valleys was Thomas Allom who, in the mid-nineteenth century, made drawings to be reproduced as book engravings. An intriguing picture is of Honister pass and crag showing a gun battle in progress; not at the time but taken from an event around 350[8] years earlier. The image follows closely a description of a battle on Honister pass between men of Borrowdale and a gang of freebooters from Scotland, the Graemes. The Scottish family were like pirates raiding to take cattle, sheep or whatever they could find. The Borrowdale men lay in waiting above the track and can be seen in the picture. As the battle continued some of the gang fled down the Buttermere side which again can be seen by anyone looking closely at the picture. The son of the clan leader was killed and buried close to the track. A picture of a well-known view of Gable from Stickle Tarn was presented to the Tate Gallery by Lady Holroyd in 1918; the image was painted in 1912 by her husband Charles Holroyd.

Artists over the past fifty years have given Gable far more attention; being painted or sketched purely as a mountain. Sketches by Wainwright, in his guidebook to the Western Fells, show Gable from north, east, south and west and in great detail from the summit and along its ridges. It seems possible that if Wainwright had been inclined towards rock climbing he, like William Heaton Cooper, could have provided illustrations for the guide books to rock climbs published by the Fell and Rock Climbing Club of the English Lake District. William Heaton Cooper's accurate, detailed line drawings of climbs on Gable are one of the highlights and pleasure of *A Rock Climbing Guide Book to Great Gable, Green Gable, Kirk Fell, Yewbarrow and Buckbarrow.*[9] Cooper's drawings of The Napes, East Napes, Kern Knotts, Tophet Bastion, Abbey Buttress and Gable Crag provide a fine collection of images, illustrating Gable's rock. They offer a detailed pictorial record of rocks which have been a delight to generations of climbers. A rock climber himself, if the rock is climbable in Lakeland there is a good chance that William Heaton Cooper will have drawn it. He captured better than anyone the splintered nature of Gable's rock faces, both in drawings, like that of Tophet Bastion, and as water colour in the view between the steep side walls of Needle Gulley.

Gable sits still for hours to be painted from all points of the compass which, when done, produces numerous views, all quite different. Gable in its fine isolation provides the one and only subject in a scene which is strongly characteristic of the sublime view of landscape. Gable has no need of props in the form of animals, forests, cottages, streams or people.

Over the past 100 years, artists in oil or water colour have frequently produced work where Gable is the sole subject. A prolific artist of landscape, George Graham, produced *Great Gable* described in The New Age magazine of 1918 as, 'clean rain-swept landscape, quite beautifully done'. Scenes of Gable from Wastwater come from Jim Ridout and his daughter Emma. A particularly fine watercolour is of Gable in winter from near Esk Hause by Neil Barlow.

Now photography as art brings us a very high standard of Gable images, which build on those magnificent black and white masterpieces from the plate cameras of George and Ashley Abraham, taken on the Napes and Ennerdale face of Gable. Equally good black and white images come from the camera of the late Fay Godwin, in particular a fine view of Gillercomb Head from Green Gable. The internet now gives mountain-lovers an almost daily 'fix' of views; in Lakeland we can rely upon Ann Bowker and Andrew Leaney to produce fine images, and occasionally either photographer will provide a treat of photographs from one of their days on Gable.

Writers' influence
When the work of early artists became more generally known, visitors came to witness these scenes at first hand and a few were brave enough to walk among the mountains and even go to the top of Skiddaw or Helvellyn. Among these visitors came writers and poets who collectively could be said to move from the picturesque to the romantic. Writers and poets settled in Lakeland either permanently or for extended periods. At any one time there could be locals Dorothy and William Wordsworth with residents De Quincy at Grasmere, Coleridge and Southey at Keswick and John Wilson at Ellery, Orrest Head. Some romantics came from outside Cumberland and Westmorland, similar to the earlier artists, each a stranger and foreigner. There were exceptions: Susannah Blamire and Catherine Gilpin who collaborated in writing verse, Dorothy and William Wordsworth and William Gilpin all belonged to the Lake District.

The romantics had arrived; there were still pictures conforming to what represented the picturesque in the appreciation of landscape, but the words of prose and poetry added more to the natural ideal of wildness. The early artists, and the romantics who followed them, wandered around the Lake District and could be said to be the first people to view wild places as subjects of beauty, or at least be the first to make such ideas accessible to the general public. One of the earliest travellers to the Lakes, who made a brave attempt to see the wilder mountains to the west of the area and write about the experience, was Ralph Thoresby in September 1694.[10] Though well before the romantics, he helped, through his writings, to make the wilder western features of the district more accessible. Thoresby crossed both Wrynose and Hardknott passes and was surprised to find a castle, later known as a fort, where he thought the Romans had never visited. Both passes were described as, 'really mighty dangerous, terrible and tedious'. Thoresby writes that Fell Foot, at the approach to Wrynose, should be called Hell-Foot. Despite these feelings he did confess to findng the country beyond Hardknott, at Dalegarth, at least, pleasant.

Soon after Thoresby's adventure other early travellers who recorded their views on Lakeland were Celia Fiennes and Daniel Defoe. Fiennes saw the district, while riding from Lancaster to Carlisle in 1698; the country was described as 'desart and barren rocky hills' and 'very terrible'.[11] Feines, on seeing the rough dwellings where people lived thought them more suitable for cattle, 'sad little huts made up of drye walls' and interpreted what she saw as showing the laziness of locals. This can be taken as an inexcusable comment coming from someone who knew only wealth and travelled with servants and had no idea of what life was like for these people; her father held a high position in Cromwell's army. No attempt was made to visit the wilder Lakeland; observations from this Lady on dwellings at Wasdale Head, as Harriet Martineau did many years later, would have been interesting. Defoe who passed through the eastern part of Lakeland in 1724 recorded feelings similar to Fiennes but without the criticism. He simply felt the hills had an 'inhospitable terror in them'.[12] Ideal landscape for Defoe was one that had some productive use, where he could see people at work. If Fiennes and Defoe had viewed Gable, there is little doubt that both would have been repulsed by the mountain.

A number of well-known writers and poets visited Lakeland, in the eighteenth century but, unlike Thoresby earlier, they avoided the central area. Like artists at the time their focus was on the valley running north from Ambleside over Dunmail Raise and sometimes they would venture up Helvellyn or to the top of Skiddaw by pony or mule. That Gable had to be ascended on foot must have been a strong deterrent to the early traveller. Even maps in use, especially older versions by John Speed, did not show the main summits, some showed only Skiddaw. Donald's map of Cumberland in 1774, showing the area around Sty Head, does not name Gable, even though it is shown clearly in relief on the map. A few visitors would travel down Borrowdale to the graphite mine and the really adventurous would go up to the Honister slate mine. The writer of a best-seller *The Mysteries of Udolpho*, Ann Ward Radcliffe rode up and down Skiddaw, in 1794, when the mountain held fear for many people and before any pathway existed. She was a brave woman but still not one who would venture into the heart of Lakeland.

One of the first descriptions of the central district, and in particular Borrowdale, available to the general public was from George Smith of Wigton. Among over 100 articles for the *Gentleman's Magazine* was one, in 1749, describing a visit to the graphite mine. He referred to the 'black lead mine' and described the ascent from Seathwaite in a dramatic way, 'the scene that now presented itself was the most frightful that can be conceived; we had a mountain to climb for about 700 yards in a direction so nearly perpendicular, that we were in doubt whether we should attempt it'. He did reach the mine and witnessed a group of locals gleaning what graphite they could find among the waste tips. George Smith said that the inhabitants of Keswick subsisted chiefly by stealing, the black lead (graphite) or clandestinely buying off those that steal, to sell later to Jews or other hawkers.

Smith could hear explosions from the Honister slate mine and commented about, 'the dreadful solitude, the distance of the plain below and the mountains heaped upon mountains that were piled around us; desolate and waste, like the ruins of a world which we only had survived, excited such ideas of horror as are not to be experienced'. We can only imagine Smith's reaction if he had been taken beyond the mine for an hour or so to Green Gable and Gable itself. He was only too pleased to retrace his steps, to reach their horses and get back to Keswick. Smith's view at this time was not unlike the attitude of people before the time of industry in the valley, when it was common practice to hide cattle in Borrowdale for safety, so few outsiders ventured into such wild inhospitable country. Later writings of Smith indicate a real liking for the high places.

Among the more adventurous writers were Thomas West, Dr John Brown and John Keats. For many writers at this time mountains were described using words such as warts or wens on the Earth's surface. None came near to Gable, Scafell or the wilder western landscape. These early writers could not be described as fell walkers; they drove around the district by carriage or rode by horse or pony. Father Thomas West, real name was not West but Daniel, worked as a Jesuit Priest and wrote one of the first guide books to the Lakes, published in 1778. The book was dedicated to, 'the lovers of Landscape Studies and to All who have visited or intended to visit the Lakes in Cumberland, Westmorland and Lancashire'. The guide is rather bland; being simply what to see and how to get from one place to the next, but it did help introduce the idea of going somewhere to enjoy and appreciate landscape. West was a good example of someone who had leisure-time to enjoy; he could rely upon income from three small farms in Furness.

Eventually writers arrived who would view mountains in a mystical way, showing a reverence and even love for what they saw and have been described as 'Romantics' with strange ideas about mountains being attractive and even having personalities. Dr John Brown bridged the gap between being fearful and in raptures about scenery. Although expressing horror at seeing the cliffs in Borrowdale he was able to write about that valley in moonlight, 'among these enchanting dales, opens a scene of such delicate beauty, repose and solemnity, as exceeds all description'. John Keats with Charles Brown passed through the eastern Lake District in June 1818, starting from the Salutation Hotel in Ambleside. Thick mist prevented an ascent of Helvellyn, but Keats did reach the top of Skiddaw, starting at 4 am. A circuit of Derwentwater was also made and their recorded tour added to general knowledge about the area.

Dorothy Wordsworth, her brother William and Coleridge were among the first to awaken the public to the romantic view: William in his *Guide Book*, with contributions from Dorothy, and from Coleridge through his letters and notebooks, and Dorothy with her diaries giving us day by day kaleidoscope-like changes to her surroundings above and around Grasmere.

Coleridge had a strong influence during the early days of the Romantic Movement; Simon Schama describes Coleridge as a shining light of the Romantic Movement as both philosopher and poet. Together with William Wordsworth, the *Lyrical Ballads* are credited with signalling the start of the movement. Despite poor health Coleridge could claim to be one of the first fell walkers with a genuine love of the mountains. In a letter to Thomas Wedgwood in 1803 after an extensive tour of the Lakes including the first recorded descent of a rock climb, Broad Stand on Scafell, Coleridge wrote, 'the farther I ascend from animated nature, from men, and cattle, and the common birds of the wood, and fields, the greater becomes in me the intensity of the feeling of life'. He made an extensive tour of the district in 1799 with William Wordsworth, and alone in 1802 on foot all the way from Portinscale visiting the valleys of Buttermere, Ennerdale and Wasdale before going over Scafell to Eskdale. Apart from taking risks on Scafell and at one time descending Helvellyn in darkness he completed an impressive round of the Coledale tops, Grisedale Pike to Causey Pike taking in Eel Crag, Crag Hill, Sail, Scar Craggs in what would be the first traverse by a walker rather than a shepherd visiting these tops to gather sheep. Coleridge on his many visits to friends would try to persuade them to buy property in Lakeland so that he may have congenial base camps around the district. Robert Southey, while not so active physically as Coleridge, did have deep feelings towards mountains, 'who sees them only in their summer hour, Sees, but their beauties half, and knows not half their power'.

William Wordsworth came nearest to Gable when passing over Sty Head with Coleridge but from his writing an impression is gained that he preferred to walk the valleys and passes, to admire the mountains while stood at their feet. He made the most of what could be seen around him during these journeys and stored images for use later in poetry and prose. The yew trees in Lorton Vale moved him to a poem, but in writing the words, recalled also the yew trees near the graphite mine at the foot of Gable which he and Coleridge passed on their tour in 1799:

> But worthier still of note,
> Are those fraternal four of Borrrowdale,
> Joined in one solemn and capacious grove.

There does not appear to be any record of climbs done while William Wordsworth camped at Wasdale Head. Yes, Wordsworth did camp there in 1809. He joined friends on what was planned to be a fishing trip. The organiser was John Wilson, who was the son of a wealthy Scottish banker. Wilson alias Christopher North could be considered one of Lakeland's minor poets, who wrote a poem *The Angler's Tent* to which Wordsworth added a few lines while at the Wasdale Head camp. Four years earlier Wilson must have been one of the first, if not the first, people to camp at Wasdale Head. Wilson set up a large tent near Wastwater and stocked it with food as well as rum and ale; he may have avoided excise problems at the time by giving the drink to locals. The main families of the valley were present: Tysons, Fletchers, Stables and Ritsons. All had a good time, eating, drinking, some wrestling, and fishing from a boat.

Another literary man at Wasdale Head in 1809 was Thomas De Quincey who generally preferred a quiet life, unlike the more gregarious, bold and ostentatious Wilson, yet the two men continued a long friendship afterwards when Wilson lived in an estate called Ellery above Windermere. The party had ample provisions because it has been estimated that thirty two ponies were needed to carry the baggage.[13] Apart from fishing the main entertainment seemed to be mixing with the few local families at Wasdale Head who could not have been accustomed to people camping on their fields. Up to that time the first sign of visitors would be knocking on a cottage or farmhouse door and a stranger asking for a bed and some food. One of the farmhouses where accommodation could be found was known as Rowfoot, described at the time as 'primitive'. When Hugh Walpole wrote about an Inn at Wasdale Head in 1760 he was working from imagination, there were only cottages and farmhouses at that time.

Not until 1856, when Rowfoot was adapted by Will Ritson and his wife Dinah, with extension added to became 'The Huntsman's Inn', was there room for official paying guests, then the inn was described as 'astringent'. The old farmhouse much-extended then became the Wastwater Hotel, now the 'Wasdale Head Inn'.

One of the earliest visitors to this newly-opened inn was Edward Whymper who climbed extensively in the Alps and Andes, making a number of first ascents including the Matterhorn. For Whymper, romance was to be found among the mountains of Switzerland, France and South America, where he could carry out his artistic work, which was also his occupation as a producer of book engravings. Our artistic record of nineteenth century mountain Lakeland would have been richer if Whymper had applied his talents to Pillar, Gable or Scafell. Like a number of Victorian Alpinists he was not particularly drawn to mountains in Britain.

Dorothy Wordsworth ventured into the high places of Lakeland and was among the first walkers, through their writings, to express a real love for the grandeur of the mountains around them. From Dorothy's writing an impression is given that she wished to climb more mountains in the central area. Dorothy admired Gable greatly and it is highly likely an ascent would have been made given the opportunity away from domestic duties. A great deal of walking up hills was done around the cottage in Grasmere but not too far from the work to be done at home. Thomas De Quincey said: 'Dorothy was always ready to walk out wet or dry storm or sunshine night or day'. What did give her great pleasure was the ascent of Scafell Pike with Mary Elizabeth Barker and a local guide described as a statesman shepherd of the vale. In writing of the day Dorothy gives, in her description, an interesting view of Gable. The ascent of Scafell Pike was made on Wednesday October 4, 1818 and described by Dorothy in various letters to friends. The description used here comes from a letter to William Johnson, held in the British Library, who for a while was Curate and Schoolmaster at Grasmere.[14] Contents of this letter and others which included accounts of the climb was used by William Wordsworth in his published *Guide to the Lakes*.

It is curious that Wordsworth in introducing the description of climbing the Scafell Pike wrote: 'The reader may not however be displeased with the following extract from a letter to a friend giving an account of a visit to a summit of one of the highest of these mountains'. Why did he not write: 'The following account of climbing Scafell Pike is taken from letters written by my sister Dorothy to friends after the ascent made with Mary Barker in October 1818? To this day some writers refer to Wordsworth's description from the summit of the Pikes, automatically meaning William and giving the impression that he was there.

Stockley Bridge
William Green, 1814. University of Cambridge Library

Before making the climb both spinsters had entertained the Wilberforce family to lunch in Borrowdale. Next day while Dorothy, Mary and a Maid travelled down the valley in a cart to Seathwaite, the Wilberforce family were preparing to climb Skiddaw and were on the summit around the same time that Dorothy and Mary reached the top of Scafell Pike. The ascent, after passing through Seathwaite Farm, was made past Stockley Bridge and up Grains Gill to Esk Hause. The bridge over Stockley Beck at this time would be as shown in a sketch (reproduced here) by William Green, done four years earlier. The bridge would be built between 1650 and 1750 (pack-horse bridge building is very difficult to date precisely) and was very simple and far less robust than it is today. The bridge was widened from its original three feet around 1853 and almost rebuilt after a severe flood in 1966. Green the artist had close association with the Wordsworths, he lived in the square at Ambleside only a short distance from where William worked at the stamp office.

Dorothy said they were going to Ashley Course but did say it was a corruption of Esk Hause. The original plan as suggested by Mary was to go only to the Hause, 'to see a magnificent prospect'. On that day they did indeed see such a prospect. Dorothy described Gable as looking very grand and added that they had attained the object of their journey but that their ambition mounted higher. With their Guide they did mount higher until the summit of Scafell could be seen with, immediately in front of them, a descent to Mickledore, and realised that any attempt to reach Scafell summit that day would mean being benighted on the mountain. No doubt, a few years earlier, Coleridge would have described to Dorothy and William how he had taken a considerable risk when climbing down what we now realise was Broad Stand to reach that Mickleldore ridge. The two ladies would not attempt to climb up that way to reach Scafell summit. Unwillingly they resolved to ascend a pike of the same mountain. Only later did Dorothy discover that they had been up the highest of Scafell's summits; highest in England. From this place Dorothy writes in her letter, 'we now beheld the whole mass of Great Gavel from its base – the den of Wasdale at its feet, the Gulph immeasurable'. The pair and guide had lunch on that perfectly still day, and they had thoughts about the water supply on Gable, 'we sat down to our repast, and gladly would we have tempered our beverage (for there was no spring or well near us) with such a supply of delicious water as we might have procured had we been on the rival summit of Great Gavel; for on its highest point is a small triangular receptacle in the native rock which, the shepherds say, is never dry. There we might have slaked our thirst plenteously with a pure and celestial liquid, for the cup or basin, it appears, has no other feeder than the dews of heaven, the showers, the vapours, the hoar frost, and the spotless snow.' Dorothy and Mary wrote letters to Sara Hutchinson, then living in South Wales; possibly the first correspondence from Scafell Pike; just as Coleridge did sixteen years earlier when writing, almost certainly, the first letter from Scafell summit. The correspondence was to Sara Hutchinson, which was in the form of an extended letter during his tour.

When the party arrived back at Esk Hause they turned left instead of going back down Grains Gill because Dorothy wished to see the view down Wasdale from Styhead which she had heard so much about. On reaching Sty Head Dorothy wrote, 'we were now upon Great Gavel which rose high above us'. From this description it can be assumed that the party moved across to the Gable-side of Sty Head Pass near where a path now leads to Kern Knotts and the Napes. From here Dorothy would get the view she wanted of Wasdale. Here was clear indication of a lady who, though tired, would go that extra distance to see yet another view; someone who loved being among mountains. It must also be remembered that Dorothy and Mary would be making the climb wearing long heavy skirts to their feet and lace-up boots far removed from the clothing and stouter footwear of the Guide, who dressed in his shepherd attire would be far better prepared for such a long tiring day. Dorothy, it can be said, was better at writing about landscape than her brother William; an example comes from her observation of rocks on Scafell's Pikes, 'no gems or flowers can surpass in colouring the beauty of some of the masses of stone'. Dorothy had a gift for bringing mountain scenery to life describing this day with Mary as, 'sun shone, sky clear blue, light and shade fell in masses upon the mountains'. A comment was made that every little stream tumbling down the hills seemed to add to the cheerfulness of the scene. From reports of Mary Barker's extensive walking, they made good companions. Clear sky and not a breath of wind must have encouraged them to linger because the final part of the journey by cart along the Borrowdale valley was made by moonlight. The maid, it is assumed, stayed in Seathwaite or returned home by cart, to return later to meet the returning party.

The appreciation of wild places by some early romantics can be seen as a luxury enjoyed by people who find themselves with the time and resources to wander, look and write; mainly free from any need to make a living or care for others. This could not be said of Dorothy Wordsworth; she had to grab what mountain-time she could, as many walkers and climbers do today.

Eliza Lynn Linton, writer and journalist, who was born at Crosthwaite vicarage near Keswick, wrote in graphic detail about working life in Lakeland and the beauty of its mountains.[15] Linton embraced many diverse feelings when writing of Gable. Sty Head could be to her terrifying in certain aspects as when the clouds hang low over Wastwater. 'Literally terrifying as if the road was going down into the home of eternal death'. Yet, when turning her eyes to Gable could write, 'a wonderful effect of form and colour is shown in Great Gable and its crags. Hollowed in the centre and buttressed with grey pillars on each side – a whole cascade of immense boulders pouring from that sweeping curve to show what wind and rain have done, and the jewelled brightness of its sides shining many coloured and glorious if the sun lights on them – it is the most picturesque of the Wasdale mountains, though not the most sought after. But the centre, as it is, of the Borrowdale system – the nave of the nave – the key-stone of the arch and point of pivot – with Wasdale, Ennerdale and Borrowdale branching out from its feet, it deserves all manner of recognition and will repay all manner of research. It is one of the finest mountains to ascend, giving some of the grandest views and most glorious effects; not to speak of the natural basin in a rock on the summit, always full of the purest water.'

There is no real unity to natural surroundings; there are many different forms of wildness which has been described as 'the promiscuous natural landscape'. One Victorian mountaineer said, 'nothing is less like a mountain at one time than the same mountain at another'. Certainly, Gable can be very different at different times. The idea that mountains can be loved universally and always be capable of being seen in a romantic way should be questioned. Whether a scene is beautiful, no matter how fearsome to some people, is dependent upon the perception of that individual who describes it as beautiful.

At a personal level I love mountains, but not all mountains. After climbing around the Cairngorms, the mountains leave me with as much longing as a northern industrial town on a wet Sunday afternoon; yet I can appreciate the view of Adam Watson, who writes about the Cairngorms, in the way he can perceive the rolling mountains' subtle attractions.[16]

When historians attempt to explain why there was a change in Western peoples' attitude towards mountains, they normally look for changes in people themselves instigated by artists, poets and writers, when a more likely source of a shift in attitude is to be found in changed circumstances. Most people over the years before and during the nineteenth century either worked all their waking hours or were fighting somewhere at home or abroad; life in general left little time for musing about the wilder places around them. In such circumstances it was easy for over-worked men and women to view mountains, which had not been experienced directly, in a fearsome way; a view also described as a superstitious fear of the unknown. There is little or no evidence that most people at this time, given the opportunity, could not have appreciated wild scenery. Indeed it is quite possible that some Neolithic people sat in awe when looking across to Gable from their workplace on Broad Crag. Some among these early people and among those who followed were likely to have a deeper feeling for the mountains and valleys within their view; they simply did not have the means of recording these feelings. Historian G.M. Trevelyan wrote that, 'it is quite possible that our ancestors were as fond of natural beauty as we are, but they talked less often and less elaborately about it'.[17]

The arrival of early industrialists with money to spare could provide their offspring with the means to enjoy free time for wandering and venting their innermost feelings. Some industrialists or their offspring were also able and willing to help support writers, poets and artists during their discovery of wild places and can be seen as contributors to the enlightenment which came from these experiences. We owe much to Coleridge and the Wordsworths for their writings about Lakeland but we should be equally grateful to their financial supporters like sons of industrialist families, Tom Wedgwood and Raisley Calvert. There does appear to be more than a coincidence that years of the romantic period match those of the machine age otherwise known as the industrial revolution. Famous artists, writers and poets, of a richness we have not witnessed since, lived alongside equally famous engineers and industrialists.

Following on soon after the early romantics, Gable and its valleys attracted a number of literary figures to visit and add their thoughts to what had been said over the previous 150 years. The view from

Gable was said to inspire Scottish writer Thomas Carlyle to write a well-known description of mountains, said to be inspired by a visit to the summit of Gable. The description is in Book II, Chapter VI of *Sartor Resartus*, published in 1832.

One of the most interesting literary figures to climb Gable was Charles Lutwidge Dodgson, better known as Lewis Carroll. The mathematician and writer would arrive at Seascale railway station and travel to Holmrook Hall, the home of the Lutwidges. Present visitors may stay at the Lutwidge Arms in the village of Holmrook, described as a Victorian roadside inn dating back to 1850. On the day Dodgson climbed Gable, August 18, 1856, he was staying further north in Portinscale with four friends, and they rowed down Derwentwater to Lodore on the east bank. From there they walked to Seathwaite and up to Sty Head before finally reaching Gable summit.[18] Very little could be seen as mist swirled around and a strong wind was biting to the skin, even though the month was August. Later, Dobson's face became swollen; he said caused by the icy wind they met at the top. From Sty Head, Dobson and John Martyn Collyns went down to sleep in a cottage at Wasdale Head while the others returned to Borrowdale. For some reason, next morning, Dobson and Collyns measured the external walls of Wasdale Head church, St Olaf (Patron Saint of Norway) and Dobson recorded the dimensions in his diary. Being a mathematician he probably wanted to prove that it was small: thirty seven feet long, nineteen wide and five feet to the eaves. Not the smallest in England, that is at Culbone in Somerset. When Dobson and Collyns wandered round the church there was no door and only a bush pulled across to keep out sheep because there was no surrounding wall or fence. There were no burials at Wasdale Head church at this time; rights were not granted until 1889. Will Ritson, then at Rowhead Farm said people do not die around here, they live to be very old then wither and wither and get so thin that the wind blows them away. There were no other references to the church as would be expected from such an observer and writer as Dobson. There is a date of 1687 in the church with the inscription of JS, believed to be John Stanley of Dalegarth who owned the tithe of Wasdale Head in the seventeenth century. The church is said to date from the sixteenth century.

Collyns who became Rector of Daventry no doubt saw the old church among the yew trees in a different light to Dobson, occupied with his measuring. Dobson visited the Lake District many times but there is no record from his diaries that he attempted again to see a view from the top of Gable; though some diaries around this period appear to have been lost forever.

One year after Dobson's Gable ascent two other famous writers visited Lakeland intending to walk and climb but Carrock Fell was all that could be done by Charles Dickens and Wilkie Collins. Their attempted adventures in poor weather were recorded in *The Lazy Tour of two Idle Apprentices.*

Four writers together stayed at Wasdale Head in 1915; they were referred to locally as 'The Socialists'. Sidney and Beatrice Webb with Bernard and Charlotte Shaw; Charlotte wrote mainly supporting women's rights as Charlotte Payne-Townshend. There does not seem to be any record of them going beyond the head of the valley.

Hugh Walpole in his fiction writing could weave a romantic tale into the fabric of the landscape. Walpole knew Gable well, the first time with his father and a lady they bicycled to Wasdale Head from Gosforth in the moonlight and hoped to see the sun rise while on the summit. There was only wet mist, but said of later visits that he had finer views from Gable than from anywhere else in the world. Among other ascents of Gable during his lifetime was a June day in 1924 when the memorial plaque was unveiled. Lakeland meant a great deal to Walpole who settled on the west side of Derwentwater. Writer Arnold Bennett on hearing about Walpole's planned move from London to Lakeland said, 'Why the Lakes my misguided friend? You will get wet through and it is a hell of a way from London'. Despite the many wettings he did get, I feel sure that he regretted being born in New Zealand rather than in Cumbria, but through his writing he became for many locals an adopted son. An actress of stage and film, Nancy Price, expressed her love for Gable and made several ascents and said she could not describe the delight experienced from the discovery of a new approach.[19]

We are fortunate in still being able to enjoy the work of present-day writers and artists who give Gable greater prominence than the mountain has received in the past. The many monthly outdoor magazines can be relied upon to feature Gable regularly and for particularly well-written work we have the reliable red journals of the Fell and Rock Climbing Club.

There is a debateable point about how far a well-rounded non-specialist education is a necessary preparation for the full appreciation of wild places. Wordsworth felt that a long course of aesthetic education was needed to instil a liking for barren rocks and mountains. In the twentieth century some educationalists introduced a curious reversal of this idea, seeing wild places as making a major contribution to a sound all-round education. The chicken and egg quandary comes to mind here; if education can promote an appreciation of mountains and wild places, many young people should come to experience the insight for themselves. The reverse order of mountain-influence upon education was promoted by Kurt Hahn who laid foundations for the establishment of Gordonstoun School and five Outward Bound Schools in Britain. Also active in this direction were: climber, poet and writer Geoffrey Winthrop Young, also Bertrand Russell, philosopher and chairman of The

Mountaineering Association, and climber, educationalist Dr Mabel Barker. Rather than let enlightenment from education lead to an appreciation of wild places, as envisaged by Wordsworth, Kurt Hahn saw value in young people being impelled into the great outdoors. The outcome so often is to see caterpillars of around twenty bored youngsters trailing behind Teacher over Gable. There is great value in Gable becoming an outdoor extension of a classroom, but this has to be done with far more sensitivity than is normally displayed at present. Numbers should be small within any group and the person responsible should be a practised walker or climber who loves wild places and who has the enthusiasm to impart their feelings and not be doing so as part of some job description. These thoughts seem far from any debate about the picturesque and romantic but should not be; sensitive education ought to bring some young people to a discovery of the sublime in landscape. We can still hold a romantic view of mountains and moors, but not too easily if these wild places are looked upon as little more than outdoor gymnasiums.

For people who love Gable there is great comfort in reading about the mountain and its many rocky neighbours, or by catching an image in a gallery or magazine, but the greatest satisfaction comes from memory; images of summer days when the rock is warm, or winter and Gable white with snow come flooding through. A romantic view is surely as real now as it was for the Wordsworths and Coleridge all those years ago.

References

[1] Unsworth, W. 1972. *The High Fells of Lakeland.* London: Robert Hale.

[2] Shepard, P. 1967. *Man in the Landscape.* New York: Knopf.

[3] Gilpin, W. 1791. *Remarks on Forest Scenery and other Woodland Views Relative to Picturesque Beauty.* London: R. Blamire.

[4] Stainforth, G. 1991. *Eyes to the Hills.* London: Constable.

[5] Bicknell, P. 1981. *Beauty, Horror and Immensity: Picturesque Landscape in Britain 1750-1850.* Cambridge: Cambridge University Press.

[6] Heaton Cooper, W. 1984. *Mountain Painter.* Kendal: Frank Peters.

[7] Bicknell, P. 1987. *Gilpin to Ruskin.* Cambridge: Fitzwilliam Museum.

[8] Walker, P.N. 1993. *Folk Stories from the Lake District.* London: Robert Hale.

[9] Cooper, C.J.A. Peascod,W. Rossiter, A.P. 1948. *Great Gable, Green Gable, Kirk Fell, Yewbarrow, Buckbarrow.* Fell and Rock Climbing Club of the English Lake District.

[10] Hunter, J. (Ed.) 1830. *Diary of Ralph Thoresby 1677-1724.* London: Henry Colburn and Richard Bentley.

[11] Fiennes, C. 1888. *Through England on a Side Saddle, in the time of William and Mary.* London: Field and Tuer.

[12] Defoe, D. 1962. *A Tour Through the Whole Island of Britain*, 2 Volumes. London: Dent.

[13] Lindop, G. 1993. *A Literary Guide to the Lake District*. London: Chatto and Windus.

[14] Owen, W.J.B. and Smyser, J.W. (Eds.) 1974. *The Prose Works of William Wordsworth*. Oxford: Clarendon Press.

[15] Linton, E.L. 1864. *The Lake Counties*. London: Smith Elder & Co.

[16] Watson, A. 1975. *The Cairngorms*. Reading: Scottish Mountain Trust.

[17] Trevelyan, G.M. 1849. *An Autobiography and other Essays*. London: Longman Green & Co.

[18] Carroll, L. 1994. *Lewis Carroll's Diaries. The Private Journals of Charles Lutwidge Dodgson*. Luton: The Lewis Carroll Society.

[19] Price, N. 1953. *Into an hour glass*. London: Museum Press. p.126.

X. Serving Climbers and Walkers

A mountaineer's mountain

In England, Gable is almost unique in being able to bring walkers and climbers closely together in a way that it can justly be called a mountaineers' mountain. Rock climbers and walkers can share Gable. Walkers who welcome scrambling on rock as part of their walk and rock climbers who enjoy combining a good mountain walk with their climbing are both served well by Gable. This coming together happens most often amid the crags of the Napes. As a major climbing ground, the Napes ridges are unusual because they face south, unlike most large crags in Lakeland. Gable has its north face but can also boast of having rocks on the other side of the mountain which, in summer, warm quickly for the climber.

A walk full of interest, below the Napes, can be made by following the Gable traverse path which leads from the top of Sty Head Pass. Near to where the path begins its descent into Wasdale, another path leads off level at the height of the pass to traverse the south side of Gable at around 2,000 feet. I must confess that selfishly, in the 1950s, we harboured ideas about obliterating the start of this path to keep walkers away from the climbing ground ahead. Feelings about walkers and climbers together, expressed here, were not commonly held in those days.

Lake District Guide Jim Cameron on Gable's Kern Knotts Crack
Tom Stephenson,
Courtesy of The Ramblers

Traversing below the Napes ridges can be enhanced by knowing something about the climbing history of the crags, or you can simply enjoy an exhilarating experience among dramatic scenery while thinking of nothing in particular except where to put your feet. A very large volume would be needed to do full justice to the history of climbing on Gable, but here are laid out a few highlights.

A few minutes after leaving Sty Head some scrambling around large boulders brings you to the first of the crags, Upper Kern Knotts, called 'upper' because there is a smaller crag below the path known as Lower Kern Knotts. The upper crag is imposing, though not particularly high at around 70 feet; the face, in approach, looks vertical but leans back by around fifteen degrees. A major step forward in the development of rock climbing in Britain took place here when a first ascent was made on the face in April 1897. Up to this time, most rock climbing had been done in gullies or chimneys where side walls gave some sense of protection. Haskett Smith used to say that one great merit of a climb in a gulley is that it can clearly define itself from bottom to top. Only the Ennerdale face can provide self-defining routes of this kind on Gable. Exposed open rock faces like Kern Knotts, which the formation of the Napes has offered climbers, were considered too dangerous. The climb follows an obvious crack, wide at the bottom narrowing higher up with what can be a strenuous section in the middle. A climber, based in London, Owen Glynne Jones was thought foolish for even considering Kern Knotts Crack as a climb. George Abraham described an incident between Jones and one of his climbing colleagues John Wilson Robinson, who lived some distance to the west of Wasdale at Whinfell Hall; he knew Gable very well, going to the top around forty times. Abraham wrote[1] 'Robinson's last Parthian shot as he turned towards Borrowdale, 'Well Jones', he said smiling, 'if you climb that crack, I'll never speak to you again'. Whether he said this fully expecting Jones to kill himself is not known, but he was concerned that doing this climb may lead to climbers, less-skilled than Jones, attempting the route, leading to serious accidents.

Jones was an ambitious, determined climber who had inspected the upper half of the crack one winter's day with the protection of a rope from above. Then on that day in April he led a climbing colleague, and alpinist, Hubert Cecil Bowen, up the crack, not from the very bottom but by traversing into the widest part from the right. This was a break-through in what was thought possible and wise for rock climbers to attempt. After Jones had climbed the crack and probably upset some of his colleagues, they continued to climb chimneys and gullies in Britain.

Jones appears to have made much of his Kern Knott Crack climb and in response to what some would, and did, call boasting, a fellow climber Oscar Eckenstein took a young lady, Miss Nichols, to the foot of the climb. In the previous year she had climbed it on the end of a rope and on this occasion promptly led the climb followed by Oscar giving support to the half-way stage then he descended and climbed Kern Knotts Chimney to meet Miss Nichols at the top of the crack. In an Abraham photograph, taken at Easter 1897, Miss Nichol and Eckenstein can be seen seated among a group of climbers outside Pen-y-Gwryd hotel in Snowdonia. The Innominate Crack immediately to the right of Kern Knotts Crack, first climbed in 1921, and, further to the right, deep in a corner, the well-named Sepulchre Climb that was done nine years later stand witness to the development of rock climbing during this period.

The Sepulchre climb is at the site of a major rock fall triggered by an earthquake on December 26, 1979. The fall changed the first pitches of two rock climbs, Sepulchre and Cenotaph, when a large block came out of the corner leaving a cave-like hole.

The epicentre of the quake was between Carlisle and Longtown; described as one of the most significant British earthquakes of the second half of the twentieth century at around 5 EMS (European Macroseismic Scale).[2] Longtown is near the site of a subduction when two land masses came together closing the Iapetus Ocean, described in Chapter II, which is a sobering thought for those who plan to bury atomic waste in Cumbria, or site anything 'atomic' in that county. The path continues, still level beyond the crack and shortly before the track begins to climb, a spring can be found deep in a recess to the right. Over the years I cannot recall it ever being dry so assume the supply is reliable. The rocks above form the buttress of Kern Knotts and here lies Kern Knotts Chimney; the cracking of the rock forming this chimney is said to go through to Kern Knotts Crack on the other side of the buttress. In time, no doubt this whole buttress will join the scree below.

The relatively-sheltered chimney was a popular climb in poor weather. As a teenager at Christmas 1954 I climbed up the chimney with a middle-aged Austrian lady who was staying in the hotel at Wasdale Head. We had more ambitious plans but sleet and snow swept across the Napes all day. There was much speculation in the bar of the hotel among local farmers about what this lady did for a living in London, and about what brought her to Wasdale Head, alone at Christmas. We were all too polite to ask in those days and I never discovered. There were many interesting people at the hotel or sleeping in a nearby barn; there to walk or climb. Arriving one winter day wet to the skin I was met by a retired medical doctor who took pity on a young lad and loaned me a pair of trousers and sweater while my clothes dried. He was a very large gentleman so the trousers were gathered in around the waist and the sweater fitted like a too-big dressing gown. The doctor spent his years of retirement living in hotels, moving from one to the other in the Lake District; I envied him greatly. When ready for the next change of scene his plan was to go over by Sty Head Pass to the Ladore Hotel in Borrowdale.

Beyond Kern Knotts Chimney, you reach a wide scree shoot called Great Hell Gate described by poet Thomas Blackburn as:

> *It's called Hell's Gate where Great Gable*
> *Plunges down in Carmine scree*
> *Through rock pillars to Wastwater*
> *And the heartbeat of the sea.*

This river of stone has not only inspired poetry from Thomas Blackburn, and from writer and mountaineer Wilfred Noyce, but made walkers sweat and toil in ascent. The loose stones provide an exhilarating and rapid descent off the mountain. As youngsters in the 1950s we would run and make jumps, while at each contact with the ground our feet would make rocks roll and rattle a short distance before coming to rest. On a hot day, dust would rise behind us and boots would suffer wear we could ill afford. Geologists recognise that far more scree movement happened in this way than in millennia of natural erosion.

There is good reason to believe that the huge fields of scree on Great Hell Gate and across below the Napes made early walkers avoid Gable; they were fearful of what lay above. Crossing Sty Head Pass they would see the splintered crags towering above and rocks lying below; a dangerous place to be passed quickly. In 1779 William Wilberforce, the politician, wrote about his feelings when seeing Gable from this side.[3] 'Great Gavel, the mountain itself looks dreadful as it stands bristling up in spiked columns above the Shivers and Ruins which it has made. It is reckoned dangerous to cross in frost as the rock then cracks and rolls violently down in huge fragments.' Now people aged from eight to eighty can be seen walking happily along over this area, thought so dangerous in the past.

The retaining wall on the far side of Great Hell Gate is known as Tophet Bastion where most of the climbing is at the severe standard and above. The first climbs were not done until the 1920s and up until the late 1930s only around eight routes had been recorded on the Bastion. Now, at the time of writing, there are around thirty routes criss-crossing the face. In 1985 one of the most extreme climbs in the country at that time, graded E6, was done by Pete Whillance and Dave Armstrong up the centre of Tophet Bastion called Incantations which was included in a Border Television series about Lakeland rock, presented by Chris Bonnington.[4] Near the top of this crag, overlooking Great Hell Gate, can be seen an overhanging wall, up this runs a climb called Breathless, the route had been thought possible for a number of years, but was not achieved until a June day in 2000 when John Dunne made a daring climb, which at the time could claim to be the most difficult in Britain and graded E9 or E10.

The grading of rock climbing difficulty had been steadily creeping upwards. Traditionally the grading of rock climbs has gone from moderate to extremely severe with no use of numbers. Robert Irving who wrote a history of British mountaineering said, 'numbers are as inadequate to give the valuation of a climb as they are of valuing a dinner'. Words seem to be more appropriate and sensitive for expressing difficulty than do cold numbers, but numbers we now have. At a level of around E10 it is reasonable to suppose that the ultimate has been reached in what Gable has to offer the climber. The mountain could be saying: 'So you can do this can you, well here is another bit of my rock see what you can do with this'. Each time, young climbers armed with elaborate artificial aids manage to force a route up the rock. Until the 1960s most climbers were hostile to the use of pitons and any artificial means apart from a rope and one or two karabiners on rope slings. Beyond these simple aids one practice was to have sticky fingers from eating honey sandwiches or barley sugar before a climb to help adhesion; now chalk is used. There was an early saying that 'a man who would put a piton into British rock would shoot a fox'. I remember doing a climb named Centipede in Langdale, where rumour had it that someone had actually put a piton into the rock, and while below an overhang with Jim Cameron, he removed the offending piton, muttering 'tut-tut' or words to that affect. Attitudes towards using climbing-aids have changed greatly over the past fifty years but to Gable a climber's hammerings are mere pin-pricks.

Napes or Gable Needle

The traverse walk brings you to the famous Napes Needle or Gable Needle. Approached from Sty Head the side first seen is not the most often painted or photographed so some walkers feel they will not find it among the crags until the rock is only a short distance away. Local attention was first drawn to the Needle when it was sketched in 1828 by Wilson Robinson whose son, John Wilson Robinson, climbed with Haskett Smith. The general public first became aware of the Needle by visitors to the Lakes seeing Abraham's photographs in his Keswick shop window. A photograph of the Needle was also seen in a window of the Strand and an illustrated article about the Needle appeared in the magazine *Pall Mall Budget*. Later, an artist's impression on railway station posters reached a wider population, as illustrated in the previous chapter.

The Needle has been shown with the title of Aiguille du Nuque as an alpine needle said to be one of the Chamonix Aiguilles in the French Alps.[5] Around 1909 George Abraham also commented on post cards in Chamonix showing Napes Needle as Aiguille du Nuque.[6]

For some reason the Needle irritates a few modern climbers, though it is still a delight for walkers who see it for the first time. The Needle has strong associations with the Fell and Rock Climbing Club, a body viewed by some, unjustly, as rather archaic. The irritation could also come from the Needle getting so much attention; almost the celebrity of rock formations. Possibly modern detractors feel other rock features deserve more prominence.

The Needle deserves to be seen for what it is, a beautiful naturally sculptured edifice. There is good reason to suppose that other needles existed on Gable among the Napes long before humans arrived. To see the Needle as the sole survivor from the ravages of nature gives it a very special place among our mountains. The old Needle too will fall eventually so let us enjoy its image from every angle possible. I have climbed it many times, apart from once facing Lingmell, always by the conventional route on the Wasdale side and as simply a one-pitch climb from bottom to top with no belaying half-way and with no artificial aids as protection.

The Needle has suffered indignities over the years; one came from Jeremiah Ernest Benjamin 'Jerry' Wright, who was like a second father to me. Jerry raced up and down in 65 seconds to set a record. Another possible record claimed by Jerry was to have made ascents of the Needle numbered in the hundreds. *The Times* newspaper reported two records, a 100th ascent in September, 1928 and 900 ascents reached in August, 1946. G.F. 'Bobby' Woodhouse, a master at Sedbergh School, claimed fifty seven ascents. Other climbers would see how many could sit on the top; three can be accommodated with reasonable comfort, trying to go beyond four is not wise. With three people on top, the upper block, it is said, can be made to rock but not something I have experienced. Also head-standing on the top was a favourite trick.

Possibly one of the most surprising people to climb the Needle, and climb a new variation on August 18, 1893, was Aleister Crowley. He was a man of many parts, of independent means, who later in life indulged in the occult, even to the extent of practising evil and making a pact with the Devil. After climbing the Needle alone he went up Needle Ridge or Needle Gulley; he wrote 'not remembering which,'[7] and from there to the summit of Gable. The day was very hot and Crowley described being, 'almost insane from heat, thirst and exhaustion' and almost crawled down to Sty Head for water. He did not know about the water supply on the summit at that time. Crowley climbed with some of the early rock climbing pioneers based at Wasdale Head. After an experience descending Gable Crag with Owen Glynne Jones and a large gentleman from Poland, who had no experience of climbing, he did not climb with Jones again. At the bottom of the crag he untied the rope and walked away in disgust; his opinion of Jones as a climber was not high and he expressed no surprise when Jones was killed shortly afterwards in the Alps. There can be little doubt that Jones, had he lived, would have had words to describe Crowley too. Jones, at times, according to colleagues could have a brusque manner towards those he did not know well but to friends he was generous, kindly and modest.

Two climbs on the Needle which are still classed as severe and very severe, and respected by climbers today, were done as long ago as

Tophet Bastion, the Napes on Gable
William Heaton Cooper. Cooper Gallery Gasmere

1912 and 1928; they are variations of a climb called The Obverse Route. In 1912 the climbing began from the lowest part of the Needle on the east side and a direct alternative was done in 1928 from the gap between the needle and the main face. Like Tophet Bastion, the Needle has spawned numerous climbs at a time when all possibilities seem to be exhausted. Climbers come along and find new ways of getting to the top, each one being more difficult, otherwise they would feel it not worth doing. A common charge is that modern rock climbing is mere gymnastics, but a similar charge was made almost 100 years ago at a Fell and Rock Club dinner, 'it is said sometimes of the rock-climber that he is not a real mountain-lover, only a mountain gymnast'. Two typical new routes on the Needle are Wasdale Roof going directly up the overhang on the Wasdale side; another route, Sick Heart River, is near The Obverse Route on the other side of the Needle; both at grade E3. As a spectacle for passing walkers the roof climb must provide a good deal of entertainment. Walkers, with care, may caress the Needle by climbing up and through the gap, where the Needle joins the main wall. The descent is normally done on the Wasdale side.

Moving on a few yards a good viewing place or 'Station', missed by Thomas Gray (see the previous chapter), is called the Dress Circle below Eagle's Nest Ridge. On most days walkers will be seen gathered there; not only to see the Needle but for the splendid views across to Lingmell and down to Wasdale.

The first ascent of the Needle on June 27 or 30, 1886 was done by Walter Parry Haskett Smith, a classics scholar who was at Eton and Trinity College Oxford and in a position to spend many weeks at Wasdale Head. Haskett Smith wrote two versions of the ascent, one in 1914, twenty eight years after the climb and again in 1936, both in the *Fell and Rock Climbing Club Journal*. An event in both accounts I have never fully understood was why Haskett Smith threw two or three stones up on top of the Needle to check whether it was flat. Two years before the first ascent Smith had already climbed the Needle Ridge immediately above the Needle from where the top is clearly visible. On the day that Haskett Smith first climbed the Needle he was approaching it by descending the ridge and would have been looking down on the relatively flat top.

Four years after this ascent a young lady always referred to as Miss Koecher, without any other details, climbed the Needle at Easter, March 31, 1890. Also on this fifth ascent of the Needle was Miss Koecher's brother Otto Julius Koecher a member of the Alpine Club. They were members of Professor Arthur Milnes Marshall's party; the Professor was a prominent zoologist who lectured on Darwinism and wrote many papers on his subject. Miss Koecher, being the eldest sister, was Frida Emilie who had German parents, naturalised English citizens, living in Rusholme near Manchester. Frida had a background similar to that of a number of women who climbed both in Britain and the Alps at this time. Details are not clear about how she joined the Professor's party but what is known is that Frida's climb of the Needle was not only the first ascent by a lady, but making the climb dressed in a long skirt was a major achievement. By the late nineteenth century women climbers could wear an alpine skirt over trousers or bloomers. Earlier, they normally attached ribbon or cord to the hem so that it could be gathered up to see their feet while climbing. A photograph reproduced (see following page) of the Needle, by Alan Craig a founder-member of The Fell and Rock Climbing Club, shows a lady standing on the top which could have been taken at Easter 1890. There is also an Abraham photograph, taken around the same time, of a lady on top.

The restrictive clothing, worn by women climbers, is well illustrated by Dr Mabel Barker describing an early climb with Millican Dalton who called himself a Professor of Adventure and lived in a cave near Castle Crag in Borrowdale during the summer months, and in a hut in the Epping Forest during winter. Lakeland writer Harry Griffin said that Millican Dalton opted out of the rat race before it began. Standing below the Needle in 1913 Mabel was about to rope-up with Millican when he said 'skirt detachable?' Mabel said 'yes' 'take it off' said Millican. Mabel said, 'I obeyed and knew the feel of rope for the first time'. Dr Barker went on to become a fine rock climber being involved in numerous first ascents, including three on Gable. She made the first female ascent of Central Buttress on Scafell, one of the most difficult climbs in Britain at the time and was in the party to make the first descent of that climb. Milligan climbed the Needle many times because one of his adventure roles was as a local Guide. He too contributed a Needle stunt by taking kindling to the top, made a fire and brewed coffee.

Not the birthplace of rock climbing in Britain

Haskett Smith has become known as the father of rock climbing in Britain and the Needle has become known as the birthplace of rock climbing in Britain. Both statements are erroneous. It was a local Lake District man who, in the words of H.M. Kelly[8] in making the first ascent of Pillar Rock 'can be recognised the first seed of English rock climbing'. Unlike the first Needle climb there can be no doubt about the date of this first ascent. It was on July 9, 1826 sixty years before the claimed 'birth of rock climbing in Britain'. The climber was John Atkinson who lived at Croftfoot in Ennerdale, and worked as a shepherd and sometimes as a cooper. Pillar Rock, or Stone as it was known at that time was far more obvious from the valley than it is now; rising up from rock and heather slopes as an integral part of the valley. Locals had talked of climbing to the top but the general feeling after a few attempts was that the climb was impossible and

Jonathan Otley in his Guide of 1823 said the rock was un-climbable. The press said a thousand attempts had been made, but that was simply exaggerated newspaper-speak. As can be expected, the first ascent gained a good deal of coverage in a local newspaper *The Cumberland Pacquet*' but does not appear to have spread beyond the area. John Atkinson set out to climb a rock to reach a top that was not the summit of a mountain, he had to use all four limbs and work out the most feasible route by climbing rock; to most people this amounts to rock climbing. This was the first officially recorded climb in Britain: rock climbing as an activity in England had begun.

Leslie Stephen, who became a well-known Alpinist (and father of Virginia Woolf), completed a climb on Pillar with variations as early as 1854, with a university party. Alderman Grave of Manchester climbed the Pillar in 1870 with his son and left a slab of slate carved with names. On the summit they found half an alpenstock and what looked like portion of a petticoat, also a bottle with four names including that of a lady. Later other names were added to the slate, one being that of Charles Pilkington, a President of the Alpine Club. The slate remained on the top for almost ten years. Haskett Smith himself did Central Jordon and West Jordon Climbs in 1882 and East Jordon Climb on Pillar in 1884. Just over 100 ascents were made of the Pillar including four by women before the first Needle ascent. Many of the early routes on Pillar were summarised by Charles Dickens in his magazine *All The Year Round* in November, 1884.[9]

Four years before the Needle's first ascent, a climb was attempted in Snowdonia and a successful climb made one year later. The first attempt was made by a member of the Alpine Club T.W. Wall with a colleague A.H.

Napes Needle, Great Gable
. Alan Craig by permission of the Fell and Rock Climbing Club

Stocker. The climb followed a line up the main cliff of Llewedd in Snowdonia, they climbed 150 feet up Central Gulley before returning; the climb is so difficult it was not finally ascended until 1938. The following year, in January, the two climbers completed a route, using a rope, to the west of central gulley. An account of the climb, by T.W. Wall, is in the 1883 *Alpine Journal*.

The climbing of rocks in Britain for interest, as a challenge or curiosity began in the Lake District in the 1860s and was well established by 1880, six years before the assumed birth of rock climbing on the Needle. Pity to take away from Gable its claim as the birthplace of rock climbing in Britain but to Pillar Rock the distinction must go.

There can be little dispute that Wasdale Head became the first centre of rock climbing in Britain, our own 'Zermatt', with Gable our 'Matterhorn'. Ennerdale, below Pillar Rock, could have been given this distinction, but it can be argued that three main factors made Wasdale the Mecca for early rock climbers: easy access to a wide range of rock climbs on both Gable and Scafell, climbing on Pillar is also accessible from Wasdale and accommodation was more easily accessible at Wasdale Head than in the Ennerdale Valley. There is a

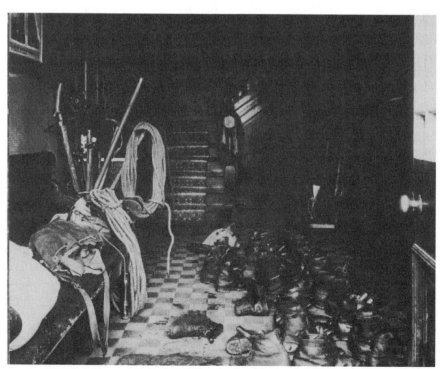

Entrance Hall Wastwater Hotel (now Wasdale Head Inn)
Abraham Brothers by permission of Susan Steinberg
©abrahamphotographics

vague similarity with Zermatt when, a few years earlier than the establishment of Wasdale Head as a climbing centre, people of Zermatt, in Switzerland, competed with those of Breuil, in Italy, to be the main centre. The first ascent of the Matterhorn from Zermatt swung the distinction in favour of that village. The hotel at Wasdale Head had a climber's equivalent too in the Hotel Monte Rosa in Zermatt, where Victorian climbers met Swiss Guides to discuss planned ascents. The Wasdale hostelry had in those days a stronger climbers' presence. Often there would be rows of nailed boots lying in the entrance hall (which can be seen in a famous Abraham photograph, reproduced on the previous page) and climbers could identify their pair quickly by the nailing pattern and gaps where nails had fallen out. Hemp climbing ropes draped the settle or banister and an odour of damp clothing filled the hall, mainly of wool and tweed. Any casual visitor to the hotel was soon left in no doubt that indeed this was a main centre for rock climbing.

Many early climbing visitors to Wasdale Head thought of themselves as mountaineers rather than rock climbers, and found that the Napes ridges provided excellent practise in climbing down at pace in preparation for a season in the Alps. Even years later, this distinction between rock climber and mountaineer persisted. Jerry Wright told me about being turned away from the Ladore Hotel in Borrowdale when wanting tea, with the words that 'rock climbers were not allowed'. He replied, 'rock climber madam? I am a mountaineer'. Jerry got his tea but only when it was discovered he was a friend of the owner.

Wasdale Head can rightly be called the first rock climbers' centre in Britain but I suspect that Gable would prefer to be known as the first mountaineers' mountain in Britain. Mountaineering in the early days was known as a healthy blend of exercise, pipe tobacco, friends and good scenery; with the odd drop of wine, spirits or beer thrown in.

At this point we can leave the Needle behind, after raising a little controversy. Before walking along the next section of path you should look upwards from the Dress Circle where lies one of Gable's most famous climbs, Eagle's Nest Ridge Direct. Named, not because the bird was around there, but by the climber who led the route, Godfrey Solly, who said he looked like an eagle perched on a nest while on a narrow part of the ridge. He added that, 'no bird would nest on so windswept a ledge'. The climb is famous mainly because it is a severe and very exposed climb done in April, 1892; the climbers were many years ahead of their time. One reason for this bold early ridge climb on Gable could be that the Napes did not offer Victorian climbers their preferred gulley climbs. Fifteen years later, George Abraham in his book *The Complete Mountaineer* described Eagle's Nest Ridge as representing the high–water mark in human climbing. There were four in the party led by Godfrey Solly and included a well-known alpinist Cecil Slingsby. The route was done in nailed boots; normally on Gable soft iron clinker nails were used. The alternative was to use Tricounis, harder steel nails with serrated edges. The doubtful theory was that soft nails suited hard rock and hard nails suited softer rock. There were even Gable Nails, sold by Robert Lawrie in his shop at a prestigious address, Seymour Street, behind Marble Arch. On Eagle's Nest Ridge there is a long section on small holds where good balance is crucial. Wearing nailed boots, as I did, the climber places one nail on the smallest of footholds, sometimes little more than a wrinkle on the rock, and moves upwards. The skill was in keeping the nail still in place while straightening the leg, before gently placing a nail of the other boot, again on a very small hold. Progress upwards was made and movement had to be delicate and precise. Few climbers at the time would lead the route, even when climbing in stocking feet.

When climbing in nailed boots was done skilfully almost no damage was done to Gable's rock, but eventually climbers arrived who scrabbled their way up climbs, protected by a rope above and caused considerable wear to the few holds available. Later, the first rubber footwear to be used was plimsolls, often bought from stores like Woolworths. I used plimsolls before boots became more readily available with rubber 'Vibram' soles and a general guide was that the cheaper the better, with soles of pure rubber rather than being made from composite material.

As you leave the Needle, look up once more at Eagle's Nest rocks and imagine Solly and his friends moving delicately up that very exposed ridge, placing their nails carefully, a heavy hemp rope between them and with no artificial aids. This climb was also a challenge for a party of German climbers, some with wide Alpine experience. The party was organised by Jerry Wright through the Worker's Travel Association in 1937; as can be imagined the venture was quite controversial. Jerry was well accustomed to controversy and revelled in taking these climbers around some of the main rock routes.

Gable traverse and Kirk Fell

The next landmark along the path is the distinctive rock formation almost as frequently photographed as the Needle, known as the Sphinx Rock or Cat Rock depending upon your viewing position and perception. The Sphinx is reached after passing a climb known as the Arrowhead Ridge, again named because of its image against the skyline. Many years ago I was told of a rock in a nearby gulley looking like Queen Victoria but was not able to locate its position or find a photograph. Beyond the Sphinx, which also forms part of a rock climb the Sphinx Ridge, is another scree shoot smaller this time and called Little Hell Gate. The traverse of the Napes is now complete with only a rock buttress known as the White Napes across the scree. There are only easy ways for climbers on this piece of rock but it can be a useful landmark when descending from Gable into Wasdale in poor weather. Gable may be traversed completely from this point by going around the White Napes to join Moses Trod over Beck Head and below Gable Crag to Windy Gap, and so back to Sty Head.

If crossing Beck Head, look up to your left at Gable's neglected neighbour Kirk Fell. The mountain will not complain about being neglected but the top is one of the finest places in Lakeland. When walkers think of 'doing' Kirk Fell from Wasdale the long steep grass on that side encourages people to walk around to the top of Black Sail pass, or follow the track of Moses on the other side to Beck Head. Approaching Kirk Fell from Ennerdale the crags on the north side make a direct route even less inviting. Compared with other Lakeland tops, few feet tread the summit of this mountain. Those that do are normally passing over the top as part of a fine ridge walk from Honister to Steeple or in the reverse direction. This walk has been described as one of the finest watershed routes in Britain. For skilled rock scramblers there is an excellent route up Ill Ghyll on the Wasdale side, which cuts into the flanks of Kirk Fell. Even for walkers in this ghyll it is wise to take a rope and know how to use it. The route begins above Wasdale Head beside waterfalls where the ghyll joins Gable Beck, and provides around 400 feet of scrambling in its height of 1,200 feet, with occasional detours to avoid rock only suitable for climbers. Eventually one of the small tarns is reached between Kirk Fell's two summits, the one on the left as approached from the top of the ghyll is the highest. Like Haystacks, across the Ennerdale valley, this summit is a place to dawdle, to wander around between rocks, to look down into the northerly combe and across to beloved Haystacks. The view of Gable from here is one of the finest to be seen. Ill Ghyll should be done after a spell of dry weather (only joking) and ideally Kirk Fell top should be explored on a dry warm sunny day.

On Kirk Fell there is much for the climber too on a crag overlooking Ennerdale. Climbing here was first done in 1925, many years after climbing began on Gable. Graham Brown and George Basterfield made the first routes; Brown, in 1925, was still recovering from service in Macedonia during the war. Like all crags on Gable, new climbs are still being done on Boat Howe; a new very severe climb was done as recently as 2008.

Continuing across Beck Head, the traverse path passes below the impressive Ennerdale face of Gable. This is another place where walkers and climbers come together, though walkers who venture into the recesses of the crag itself need to be very experienced scramblers and should have done some rock climbing previously. The start of any climbing on this face is important too because identifying the routes which can be safely attempted is not always easy; well-known and recognisable landmarks as on the Napes are few. An exception to gulley climbing in the early days of exploring this face, are two climbs on the left near Windy Gap called Mallory's climbs, done by George Mallory and Geoffrey Keynes on September 21, 1908. Both climbers were at Wasdale Head for nine days with a party of students from Cambridge. During this holiday the students completed many climbs on the Napes Ridges.[10]

Over the years a general feeling seems to be that Gable's Ennerdale side has been neglected but new rock climbs are still being created. When a climb Engineer's Slabs was done in 1934 it was said that the crag was exhausted but around seventy years later a climb at E2 called Snicker Snack (imaginative names for climbs is largely a thing of the past) was done as an extension of the slabs. Another climb, Dream Twister, at E3 was also done nearby at this time.

Good challenging winter routes are to be found as expected on a north-facing crag where a long steep gulley and chimneys can be found. The first recorded winter climb on Gable was Eagle's Nest Gulley, in summer an easy scramble, but in snow and ice on December 29, 1890, a new challenge. A year later the snow was in good condition on Gable's Ennerdale face as late as April 1st when the Central Gulley became the first recorded climb in winter conditions on that crag. On the same crag, Owen Glynne Jones and party climbed the Oblique Chimney on January 6, 1893. Unfortunately seasons seem to be fast approaching when winter climbing with ice axes and crampons will be only a memory, especially in England and Wales. There was a time when it was not uncommon to find an igloo at Esk Hause, where the snow conditions were particularly good for building with blocks of snow. Climbers would be cutting steps in ice on the path from Sty Head to Sprinkling Tarn as reported in the climber's book of the hotel at Wasdale Head. With other climbers I have built an igloo in the Cairngorms but cannot foresee a time when this could be done again on Esk Hause. Similarly we could guarantee good snow and ice climbing in the gullies of Great End above Esk Hause, but unlikely in future. Epic struggles took place in winter on Gable's north crag but now climbers count themselves lucky to meet similar conditions.

Returning to our traverse of Gable, there is a good view of Gable Crag from Windy Gap, but better still, seen from Green Gable's top just behind you. To complete the traverse of Gable the route goes down Aaron Slack to Sty Head Tarn. I can never see this tarn without recalling an account by climber John Bechervaise of camping by its shores for one week in January, 1939. On the last day of the year he had a tent and provisions taken up to the tarn and spent New Years Eve at the Scafell Inn over tankards of good English ale, with everyone wishing him well for the week ahead. From New Year's Day he was then alone. One of my great joys is to walk and camp in winter on the Rhinog mountains in Mid-Wales, so I fully appreciate his sense of independence and satisfaction in being able to survive, alone, in below-zero temperatures with only a tent wall as protection from the elements; though now I have a much easier task with a very robust one-person Hilleberg tent for shelter. Bechervaise describes days walking on Gable, and later climbing on the Napes when a friend arrived. John Bechervaise gives a fine description of skating alone on Sty Head Tarn when, 'only the ring of steel on the hard ice broke the peace of the fells'. He skated during the day and after dark when the moon could give him light enough to glide around the tarn against the backdrop of mountains.[11]

The walker's traverse just described begins and ends at Sty Head. Owen Glynne Jones suggested an alternative traverse for climbers, combining a walk and three climbs. Descend from the summit of Gable by the Westmorland Crag then down Needle Ridge, walk around to the Ennerdale face by the traverse path and climb the Bottle-Shaped Pinnacle Ridge. This traverse of Gable O.G. Jones likened to traversing from the Dom, highest mountain entirely in Switzerland, to its neighbour the Taschhorn.[12] Jones had made this traverse in 1895, and again 1898 in the reverse direction.

Up to the 1930s most rock climbing on the crags of Gable had been done by what can best be called professional classes. One of the first signs that this trend was about to change came from man and wife climbers Sid and Alice Cross, who began their climbing while working in a Kendal shoe factory. They made a formidable climbing pair in the years leading up to the war, especially making first winter ascents of some major climbs including the direct finish of an ice-packed Central Gully on Gable Crag. In later years after the war Sid and Alice became well-known while managing the Old Dungeon Ghyll hotel in Langdale.

Summit views and reflections

Beyond the Napes an alternative way to the top of Gable for walkers is to clamber up past Westmorland Crag. It is at this point that the crags of the Napes join the head of Gable: the ridge joining the two is like a neck though it is possibly too fanciful to imagine this being linked to the name 'Napes'. It was around here that C.E. Montague Writer, Journalist and Editor of the *Manchester Guardian*, recalled, 'sandwiches eaten with grimy fingers at the top of the Napes on Great Gable attain a strange quality of pleasantness; the meal, like every meal that has somehow gone wrong, achieves a touch of sacramental significance'.[13] The Westmorland Crag stretches across the upper part of the mountain and further towards the direction of Sty Head lies the shattered crag of Tom Blue, and beyond this, lower down is Raven Crag above Kern Knotts. In recent years, both Tom Blue and Raven Crag have had new climbs established up to the grade of severe.

For walkers, above the Napes, the way skirts Westmorland Crag until near the summit Westmorland Cairn is reached. Here along with other ashes lies Lt Colonel Horace 'Rusty' Westmorland, a well-known Lakeland climber, laid to rest here in 1984 at the age of 98. Rusty's father Tom and his brother Ned from Penrith built the cairn in 1876, which has been named after them.

There are mixed views about the building of cairns; a make-believe 'club' was formed with the aim of destroying as many as possible,

Professor Arthur Ernest Field on Eagle's Nest Ridge Direct Great Gable
Abraham Brothers by permission of Susan Steinberg ©abrahamphotographic

named the Gadarene Club. A member, and possibly the only member, P.J.H. Unna (Percy) claimed to have levelled 300 to 400 ugly piles on only six Lakeland fells. I kick cairns flat in places where they serve no purpose, other than to indicate that another human has been there. There are far too many smaller cairns around the summit of Gable possibly because the block-field summit provides ample material for the strange hobby of cairn building. In an ideal world walkers would visit our mountains and not leave the smallest trace of them ever being there, but this is rather too much to hope for. Anyone who needs cairns to guide their way on mountains should not be there.

A short distance to the east of the top is a water supply known to Dorothy Wordsworth and after her writing appeared in William's Guide the pool became better known to the general public. Jonathan Otley, local watchmaker and amateur geologist, when on Gable's summit, in 1812, took careful measurements of the water-holding cavity. For some time Otley corresponded with the Astronomer Royal about the unusual water supply and when the Royal Observatory planned to put a survey pillar on top of Gable he persuaded them to move the object ten feet to the west. John Jackson, postmaster at Rosthwaite, in Borrowdale, and a Dr Lietch went to the summit to supervise the 'Sappers' of the Survey during the building work.

From Gable's summit can be seen seven lakes and around seventy hills and mountains. Looking down to the east can be seen the serpent-like form of Piers Ghyll, a deep ravine in the side of Lingmell. There on June 21, 1921 a tourist, from London, named Cornelius Crump lost his way in the mist while walking from Coniston. He wandered into the ghyll, seriously hurt his leg and could not get out; he lay for eighteen days until July 10. Fortunately he had water to drink which was trickling nearby, and the summer of 1921 was one of the warmest and driest on record. He would have died if not discovered by a group of climbers attempting the first descent of the ghyll. There had been only two ascents up to this time. The first was done by Dr Collier in 1893, but not again until 1911 when H.R. Pope led a party to the top. The main climber to find Crump was Arthur Thomson[14] who despite being handicapped physically was able to climb. On that day he had gone from his home, Lonning Garth in Portinscale, with Walters his chauffeur and a climber W. A. Wilson; together they rescued Crump.

Still looking east from the summit a great fault can be seen passing to the north of Great End, past Sprinkling Tarn and on into Great Langdale. The path following this fault was the one taken by stone axe makers described in Chapter V. The Langdale Pikes can be seen clearly, the site of the largest Cumbrian stone axe factory, and in the foreground Broad Crag and the Pikes, the site of a smaller axe factory. The view east from Gable has changed little over the past 4,000 years.

On the other hand, looking south many changes have been made. Walkers on Gable for the first time can be fascinated by the pattern of dry-stone walls as they look down on the intricate pattern of fields at Wasdale Head, what William Wordsworth called 'lawless patchwork'. There is no certainty about when these walls were constructed but from research it could have been around 4,000 years ago, to keep livestock rather than grow crops. Archaeologists have unearthed similar patterns in County Mayo, Ireland called the Ceide Fields in use earlier than 4,000 years ago.[15]

The view westward taking in Kirk Fell, Pillar and Steeple should be one of the finest in Britain; unfortunately it is blighted by a forest of non-native trees, ugly when fully grown and now leaving a far worse scar while being felled. Ennerdale without the foreign trees was magnificent, like the Long Sleddale valley to the east of the Lake District which is a continuous undeviating line. Ennerdale runs straight from the foot of Gable Crag to the lake. Near the lake there were small groups of native trees but between them and Gable was a valley exquisite in its barrenness; Pillar Rock could be seen in all its splendour, with below the river Liza with its falls and pools and remains nearby of Neolithic dwelling places. In time and with some sensitivity Ennerdale will hopefully be restored. Walkers and climbers of my generation who have had to suffer the mess of Ennerdale our entire lives are unlikely to see the valley as wildness. The 'problem' of Ennerdale and its forestry is discussed in more detail in Chapter XII. Eyes are best kept away from the southwest where towers of an atomic reprocessing plant are an imposition. A poem from Lakeland writer Norman Nicholson describes the site well:

> *The toadstool towers infest the shore:*
> *Stink-horns that propagate and spore*
> *Wherever the wind blows.*
> *Scafell looks down from the bracken band,*
> *And sees hell in a grain of sand,*
> *And feels the canker itch between his toes.*

If such a building has to exist better it be like the design of Sir Basil Spence at Trawsfynydd in Mid-Wales, where square boulder-like blocks of buildings are more able to blend into the surroundings. Some people have done their worst to bring blight to the western view from Gable. Better to turn away and focus attention on the summit or to the remaining three main directions of the compass.

The view along the north ridge takes in one of the finest walks in Lakeland; it is no exaggeration to say that a week spent walking from Honister to Gable and back every day would provide seven days of bliss. Green Gable immediately below has gentle grass slopes but a splendid rocky summit and keeps well hidden a crag for climbers of around 150 feet high on the Ennerdale side. Like Boat Howe crag on Kirk Fell, the climbs were first done around 1925.

Looking around at the very top of Gable, a bronze plaque shows a relief map of the memorial area and the names of Fell and Rock Club members who died in the 1914-1918 European War. The memorial is the subject of the next chapter.

Tales of losing the way on and around Gable are numerous: Professor John Tyndall, Victorian mountaineer who climbed extensively in the Alps, wrote in the *Climbers' Club Journal*,[16] how he thought he was on Gable, instead he was near Baysoar Slack on the way up Kirk Fell. When the mist cleared he could see Gable in front and above, it was then necessary to go from Kirk Fell summit to Beck Head and on to Gable. Even Owen Glynne Jones and party were heading for Wasdale from Beck Head in mist and instead of expecting to see something of the White Napes or the prominent rock of Moses Finger came up against Gable Crag on the other side of the mountain. I recall hearing on radio many years ago an account by Jack Longland, a well known climber and educationalist, of intending to lead a group from Gable down to Borrowdale and finding, as the mist lifted briefly, a view into Wasdale. He promptly changed course and led the group over Sty Head and eventually into Borrowdale, saying that they were none the wiser. If you do find yourself on an unintended side of Gable, comfort yourself with the thought of being in good company. Coming off Gable with my son in thick mist, various walkers were asking us directions, clearly we must have looked like we knew where we were going. We were heading for Beck Head and Moses Trod to Honister, so when we reached Beck Head, Wasdale-bound walkers were pointed into that valley, while some wanting Borrowdale followed our route rather than as they had planned, taking in Windy Gap and Green Gable on their way back to Borrowdale or alternatively, by Sty Head. Some walkers claim that cairns guide the way but so many litter Gable's summit that they are no help whatsoever.

Early walkers

So far this account of walking and climbing on Gable has described mainly the activities of rock climbers. The people who first walked Gable's valleys led to others who not only walked but looked to the rocks for climbing. The small number of people who simply walked the area is crucial to the overall story. In the late eighteenth century, mountains in the Lake District higher than Gable were ascended by people walking steadily uphill until they reached the summit; all have at least one easy way to the top and most importantly these routes look relatively easy from below. Gable was rarely climbed at this time because on sight all routes appear quite forbidding as all sides rise up steeply. To the south, there is the appearance of the gable-end of a building; giving the name. From other directions the appearance is of a dome. Coleridge could stroll up the south side of Scafell without concern, similarly he visited the top of Helvellyn from the west and even Wordsworth walked this route. Skiddaw and Blencathra could be treated in the same way. Gable for many walkers was out of bounds. There is an 'easy' way by going straight up from the top of Sty Head Pass by the breast route but even this way can be dangerous and even fatal in poor weather conditions, as Wasdale Mountain Rescue Team members will testify.

Coleridge is without doubt the best-known of these early walkers and as explained in the previous chapter made possibly the first descent of a rock climb, but he was not the first serious walker. There was someone who can rightly be called the first true mountain walker both in spirit and deed. Joseph Budworth, used the pseudonym of 'A Rambler' when writing of his tour in 1792; he made no claim to be a romantic, simply a good determined fell walker; he said that recollection of past labour was more satisfactory than past ease. Though handicapped by the loss of an arm at the siege of Gibraltar, only a few years earlier, he was the first in Lakeland to practise the kind of fell walking, we recognise today. Budworth did not reach into the central area of Lakeland but came close and opened the door to more adventurous walkers. Sometimes he was known as Joseph Palmer after he inherited the Palmer estate on the death of his brother-in-law. When on the top of Helm Crag he believed that his was the first ascent by a stranger, or rather as someone not working as a shepherd. Two guides went with him, one a local shepherd and the well-known guide from the Salutation Hotel in Ambleside, Robin Partridge. Budworth also climbed the rocks of Helm Crag to reach the overhanging highest point. He went up Coniston Old Man, which he called Old Gentleman, a mountain crowned with the deepest moss he had ever trodden. They followed the summit ridge to descend to Levens Water. On the way he drank from a spring of soft and cool water. Whenever drinking spring water he had the habit of preparing his stomach for it by 'a gulph of brandy'. That day he started and finished in Ambleside; in addition to the Old Man ascent he walked around twenty miles. For a description of climbing Helvellyn, Budworth's ascent with Guide Robin Partridge from the Salutation Hotel is one of the earliest on record. They started from Ambleside at 4am and went over Fairfield to the summit of the mountain, then along the ridge to finish in Wythburn. When staying in Buttermere he saw a young maid, who was then around fifteen years old, so Budworth must have been one of the first travellers to draw people's attention to this beautiful girl. In his words she 'looked an angel' and was a very Lavinia; 'Seeming when unadorn'd, adorn'd the most'. Eventually she became the well known Maid of Buttermere, Mary Robinson or 'Sally' as he called her.

In the year that Coleridge and William Wordsworth stayed at Wasdale Head, see previous chapter, a sturdy walker, like Coleridge, described the valley approach and life in Wasdale. James Plumtree approached the valley from Gosforth. He called the mountains here 'rude' being more beaten by storms than in Ennerdale. He seems to have planned an overnight stay at Nether Wasdale Inn but when seeing the frugal fare decided to take a chance on finding accommodation at Wasdale Head even though no inn existed. The choice was between the houses of two statesmen, Thomas Tysen and Isaac Fletcher. Tysen's house was nearest so a very tired Plumtree knocked on that door. It is surprising in a valley head so remote at the time that he found the accommodation, 'even approaching elegance: I had a basin with water and a towel set for me, and the only fault I found with the sheets was that they were finer than I liked'. Plumtree described the valley head beneath Great Gavel as a sequestered and innocent spot. There was neither public house, shop or artificer of any kind; they had to go ten miles to Gosforth to have a horse shod. One clergyman lived permanently there, performing service every Sunday and teaching a few boys at other times for a stipend of around £30 per year. Plumtree wrote of Wasdale head as though it was as remote and unexplored as a jungle village, as when giving advice to any future traveler. 'I cannot forbear adding a caution backed by entreaty, that he do not introduce luxury, extravagance and vice into these retreats of pastoral simplicity. Let him put off and forget the dissipated world before he approaches them'. He saw the valley as being totally without dissolute retinue of servants; the seducer and the drunkard. He could well have had the visit of poets from Grasmere in mind when he said: 'I hope, as yet strangers to them, the lover of the works of nature, as a humble pedestrian, will, I hope, alone traverse these delightful regions'. Jonathan Otley wrote in 1849 about Wasdale Head: 'all is peace, rusticity and happy poverty, in its neatest, most becoming attire'.

Early in the nineteenth century a very strong walker discovered the high places of central Lakeland and wrote about them in a way not previously matched, his name was Edward Baines from Leeds, newspaper editor and Liberal MP.[17] Looking at Gable from Green Gable he described the mountain as rising in frowning and fearful majesty. Baines was on the summit of Gable as the sun was setting and saw the tarns below as glittering like diamonds. He could see every considerable hill from Black Combe to the Solway Firth and from sea to Shap fells. Baines described the summit water supply and how the cloud-supplied water served to dilute the stronger liquid he had brought with him. He pointed out that the water supply never ran dry except when Thomas Tyson's fox hounds from Wasdale Head lapped up the whole contents.

An early walker to bring more attention to the pastime through his writing was John Barrow, Fellow of the Royal Society and member of the Alpine Club who made many ascents in Lakeland during the nineteenth century.[18] John Barrow, like many at this time travelled from Keswick to Seathwaite in a dogcart. After climbing up from Stockley Bridge he gave recognition to the man who provided the funds for building the next bridge on the way to Sty Head. This is the wooden construction which aids the crossing of Sty Head Beck, especially when in flood. Known as Airey's Bridge; it was paid for by Professor George Airey, Astronomer Royal.[19] The name Airey's Bridge has also been given to a rock formation on Gable by geologist Robin Langford Oliver. The bridge is now sited some yards or metres further upstream.

From Sty Head, Barrow with Guide Joseph Gash climbed up past Dry Tarn and noted the view down Wasdale from this point. He described Great Gable as a noble mountain and in some respects the grandest in the Lake District, its precipices being numerous and appalling. The view from the summit, he said was superb on such a clear day. 'While on the summit a large buzzard hawk flew close to us being on a level with the eye', they saw only two ravens and no other birds. Barrow also located the water supply on the summit, which by this time was becoming well-known, 'sparkling liquid gushing forth from the little fount'. [20] The water must have been like this until becoming brackish. From the summit they headed towards the top of the Ennerdale crags before going down to Windy Gap. It was here that Barrow recalled the accident to Rev. Pope. He too planned to go towards Windy Gap but steered too far to the left above Gable Crag and in going down jumped to a grass ledge, thinking it was the way, lost his balance and fell to the bottom of the crag. The party was on the mountain all night and it was early morning when the body was found. Barrow was passing through Seathwaite when the inquest was being held into the accident and describes being invited to see the remains, but declined.

Barrow and Guide reached Windy Gap and Green Gable safely. From the top they descended over Base Brown where observations were made on the vegetation to be seen, such as Alpine Moss, Club Moss and Staghorn Moss. Then some steep scrambling down beside Sourmilk Gill took them to where the dogcart was waiting. The adventure was over when they reached Keswick at 8 pm.

A close friend of nearly all prominent walkers and climbers at Wasdale Head, in what can be described as the golden age of Wasdale mountain activity, was Frederick Hermann Bowring. He was an outstanding walker and scrambler with a detailed knowledge of mountains and fells in Lakeland. He ascended Gable over 100 times. It's probably true to say that apart from ventures into the mountains of Wales, Bowring gave most of his life to Gable and the surrounding tops and was in a position to give advice to many of the early climbers, even though he avoided steep rock faces. His knowledge of the best gullies and chimneys was invaluable to climbers at that time. He kept equipment to a minimum and managed to put food, book, pipe, tobacco, compass and map into large pockets. A fine tall figure in a wide-brimmed felt hat, Bowring could be seen striding up Gable carrying his long spiked fell pole for yet another ascent of his mountain.

Since these early days the approach to Gable by dedicated walkers has changed little. Equipment provides much better protection against the weather but this is possibly the one main difference. The wonderment and satisfaction from a day on the mountain can still be that experienced by Barrow, Robinson or Bowring. By the end of the nineteenth century a steady interest and drift towards the mountains had already begun and Gable's peaceful days with only shepherds, sheep and the odd tourist at its base for company were coming to an end.

Recent walkers have their special memories of Gable, one of mine is described in Chapter I and I particularly like that from Peter Bicknell.[21] He describes his first sighting of Gable when, as a seven-year old, walking up from Warnscale Bottom at Christmas. On that clear frosty day he and his sister were becoming tired when suddenly there was the sight of a great white dome rising from the surrounding hills, to him like an enormous and dazzling ice pudding; the Ennerdale face of Gable. Since that day he saw Gable hundreds of times, but never again looking like that.

References

[1] Abraham, G.D. 1910. *Mountain Adventures at Home and Abroad.* London: Methuen & Co Ltd.
[2] Musson, R.M.W. and Henni, P.H.O. 2002. *The felt effects of the Carlisle earthquake of 26 December 1979.* Scottish Journal of Geology 38, (2) pp.113-126.
[3] Wilberforce, W. 1983. *Journey to the Lake District from Cambridge 1779.* Stocksfield: Oriel Press.
[4] Bailey, A. 1985. *Lakeland Rock Classic Climbs with Chris Bonnington.* London: Weidenfeld and Nicolson.
[5] Fleming, P. 1990. *Napes Needle – The French Connection.* Journal of the Fell and Rock Climbing Club 25 (1) pp.80-82.
[6] Abraham, G.D. 1948. *British Mountain Climbs* (First Published 1909) London: Mills and Boon. p.78.
[7] Crowley, A. 1969. *The Confessions of Aleister Crowley.* London: Cape.
[8] Kelly, H.M. 1923. *Pillar Rock and Neighbouring Climbs.* Journal of the Fell and Rock Climbing Club 6, (2) pp.129-183.
[9] Dickens, C. *Climbs of the Lake District. 'All The Year Round'.* November, 1884.
[10] Robertson, D. 1969. *George Mallory.* London: Faber and Faber.
[11] Bechervaise, J. 1942. *Alpine Adventure in Lakeland.* Fell and Rock Climbing Club Journal, vol. 13, pp.144-151.

[12] Jones, O.G. 1900. *Rock Climbing in the English Lake District.* Keswick: G.P. Abraham and Sons.

[13] Montague, C.E. 1925. *The Right Place.* London: Chatto & Windus.

[14] Holland, C.F. 1944. *In Memoriam. A.R. Thomson.* Journal of the Fell and Rock Climbing Club 14 (1) pp.59-61.

[15] Caulfield, S. 1978. *Neolithic Fields:* In Bowen, H.C. and Fowler, P.J. *Early Land Allotment.* British Archaeological Reports No 48, pp.137-144.

[16] Tyndall, J. 1903. *A holiday among the Lakes.* Climbers Club Journal 6, No 21.

[17] Baines, E. 1834. *A Companion to the Lakes of Cumberland, Westmorland and Lancashire.* 3rd Ed. London: Simpkin and Marshall.

[18] Barrow, J. 1886. *Mountain Ascents in Westmorland and Cumberland.* London: Sampson Low, Marston, Searle and Rivington.

[19] *Place Names of Cumberland,* 1950. English Place Names Society, vol. 21. Cambridge University Press.

[21] Bicknell, P. 1950. *Great Gable.* In Moloney, E. (ed.) *Portraits of Mountains.* London: Dennis Dobson Ltd.

XI. Memorial Mountain

I changed my ice axe for a bayonet,
Forsook the rocks and snow for Flanders mud
Remembering England, yet could not forget
The peace before the coming of the flood.
Make not my death the cause of further strife:
Peace I love dead no less than during life.

Anon[1]

They gave their lives

Between 1890 and 1914 there frequently gathered at Wasdale Head a group of climbers, most known well to each other. They would spend a week or more, and not only once a year, staying at the hotel or farmhouses below Gable. At any one time, seated around a farmhouse table, playing games in the hotel billiard room or seated over a drink at a long table in the coffee room, would be an impressive collection of individuals who were not only active on the rocks of Gable, Scafell or Pillar but also made a major contribution to society in following their professions. Any one group could typically represent: Law, Science, Engineering, Business, Medicine or Education. There were older members who had made their reputations by 1914 and younger members around nineteen years old to mid-thirties who still had ambitions to fulfil and contributions to make, both on mountains and in their respective occupations.

Among the younger climbers a number were killed during the 1914-1918 European War. There have been commentators who claim that the extent of loss to the nation by deaths in this war has been exaggerated, but a microcosm of society represented by these members of the Fell and Rock Climbing Club gives a lie to any claims of this sort. The loss created by the premature deaths of these men who have their names on Gable's summit plaque was immeasurable. Without this war they would have had a significant impact on the Nation's well-being and in turn, sons and daughters, not to be born, would have made their contributions and society would have been the richer. They would have continued to form groups at Wasdale Head and climbing history in this country would have been the richer too. Mountaineer J.P. Farrar, writing in the *Alpine Journal* about climbers lost during the war, said: 'In the wider aspect of the future staunchness of spirit of the English race they are an irreparable loss'.

When peace finally came to the country it could be said that looking back everyone would be sadder but wiser about the folly of war. Unfortunately, to this day, the 'wiser' does not apply.

The details gathered together here from climbing club journals, university magazines and family history sources inevitably vary in length, depending upon what has been recorded and what can be found. The intention in putting these details together is that characters can be put to some of the names we see on a plaque when reaching the top of Gable.

James Scott Bainbridge belonged to a farming family of Ravensworth, Richmond, Yorkshire; born in 1888 the youngest of seven children. Before enlisting in 1915 he worked as an analytical chemist.

James was commissioned from the ranks and became a Lieutenant in the 4th Battalion, Yorkshire Regiment. He was gassed during action at Arras in 1917, then killed in action on March 22, 1918 during the battle of St Quentin aged 30.

Climbers talk of 'sustained interest' on a rock climb and in a letter from the trenches to the club he wrote that the past year had surpassed all others for sustained interest.

James had already lost a brother, John Clifford Bainbridge a command sergeant major in the Yorkshire Regiment, also killed in action in 1916 aged 30.

John Gordon Bean from Birkenhead was among the first to volunteer for active service but was rejected because of poor eyesight. He did not resign himself to this rejection and kept on applying until eventually, in 1915, he was accepted into the King's Liverpool Regiment and became a Lance Corporal. Not until 1917 was he able to see the shores of England again when he returned home to marry. Soon he was back in France and only five months later on July 2, 1917 he was killed near Ypres. Most of his climbing was done in Wales and in Cumbria on Pillar, Gable and Scafell. In addition to being a Fell and Rock Club member he also belonged to the Liverpool Wayfarers Club.

Herbert Samuel Penny Blair was born in Richmond Surrey in 1890 and his name can be found on the Richmond War Memorial. Blair joined the army as Second Lieutenant in the Duke of Cornwall's Light Infantry, 3rd battalion. Wounded on the Salonika Front at a time when the campaign had been successful with the capture of an important pass, and died from his wounds, aged 26 on October 31, 1916. Blair is buried in the Pieta Military cemetery in Malta.

Arthur Joseph Clay joined the Fell and Rock Climbing Club in 1913. He gained an MA at Oxford University and at the outbreak of war was a brewery director living in Ashby de la Zouch. Like Oppenheimer, listed below, Clay at 43 was too old for active service, but joined as a territorial and served as Captain. He died on February 18, 1915 believed to be from wounds.

James Neville Fletcher was the first Fell and Rock Club member to die in the war. He had been in the club only a short time before going to France with the Northumberland Fusiliers. He was born and brought up in Gosforth, Newcastle-upon-Tyne. Promoted to Corporal he received severe injuries from machine-gun fire at the second battle of Ypres on April 26, four days after the start of fighting, and died from his wounds on May 27, 1915, aged 29.

William Henry Bright Gross was born in 1890, brought up near the Lakes at Barrow-in-Furness, and joined the club in 1915. William was the older brother of Herbert Spencer Gross who wrote extensively about Gable in the Fell and Rock journals and edited the first rock climbing guide to Gable. Working as a teacher before joining the army, he served as second lieutenant in The Queen's Royal West Surrey Regiment and is named on the Thiepval memorial (Somme) as died November 3, 1916.

Edmund Hartley's name joined that of his cousin Henry Slingsby on the Gable plaque. Hartley's war record is almost an unbelievable account of courage and fortitude; three times he returned to the front after being wounded. He went to France in April 1915 and was seriously wounded at the battle of Ypres; after convalescence he returned again to France in 1916 to be wounded at the battle of the Somme. By 1917 he was back in France at the battle of Arras where he was wounded for the third time, a bullet passing through his left lung. Part of his convalescence this time was in Windermere. As his health improved it was possible to go up Langdale to climb on Pavey Ark. From what has been written of that time I will always hold an image of this young man enjoying tea with climbing colleagues in the garden of the New Dungeon Ghyll hotel; happy and relaxed despite what he had suffered. Though distanced by many years I want to cry out, 'for goodness sake Edmund you have done enough, stay in the Lakes and get on with your climbing'. He was a brave man with a very high sense of duty and felt he had to go back to France voluntarily. The last climbing he did, before returning to the trenches, was West Climb on Pillar Rock. On May 18, 1918 he was killed by a shell. He died a Lieutenant in the Lancashire Fusiliers and lies in the cemetery of Mont Bernanchon, Gonnehem. His Uncle Cecil Slingsby writing in the Journal of the Fell and Rock Climbing Club said that the club had sustained a great loss. I feel sure we can add that the Nation sustained a great loss. Edmund was described as a comrade trusty, tried and true.

Siegfried Wedgwood Herford was from Aberystwyth in Mid-Wales, and graduated from Manchester University in 1912 with a research scholarship at the head of the Honours School in Engineering. Herford was reported to be a student of exceptional ability and after his death lengthy tributes were printed in the *Manchester University Magazine*. In one tribute a climbing partner John Laycock wrote that Herford said to him, 'I'll write your obituary for the *Fell and Rock Climbing Journal*. You can do the same for me'. Laycock did fulfil the request. Following University-based research he went to the Royal Aircraft Factory to work on problems connected with the design of aeroplane engines. At the outbreak of war in 1914 he went to France with climber, poet and educationalist Geoffrey Winthrop Young and served as an ambulance driver. In 1915 he enlisted in the 24th Battalion of the Royal Fusiliers and on January 28, 1916 was killed by a rifle grenade at Festubert near Bethune.

The greatest loss is summed up in the few lines above, there was too a great loss to climbing. A general feeling among fellow climbers was that Herford could be described as the finest rock climber up to that time. Haskett Smith wrote in the *Manchester University Magazine*, 'having known nearly all the finest English rock climbers over the past thirty years, I should be at a loss to name a single one who could be classed above Herford'. Siegfried was climbing at the highest grade of exceptionally severe, initiated by Owen Glynne Jones, with a wide margin of safety. Herford's first ascents ranged across all grades of difficulty, from a climb hundreds of beginners know well, Middle Fell Buttress behind the Old Dungeon Ghyll hotel in Langdale to Central Buttress on Scafell, which for many years was the most severe route in Britain. After returning from the Dolomites in 1912 he made what was most likely the first free descent of Eagle's Nest Ridge on Gable, something Godfrey Solly, who led the first ascent, said should not be attempted. Possibly his greatest contribution to the history of British rock climbing was leading the first ascent of Central Buttress, Scafell, with George Sansom and Cecil Holland in April 1914. In November of that year he was in the army. John Laycock a climber who knew him well, wrote that to his intimates, 'he was the truest, kindest and most generous of friends, our idol and our pride'. In the year 2000 a biography of Herford was published.[2]

Stanley Ferns Jeffcoat, 'Jeff' to his friends, he served as Second Lieutenant in the Royal Fusiliers (City of London Regiment). So well known, liked and respected it was said that a letter, addressed to Jeff, Buxton would reach him. He was brought back from the front riddled with shrapnel and taken to the Military Hospital in Newcastle. So badly wounded was he that friends expected that there would be no return to France but like Edmund Hartley he did return and, in 1917, was fatally wounded in an attack on the 'Oppy' line. When most of the Officers were wounded or killed he led the remaining men. He was wounded after taking a German trench and died on April 29, 1917, aged thirty three. He left a wife and son.

Jeffcoat climbed in the Alps but he is best known for exploits in Cumbria, climbing with Siegfried Herford on his direct finish to Woodhead's climb on Scafell. There is too the eponymous Jeffcoat's ledge, around half-way up Central Buttress on Scafell. A keen climber of gritstone, he joined Herford, Archer Thomson and John Laycock on climbs in Derbyshire; he was a pioneer of rock climbing in that county. There is a fine description of 'Jeff' at the Needle Gap on Gable, 'a genial young giant with fair curly hair and the jolliest pair of laughing blue eyes'.

Eric Brown Lees was one of the longest serving members of the Fell and Rock Climbing Club, joining when the club was a little over one year old. Lees was born in Kensington in 1878 and afterwards lived at Thurland Castle, Kirkby Lonsdale. Being commissioned in 1909 he served in the war from the beginning with the Westmorland and Cumberland Yeomanry. He was invalided home with heart trouble and after convalescence was sent to Ireland to be in command of the Curragh near Dublin. In July, 1918 Major Lees was back at the Western Front where he was killed in action on the last day of that month.

Stanley James Linzell born in Newmarket in 1888. Educated at The College, Bishop Stortford before qualifying as a doctor at Edinburgh University and later worked as a physician at the Royal Infirmary, becoming President of the Royal Medical Society in Edinburgh. At the outbreak of war he was posted to France attached to the Second Bridging Team, Royal Engineers. Six months later he was wounded and after recovery, worked at hospitals in England, mostly in Eastern Command. Linzell was posted again to France in May, 1916, only after he had made many requests to return. He became a Captain in the Royal Army Medical Corps and was awarded an MC after working under fire and in waist-deep mud, evacuating the wounded. The award citation read:

> *For conspicuous gallantry and devotion to duty in supervising the evacuation of the wounded. He continuously visited the forward Battalion Headquarters, passing under heavy fire. He set a splendid example of courage and determination throughout.*

He was also awarded the Croix de Guerre by the French for help he gave to civilians, including sick children who were described as rife with disease. Captain Linzell was killed with a shot in the head while on patrol on April 3, 1917, aged 28. He is buried at Forests Communal Cemetery, Aisne.

Lehmann J Oppenheimer or 'Oppy' to his friends was forty-eight years old when he died of his wounds in a Boulogne hospital on November 8, 1916. Far too old to be on active service, he lied about his age to join the army as a younger man and as a Private, at one stage he was saluting an Officer who was his son. He reasoned through his decision to enlist in *De Profundis* printed in the *Climbers' Club Journal*. There was guilt about the design work he was doing when the war was more important, also some shame in his German name and wanting to follow his son's example. Oppenheimer studied architecture and design at Manchester School of Art and later designed the mosaics in Lille Cathedral and completed work for Armagh Cathedral. He was an accomplished painter in oils and water colours and had three paintings hung in the Royal Academy, including one of Pillar Rock. Much of his rock climbing, including first ascents are well described in his wonderful book, *The Heart of Lakeland* a favourite among many Lakeland climbers.

Arthur Illtyd Prichard joined the club in 1915. His initials on the plaque are A.J. but both census and army records give his middle name as Illtyd. Before the war he was a civil servant being private secretary to the First Commissioner of Works. Prichard served as a Private in the London Regiment (Prince of Wales Own Civil Service Rifles) and was killed in action May 21, 1916 aged 35. He is named on the memorial at Arras, Bay 10. The J has recently been corrected to an I.

Arthur Mitchell Rimer was a member of the club from 1913 until his death in the war. Before the war Rimer was a solicitor living in Leatherhead, Surrey. He was serving as a Private in the Royal Fusiliers when he died, believed to be from wounds, on July 23, 1916 aged 29. Roy Broughton Sanderson belonged to a climbing family. He climbed regularly with his father, Headmaster of Oundle School, and a younger brother on visits to Wasdale Head. Sanderson was another Fell and Rock member who returned to the trenches after being invalided home from France. During convalescence he married but soon afterwards was in the trenches. He died of wounds on April 17, 1918. After graduating in mathematics and mechanical science at Queen's College Cambridge he joined the London and North West Railways as an Engineer. From there he was appointed to the Royal Naval College, Osborne. Sanderson could have remained there but was given leave of absence to join the army as Second Lieutenant with the Royal Garrison Artillery.

Henry Lawrence Slingsby was only nineteen when after Charterhouse school he was commissioned in the King's Own Yorks Light Infantry in 1912, as Second Lieutenant In 1914 he was mentioned in dispatches. In that year he was in the battle of Mons and then the battle of the Marne. From here Slingsby wrote a letter to William Palmer, Editor of the *Fell and Rock Climbing Club Journal* and in it said, 'Walking up Rosset Ghyll with a heavy rucksack on your back, on a boiling hot day, with the streams all dry, is bad enough, but marching on cobbled roads with Germans hard after you is the limit'. Later, in the letter, adding, 'Mile after mile we resisted, when by all military rules, we should have been overwhelmed by the great masses of all the arms which the Kaiser hurled at us'. Near Ypres, in 1915, he received a serious head wound. A bullet entered above the eye and travelled to behind the ear. Following an operation he was reported as 'progressing favourably'. When fully recovered Slingsby rejoined a reserve battalion and, in June 1916, went with the Duke of Cornwall's Light Infantry to the front. After the battle of the Somme he received his MC. In August 1917 a shell hit the headquarters shattering his thigh and he died a few hours later. In addition to the loss of Henry, three Slingsby cousins were also killed during the war.

Slingsby had so little time to follow in the footsteps of his father, well-known mountaineer William Cecil Slingsby, though he did manage to climb in Glencoe, Skye and Norway.

George Corrall Turner from Ilkley in Yorkshire, was born 1884 and is included on Sedbergh School's roll of honour. An early member of the club, he is in a group photographed outside the Sun Hotel Coniston, during a meet in June 1907. After Leeds University he became an engineer, first based at Kendal, then in British Columbia. With the outbreak of war he became a captain in the West Yorkshire Regiment (Prince of Wales Own) 62nd Division, killed in action, 1917, at Riencourt near Bapaume and lies in the Favreuil British Cemetery.

At 4am the enemy placed a heavy barrage of all calibres, artillery and trench mortars on his front. Captain Turner at once rushed up to number 1 post, and showing a complete disregard for his personal safety, he mounted the parapet and walked continuously from post to post, thus making sure that all fire steps were manned, until he was struck by a trench mortar and killed shortly before 5am. In the words of his second- in-command he made the weakest into heroes by the force of his example and perfect courage and coolness.

Benjamin Heywood Whitley was born in Staffordshire and went to Denstone College. He worked as a Master at Worksop College before joining the Royal Scots Lothian Regiment 3rd battalion and went to France in March 1916, four months later he was killed in action on July 17, 1916.

John Haworth Whitworth was, before the war, a member of the Chancery Bar in Manchester after graduating from Wadham College, Oxford. A strong supporter of the Liberal Party he had stood as a parliamentary candidate. He joined the Manchesters Regiment 6th Battalion in 1914. During action in 1917, near a place called Nieuport, Whitworth received the Military Cross for gallantry. Close to the end of the war when fighting was fierce he led his Battalion and was awarded the DSO. He died of wounds on March 31, 1918, leaving a wife Ida and four daughters.

Claude Swanwick Worthington was brought up at Alderly Edge, Cheshire, went to Sedbergh School and Manchester University, where he read law and had a successful business career in Manchester. From September 1914 to February 1917 Worthington served in Egypt and Gallipoli before returning to the Western Front in Europe. During this Middle-East campaign, in which he commanded the 6th Battalion of the Manchester Regiment, he was awarded the MC and DSO. A bar to the DSO was awarded during fighting at Oisy le Verger on September 27, 1918. With the 5th Battalion of the Dorset Regiment Worthington displayed conspicuous gallantry whilst in command of his Battalion. 'When two companies were held up he went forward in face of heavy fire and cleared up the situation on taking and consolidating his objective.' He displayed the same determined leadership when under heavy machine-gun fire on the first day of October; two days later he was wounded and died in hospital on October 14, 1918. Colonel Worthington was mentioned in dispatches three times and wounded three times. Worthington has the dubious honour of being the last club member to be killed in the war.

As a climber he ascended most of the routes on Scafell, Gable and Pillar and led the first recorded winter ascent of 'Engineers Chimney' on Gable. He also climbed in the Alps and returned from Switzerland shortly before the outbreak of war. At the time of going to Egypt he was being considered for membership of the Alpine Club. There was still much for him to do in business and as a rock climber and mountaineer. In the published war-time diary of Lieutenant Colonel Claude Worthington; *Great Gable to Gallipoli*,[3] a brother Officer writes, 'He was brave in a way very few have been, unselfish in the highest degree'. A diary of a soldier at Ypres, Robert Mackay wrote on August 1st, 1917, 'above all was their C.O., Colonel Worthington who richly merited his DSO. I saw him on the Frezenberg Ridge in the midst of a barrage, and if it had not been rather dangerous I would have lifted my steel helmet to him'.

A Note: Some years ago when reading the 1922 copy of the *Fell and Rock Climbing Club Journal*, I came across an obituary of Basil Howard Witty who died in January 1922 and after more searching realised that he was the same B.H. Witty named on the Gable plaque, this obituary was published two years before the unveiling so the error is difficult to understand. Also in the 1919 *Journal*, the Roll of

Honour shows the correct entry of B.H. Whitley. An 'In Memoriam' for B. H. Whitley was also included in a war-time Journal. Recently, the error has been corrected on the memorial plaque.

Memorial land

During 1919 there was, as can be imagined, a good deal of discussion about a suitable memorial for Fell and Rock Club members who fell between 1915 and 1918. One of the first ideas was quickly rejected, that was to have shelters of some kind below crags in central Lakeland. No matter how well hidden, the buildings themselves would too easily become sordid, like some of the refuges in the Alps without Guardians. There were even letters to the *Manchester Guardian* in protest at the idea. A more acceptable plan was to have a permanent base for the club in one of the valleys. Another idea was to issue a series of six pocket guides to each of the main walking and climbing areas of the Lakes which would also contain details of the members lost in the war.

What walkers see now on reaching the highest point of Gable is a cairn and a bronze plaque. The plaque shows the names of Fell and Rock Club members lost during the war. Above their names is a relief map of the memorial area, first created in moulding clay by author, artist and antiquary, William Gershom Collingwood, with the help of one of his daughter the sculptor Barbara Collingwood. To the casual walker at the top of Gable the bronze plaque represents the memorial. The real memorial is the mountain-area bought by the Fell and Rock Climbing Club and passed over to the National Trust for safe keeping. The mountains are: Great Gable, Kirk Fell, Green Gable, Base Brown, Brandreth, Grey Knotts, Glaramara, Seathwaite Fell, Allen Crags, Great End, Broad Crag and Lingmell. In total around 3,000 acres.

How the Fell and Rock committee negotiated the purchase of such a large area and put in place an ambitious plan is a lesson in patience and dogged persistence.[4] Firstly, the plan was to have the memorial on Pillar Rock but Lord Lonsdale the owner would not agree to a sale. In response to this refusal an interesting comment was that, 'though the rock belongs to all of us, its property for the purposes of the law is in Lord Lonsdale'. At this time the Musgrave Estate was trying to sell off large areas of mountain-country around Wasdale and the committee members tried to buy Row Head Farm which would include Gable, but were unsuccessful. Then the whole estate was bought by Herbert Walker of 'Lingmell' Seascale. The first move was an attempt to buy Napes Needle as a memorial but a value could not be agreed. By the time the committee had reached the negotiations their ambitions had increased considerably and the memorial area we have now was proposed. When the owner, Mr Herbert Walker, asked what they wanted, a map was produced and pointing to the central area, Herbert Cain, the club spokesman, said, 'all this over 1,500 feet please'. Not surprisingly Mr Walker needed time to consider the request. Fortunately he was a climber, sympathetic to the idea and described locally as a man of great public spirit and deep religious conviction who spent a fortune attempting to save the Whitehaven collieries. Finally he asked £400 for the mountains. With contributions from club members the deal was done. This deal was especially pleasing because Herbert Walker had bought the estate of John Musgrave; the man who played a leading role in planning a motor road over Sty Head. However, the door was left open for a road at some time because the memorial land did not include a strip wide enough for a road across Sty Head. The debate about a Sty road is described in the next chapter.

The outcome was the best that could possibly be imagined and we must be grateful to members of the Fell and Rock Club and in particular the negotiating group of Herbert Cain, Wilson Butler and Darwin Leighton that we have this magnificent panorama of mountains protected for all time. A comment in the *Yorkshire Ramblers' Club Journal* by J.F. Seaman, club Vice President, summed up the feeling very well: 'The Fell and Rock Climbing Club could have found no more worthy form of memorial to its fallen members. Monuments crumble and fall, but the everlasting hills stand fast and give inspiration to all who lift up their eyes to them until the end of time'.[5]

On June 8, 1924 walkers, climbers and dales-folk made the first of what was to be an annual memorial pilgrimage to the summit of Gable. Between the wars the pilgrimage took place on November 11, not as now on the nearest Sunday.

Those who were approaching the mountain from Honister along the north ridge would not realise, as they reached Windy Gap and looked across towards Mallory's climbs on Gable Crag, that almost at that moment Mallory, with Irvine, was seen alive on Everest for the last time. Mallory, who served in the war, might have had his name on the plaque too but he was able to enjoy six more years among mountains before ending his days, on Everest.

In October 1923, at Coniston, the title-deeds for 3000 acres of the memorial area were handed over to the National Trust. Now in June, the bronze plaque could be unveiled. Initially the person asked to do the unveiling was the Prince of Wales; fortunately he declined the invitation and a far more appropriate choice was Arthur Wakefield, medical doctor, enthusiastic fell walker, rock climber and President of the club. Before the war he had climbed in the Alps. He served in the war and was mentioned in dispatches in 1917. After the war he climbed in Canada and was on the 1922 Everest expedition.

William Palmer, who had been Editor of the *Fell and Rock Climbing Club Journal* during the war, described the scene as an estimated 500 people stood in, 'soft rain and rolling mist on the crest of Great Gable'.[6] The unveiling was done by removing a war-stained Union Jack which had flown from H.M.S. Barham at the battle of Jutland. The

Captain of that ship was Arthur Craig, brother of Alan Craig, one of the founders of the Fell and Rock Climbing Club and the Vice President in 1919 when the memorial was first discussed. As Commander Alan Craig, son of the founder member, points out in a letter to the *Fell and Rock Climbing Club Journal*, 'that his father would have obtained the flag from his brother and this is the most likely source of the flag used during the Ceremony'.

The flag provided the only bright colours to be seen because people were dressed in the sober hill-clothes of that time. There was the sound only of hushed voices, clinker-nailed boots on rock and the wind.

The club President, Arthur Wakefield, spoke with feeling of the climbers who had paid the last great sacrifice. In a few words he spoke of the mountains which in their memory had been presented to the nation, a possession for ever. Geoffrey Winthrop Young, who was at the battle of Ypres and later lost a leg while with the ambulance service in Northern Italy, paid a tribute to the fallen, modelling his words on President Lincoln's speech at Gettysburg. Godfrey Solly read the appropriate Psalm 121. Herbert Cain read aloud the inscription on the tablet:

> In glorious and happy memory of those whose names are
> inscribed below – Members of this club – who died for their
> country in the European War 1914-1918. These fells were
> acquired by their fellow members and by them vested in
> the National Trust for the use and enjoyment of the people
> of our land for all time.

The service was brought to a close with the sound of the *Last Post*.

One person who suffered acutely during the latter part of the war was William Palmer, author of several Lakeland books as well as Editor of the club journal. In an official capacity he had acted as a recruitment officer during the war and on realising the dreadful waste of life and loss of close climbing friends he broke down while editing the 1917-1918 Journal; he laid aside his pen in tears. The work had to be completed by his wife, Annie. Even now over ninety years later I feel acute sadness when compiling the details from war records and journals; a very upsetting experience. Having read so much over the years in the climbing literature of men who have their names on that plaque there is a sense of having known them and the loss felt at that time can be experienced still; though not in so intense a way as that felt by Palmer and his climbing colleagues.

Ennerdale memorial

Below Gable in the Ennerdale valley is another Fell and Rock Club memorial dedicated to members who were lost in the Second World War. The bridge over the river Liza was becoming unsafe by the 1950s and a new bridge was to be the memorial. The bridge was reconstructed in 1959 by the Cumberland County Council and the Fell and Rock Club bore a share of the cost with money remaining from the purchase of the memorial land and summit plaque. The fund had accumulated interest and with further donation, the weak bridge was eventually replaced.

A plaque at the north end of the bridge bears the names of thirteen members. Again like the Gable summit ceremony in 1924, many walkers, climbers and dales folk came to a ceremony on the banks of the river Liza, on the anniversary of victory in Europe (VE Day) Sunday May 8, 1960.[7] From various accounts the gathering was not the spectacle of the memorial day held at the summit 36 years earlier, but there can be little doubt that feelings of sadness and gratitude would have been no less.

It has been reported that climbers on Pillar Rock that day could hear the hymns being sung far up the valley and could feel almost part of the ceremony. Gable then carried one memorial at its head and looked down on another.

> *Have you forgotten yet?*
> *Look up, and swear by the green of*
> *The spring that you'll never forget.*

Siegfried Sassoon. MC. 1919.

References

[1] Anon. 1919. *A Mountaineer to those that expressed anxiety lest he might have died in vain.* Journal of the Fell and Rock Climbing Club, 4 (3) p.229.
[2] Treacher, K. 2000. *Siegfried Herford An Edwardian Rock Climber.* The Ernest Press.
[3] Bonner, R. (Ed) 2004. *Great Gable to Gallipoli.* Knutsford Cheshire: Fleur de Lys Publishing
[4] Anon. 1923. *The War Memorial.* Journal of the Fell and Rock Climbing Club, 6 (2). pp.240-244.
[5] Seaman, J.F. 1924. *The Fell and Rock Climbing Club War Memorial.* The Yorkshire Ramblers' Club Journal. p.146.
[6] Palmer, W. 1924. *Unveiling the War Memorial Tablet.* Journal of the Fell and Rock Climbing Club, 7 (3) 365-368.
[7] Plint, R.G. 1961. *War Memorial 1935-1945.* Journal of the Fell and Rock Climbing Club, 19 (2). pp.165–169.

XII Threats

Is there no nook of English ground secure
From rash assault?

William Wordsworth, 1844

Related threats
Over the past 200 years Gable, in its glorious position has become a sanctuary for people, if only briefly, from what can be oppressive business life and industrialisation. In the words of humanitarian Henry Salt, 'mountains have in all ages given asylum to free races. Has the time come when a free race must give asylum to its mountains?'[1] Gable has witnessed industrial workings over the years and has survived virtually intact. For this we must thank many dedicated lovers of Lakeland who have campaigned tirelessly to hold back baleful actions from people motivated by avarice and greed and prompted by certain business interests. Campaigners in particular have come from members of the Lake District Defence Society and the work of Canon Rawnsley, John Ruskin, James Bryce MP and Robert Somervell, all acting with support from members of the general public to repel the dangers, first highlighted long ago by William Wordsworth. Since 1934, generations of workers through Friends of the Lake District have followed the examples set by these early pioneers and achieved a great deal; they deserve our utmost support.

Within living memory the greatest threat to Gable has been the planned motor road over Sty Head Pass between Wasdale and Borrowdale. There have been other threats to the mountain and its valleys and threats still exist. Some people cite the various conservation bodies: Town and Country Planning, National Trust, Council for the Protection of Rural England (formerly Preservation), Friends of the Lake District and National Parks, in support of the idea that wild areas like Gable are now safe from, in Wordsworth's words, 'rash assault'. There are many examples where big business has ignored the need for conservation of wild places, irrespective of pleas from conservationists and concerned members of the general public. An area I loved as a boy suffered in this way, and as an example it is a good place to begin this chapter to serve as a warning for our mountain.

As part of a group of teenage walkers and climbers in the North-East, I can say we shared a special affection for the wild moors around Cauldron Snout in Upper Teasdale, where beer-coloured water of the

River Tees falls 300 feet in a series of cataracts. We returned time and time again in all seasons, using the old wooden youth hostel at Langdon Beck as a base. In sharp contrast, planners and bureaucrats responsible for the building of Cow Green reservoir, in the midst of these moors, clearly did not appreciate the beauty and splendour of this area; otherwise they would not have destroyed the moor and rare plants which grew there. The new reservoir covers an area of 21 acres (8.5 ha) of unique upland habitat which had developed naturally over the past 10,000 years; harm was also done to flora growing downstream from the dam because levels of the Tees river were being controlled artificially. Before the dam was built, the area had some of the rarest plants in Britain, around 75 species have been recorded and many have been known since the early nineteenth century.[2] Teesdale had vegetation closely related to the late-glacial period. In the words of Winifred Pennington 'its plants presented a record of flora and vegetation of late-glacial Britain which was unique and irreplaceable'.[3]

When Alfred Wainwright stood below the dam during a televised programme, he commented that, 'it is a crowning humiliation to the Tees', when seeing the river spurting out of a pipe. During the same visit, on looking across the moors he said, 'officialdom certainly regards the North Pennines as an area of desolation, which it isn't, desolation so called fashioned by nature is often quite beautiful, it's desolation created by man that's ugly, and they are trying to transform natural beauty into areas of industry that leave ugly scars all over the place'. Wainwright commented upon the great opposition to the proposed dam and added that despite this, 'Big Brother won as he usually does'.[4] The Romantics in Lakeland around 150 years earlier would have understood Wainwright's pleas and would be in full sympathy with his ideas. There are people today, some could be described as anti-romantic, who seem to want, as an aim in life, to instil order upon nature. The practice of imposing order upon mountainous country highlights the difference between aesthetic sensitivities shown by lovers of wild places and those who appear totally indifferent to wildness.

Wherever they look there is a wish to see symmetry and orderliness in the form of steel and concrete in angular shapes, and when they do it seems to be with satisfaction that they have removed some of the 'desolation'; they have what appears to be contempt for natural landscape.

Ironically, in the North East the major users of water, heavy industry, no longer exist and were already diminishing when the dam in upper Teesdale was built. Lessons from the damage done to Thirlmere and Haweswater in the Lake District were not heeded when planning the damming of the Upper Tees. Despite ample sources of underground water in what was described as 'the new red sandstone', close to towns and cities of the North West, the damming of Thirlmere was seen as essential for Manchester's water supply. The attitude towards wild places was well summed up when two officials representing the reservoir scheme told conservationist Octavia Hill that Thirlmere offered the only site and it would be right that the question of beauty should be dismissed.

Threat from vehicles

Many walkers and climbers seek wild places, but at times must feel that 'wild' is really an illusion; very few places in Britain can claim to be more than six miles from a tarmac road. Seated outside my tent by a frozen tarn among mountains in winter can feel like being deep in a wild place, but only if I conveniently ignore roads to the east and to the west only a few miles away. We have squeezed wild places into pockets of our imagination by building far too many roads.

To return to Gable and possibly its greatest threat, the proposed building of the Sty Head road, that has been described as the serpent of civilisation. Most walkers, climbers and indeed the interested general public would think such a proposal to be now unthinkable. Yet they drive over Honister, Wrynose and Hardnot passes cutting through some of the wildest parts of the district without giving a thought to what the area would be like without those roads, and rarely does anyone bemoan their existence. Editor of the *Fell and Rock Climbing Club Journal* in 1923, R.S.T. Chorley wrote, 'there has been great activity among the vandals during the year. Following Sty Head, the motorists have been making determined efforts to get the local councils to construct a road over the Wrynose pass, and this under the specious pretext of work for the unemployed'. Many visitors driving over Wrynose and Hardknot passes take as some kind of right that they should have a road and do not imagine for one moment that it is an encroachment. Chorley added in his editorial that the planned Wrynose road never reached a really dangerous stage. Eventually, despite many protests, the road was constructed. In time, when a conservation battle has been lost, an air of resignation passes over even those who preferred to have only the sounds of nature from wind, streams, sheep and birds when among mountains. Hugh Walpole in his house Brackenburn, below Catbells in the Manesty woodland, wrote that for a week no motor-car had passed along the road outside his cottage. The only sounds were of a mountain stream running through his garden and occasionally a woodman working nearby; lucky, lucky man.

The most recent vandalism, and a warning of what could happen to Gable has taken place below Blencathra and Skiddaw with the development of the A66 road between Penrith and Cockermouth. The aim was to allow fast commercial traffic a route from the M6 motorway to West Cumberland. Despite massive protests, clear objections and an offered alternative around the northern boundary of the National Park the planned work took place. The proposed diversion presented environmental problems too. Large amounts of plant life would be under threat on the verges of the old drove road through Sebergham. The planned road-widening or its possible alternative to the north were not sensible ideas. To develop such a road through a National Park was unforgiveable. The width of any road in the Lake District should be no more than sixteen to twenty feet if traffic is to be discouraged; to have roads of up to forty feet wide is totally unacceptable. The noise from heavy traffic on the A66 can be heard on most parts of Blencathra and damage has been done to the western shore of Bassenthwaite which will be permanent.

Wordsworth and later John Ruskin, Canon Rawnsley and James Bryce MP led objections to railways in the Lake District but if they saw the present A66 they would look upon the rail alternative between Penrith and Cockermouth as a harmless blessing.

The disturbance of peace on Blencathra would have been repeated on Gable had the Sty Head road been built; or will be, if a road is built in the future. In 1896 a plan was proposed to build a road across Sty Head. From Wasdale Head at the south end, the road would climb steadily at first into Mosedale, then around the foot of Kirk Fell across Moses Trod and ascend below Napes Ridges at a gradient of one in twelve to reach the summit of the pass. The distance by road from Wasdale Head to the summit would be four miles, when by path the distance is around two miles. The descent into Borrowdale would follow the current track to the foot of Grains Gill and then to Seathwaite, Seatoller and on through Borrowdale. The Cumberland County Council Highways Committee supported the proposal.[5] An early protester at the time, H Stanley Taylor, wrote in *The Times* that a national trustee or curator should be appointed to guard the Lake District from acts of barbarism like the Sty Head road, even if such a scheme involved the purchase of the whole district by the Government.

A driving force behind this road building was John Musgrave, lawyer and industrialist who lived at Wasdale Hall, and in anticipation of a 'commercial killing' began buying land on both sides of the pass. Musgrave could see new hotels not only at Wasdale and Seatoller but at Sty Head too. What was not mentioned during this debate was the extensive road widening necessary alongside Wastwater and in the Borrowdale valley where widening on the west side is limited by the river and on the east by extensive crags which had already been cut back by earlier widening. By 1928 the quiet centres of Seathwaite and Seatoller would have been be changed beyond recognition. On the other side of the pass a secluded community at Wasdale Head would have vanished to be replaced by large commercial ventures. One of the arguments in favour of the road was to bring in people because, 'only rock climbers went there'. Only around sixty people lived in the parish of Wasdale Head and at the school only four children attended three days a week, coming from the same house. The teacher walked five miles to reach the school from Nether Wasdale. A parish of roughly this size had been there for at least 350 years. The population fluctuated over this time but was always an oasis of peace and quiet.

There were strong allies of Musgrave on the local council, the influential County Surveyor was a keen supporter of the plan, but the main obstacle in building the road was raising funds; by 1913 the estimated cost was £30,000 with an upkeep cost of £800 per year. We can be thankful to Musgrave for one thing and that was his reluctance to finance the whole scheme himself. Canon Rawnsley campaigned strongly against the road but had Musgrave provided the resources there is little doubt that we would now have a Sty Head hotel or at least a 'happy eatery' of some kind on the eastern flank of Gable. Although the initial scheme failed when there were insufficient outside subscriptions, Musgrave moved again in 1910 to have the road built two years before his death. Musgrave was not going to let even his death spoil the plan because he left £5,000 in his will towards the eventual building of the road, if completed by the early 1920s. An obituary in *The Times* described John Musgrave as a master of sarcasm and repartee and that his force of character enabled him to carry every scheme he adopted; there was no reference to his failure with the Sty Head scheme.

By 1920 the plan was finally shelved. After reading various reports, produced at the time, I am not convinced that defeating the road building scheme was due to aesthetic reasons and for the preservation of solitude in high places. A major difficulty in raising funds seemed to arise from the reluctance of existing hotel owners to give financial support; fearing that new hostelries, serving users of the new road, would have an adverse affect upon their businesses. A Sty Head road is still a possibility as noted in the previous chapter; the area under trust as a war memorial did not include the strip of land up to 1,750 feet, where a road could go over the Sty.

A final comment on the proposed Sty road may be taken from the writing of Lehmann Oppenheimer, 'Oppy' who is named on Gable's memorial plaque. In the hotel smoke room at Wasdale Head Oppy reflected upon a conversation about the planned road 'a road over Sty Head will be the beginning; then there will be an outcry of lack of accommodation, and several well-appointed hotels will naturally follow, with a guide's bureau beside the bandstand and telescopes in the parterres for watching the principal climbs. Next a fernicular railway up Gavel Neese to an Aussichtspunkt Beer-garden on the Gable top, with a station midway for visitors to the Needle and Aretes.'[6] Oppy's words are no flight of fancy, there were serious plans to build a railway or cable system from Dalegarth station on the

Ravenglass line to the summit of Scafell, simpler they said than building a railway on Snowdon. The summits of Wansfell or Consiston Old Man were also targeted as places for mechanical access and the almost inevitable café.

Threats to upper valleys

The end of Gable's north ridge at Honister could have been the site of damaging industry if slate extraction had been done by quarrying rather than mining, described in Chapter VII, but the mine workings which do remain are slowly becoming part of the landscape. A recent practice of converting the crags into a tourist playground seems quite harmless and only the unfortunate design of slate-cutting sheds detracts from the original grandeur of the pass. We are spared the noise of cutting machinery and heavy vehicles and the stream to Gatesgarth is no longer polluted. The experience of following the ridge from Cat Bells to Gable would be enhanced by not having the road and its attendant summit buildings but we can be thankful that this is the only vulgarity on that route.

Overall, Gable's valleys have survived well: Wasdale in approach still has a primitive feel, an emptiness which draws you in towards the head, with only the ripple of water at the narrow road's edge. The geology of Wasdale has saved this valley from mining or quarrying.

Borrowdale with its broad-leaf trees is one of the world's greatest sights during spring and autumn. For climbers and walkers who have known the valley most of their lives, each bend in the valley can hold a memory. The west shore of Derwentwater is relatively unspoiled; a place to have quiet wanderings through splendid woodland, was close to being damaged in 1882 by a railway from Honister mine to the railway at Keswick; to be known as the Braithwaite and Buttermere Railway running for a distance of almost ten miles. The planned line was debated in Parliament in January 1883 and defeated in April of that year. A poem in the magazine *Punch* to Philistines about the proposed railway referred to 'locomotive's noise shall drown the murmur of Ladore'. Not long before this rail plan, the flooding of the Thirlmere valley by Manchester Corporation had been done in the face of great opposition, so the feeling may have been that no desecration was too big for the Lake District. The valley of Buttermere too, below Yewbarrow, can leave you lost for words by its beauty, and in fields by the mere outside the village is a place to make you want to stand and stare for a very long time.

Possible damage to Ennerdale in 1883 was a proposed six mile long iron-ore railway into the upper part of the valley. The plan was defeated in Parliament with the help of James Bryce MP and support from Canon Rawnsley. The decision was made 'respectable' by rejecting the proposal for financial reasons rather than aesthetic considerations. Canon Rawnsley was against the possibility that tourists would be transported up this valley to 'visit drink shops and whirligigs'. Almost 40 years later in 1921 there was talk of building a road through central Lakeland from Ennerdale to Langdale, passing over Windy Gap. The idea was described by R.S.T. Chorley, Editor of the *Fell and Rock Journal*, as 'possibly the figment of a diseased imagination'. This plan rivalled that of the Sty Head road which had been recently abandoned. Some people seemed determined to have the smell of cars and heavy vehicles around Gable and Scafell. Fortunately this plan failed too.

When some drivers cannot have their roads built across our mountains they decide to use motor bikes or 4x4 vehicles in what is called 'off roading'. Motorised vehicles have not yet become a serious threat in central Lakeland, as they have on moors elsewhere in the country where the battle to ban access is on-going.[7] There has been a private member's bill before parliament but only for control and registration of vehicles operating 'off road'; there needs to be a banning of all motorised vehicles, whether two wheels or four, from mountains, hills and moors.

An attempt was made to build a dam and raise the level of Ennerdale Water by five feet. The reason was to provide water for a planned artificial-silk stocking factory at Sellafield. Up to this time, railway, road and dam have all been fought off to help keep the Ennerdale valley as an amenity where people can go for an uplift of spirit and where sheep may find excellent pasture; until the Forestry Commission brought another threat.

Alien trees

Given that Wasdale, Borrowdale and Buttermere have largely escaped the worst that business and industry can throw at them, why did the Forestry Commission decide to desecrate Ennerdale and plan to do the same to Eskdale until stopped? A threat to Ennerdale which could not be stopped was a plan to fill the valley with a plantation of trees designed to be insensitive beyond measure. One of the earliest records of Ennerdale, in 1334, described Gillerthwaite as an unenclosed cattle farm and so remote that until 1780 the valley was the last in Cumbria to have wild red deer. Beyond this time, until the 1920s, remoteness and wildness were preserved very well.

In Britain, almost half a million acres of woodland were felled during the 1914-1918 war, most were of well-established broadleaf woodland. The plan, and reason for setting up the Forestry Commision in 1919, was to plant, throughout the country, close to two million acres of softwood trees. This business venture was to be split between the Commission and private ownership; individuals and corporate. The intention was not to replace woodland that had been felled but to plant serried ranks of non-native trees which provide quick-growing marketable timber. This threat was more difficult to oppose because the Forestry Commision operates outside normal planning regulations and are both judge and jury in the case of any conflict; only strong coordinated public protest can stop their thoughtless activities. The Commission was to be a servant of the people but from then to the present day their behaviour is high-handed to such an extent that we can be forgiven for thinking of them as our masters. Foresters will typically refer to wild upland as 'barren waste' or 'unproductive land'; by using such emotive terms they seek to justify the planting of trees in these areas. Uplands of Britain support a rich variety of wildlife which enables us to experience an environment as close to wilderness as we can ever hope to achieve at the present time. To walk across country unsullied by any mechanical contrivance or uncontaminated by any form of chemical is something to be cherished. Much of ancient, natural woodland has been lost to the practice of growing trees in plantations; more has been lost in the past 40 years than in the past 400 years.[8]

In Ennerdale, planting was done in park-like straight lines, an anathema to nature. Rev. Symonds wrote of the trees in Ennerdale as, 'goose-stepping on the hillside'.[9] Harry Griffin, writing about the harsh and knife-sharp edges of the plantation said, 'if the edges of the forest had been treated with a little more imagination the effect would not be disastrous but merely unfortunate'. Only two or three species were planted, all placed close to each other where they could grow only short branches to provide more marketable timber and all planting was done at the same time adding to the dreadful uniformity. From a distance any conifer plantation has the appearance of a green plastic cover, or when in a valley like Ennerdale as a bath of dirty green water. The purpose was entirely functional with no thought given to any conflict with nature. Within fifteen years the trees formed a tightly-knit canopy cutting off access to the river Liza. The bed of the plantation was as dark as night, any flora died and even mosses and ferns struggle to survive. This plantation-approach to producing wood and timber involves planting trees which are not part of the natural vegetation and when felled do not regenerate, and have to be replaced by yet more planting. There is a clear distinction between this approach, called forestry, and that of woodmanship which uses skills needed to look after woods; where trees replace themselves by natural growth and where other wild vegetation may flourish. Another preferred approach to tree growth is to have wood pasture where trees exist alongside grazing animals. Acre for acre sheep support more people gainfully than forest plantations, especially during the period of growing which is the longest stage in the life of a forest.

Forestry as practised by the Commission follows an attitude to nature from as early as the sixteenth century when humans began imposing order on what they saw as the disorderly world of nature.

By the 1920s this attitude had largely changed within the general public, although even now some local authorities still plant trees in straight equally-spaced lines when there is no functional reason for doing so. (The Forestry Commission at least can give 'ease of timber extraction' as a reason for planting in straight lines) Symmetry and planting in orderly patterns seems to be a way of making a distinction between culture and nature, if sometimes sub-consciously. The change in attitude can be traced to the eighteenth century; the planting of Scots Pines and Larch in the northern Lake District was planned and organised by governors of Greenwich Hospital. The land for planting had been given to the hospital after the Jacobite rebellion of 1715 and had belonged previously to the rebel Earl of Derwenwater. This early act of vandalism was carried out, as with similar acts since, by people some distance removed from Lakeland, who have little sensitivity towards the delicate balance inherent in the landscape. The new forest brought protests from people who objected to having non-indigenous species in the area at this time. William Green, eighteenth century artist, damned the planting of conifers as 'spriggery'. The aim of the hospital governors was to make money from a forest which has rapid growth, which would become one of the attractions for John Marshall, Member of Parliament for Leeds, when he bought the land from the hospital governors in 1832.

The interests of business must not be underestimated when thinking of rapid-growth trees in plantations, rather than as trees in natural re-generating woodland. Appealing to promoters of plantations in an 'aesthetic' sense is a waste of time; either they do not know what the word means or choose to dismiss it as unimportant. Investment in forestry is entirely profit-driven. Income from commercial forestry is free from income and corporation tax and falls outside the inheritance tax net. Increases in the value of timber is exempt from capital gains tax.[10] Without subsidies from the State, the planting of uplands with conifers is uneconomic; taxpayers money could be put to more productive use.[11]

The valley of Ennerdale before the plantation was a landscape that could be described as primaeval, like Gable's other valleys, there was a delicate blend of colouring; in the lower parts, where deciduous trees can flourish, there were colours from beech, ash and oak in natural woods. Only Borrowdale, of Gable's valleys, can provide a range of colouring from native broadleaf trees and lies in stark contrast to Ennerdale. Before the 1920s, the upper part of Ennerdale, without trees, had its own distinctive colouring and existed as a semi-natural environment with a little help from sheep; not wilderness but certainly wildness, Ennerdale, like Wasdale, was nearest to a valley in Norse times. A comment about wildness from Henry David Thoreau: 'In wildness is the preservation of the world', is often misquoted by using the word 'wilderness'. If left to nature without humans, as it will be one day, the upper valley of Ennerdale will have trees but not alien varieties.

In his notebooks, Coleridge saw Ennerdale in its wild state and described the scene while on one of his Lakeland tours 'no house, no tree and the unbroken line of the steep crag is tremendous'.

The wild open valley remained for farming until the arrival of the Forestry Commission. Before mass planting a walk up the valley could be described as bliss. The River Liza on your right, and at each step, the valley opening out before you. E. Lynn Linton writing about the river in the mid nineteenth century called it, 'the pretty, clear, bright little Liza starting with a laugh from her birthplace on Great Gable, and laughing to the end'. Linton described how every summer and autumn, hundreds of hives were brought up into Ennerdale for the bees to get sustenance before winter time. In the late nineteenth century, when the valley had around thirty more years in its wild state, George Abraham described a scene in winter 'it was a glorious sight. Ennerdale is grandly stern and wild at all times, but is seldom seen so well as when the winter's sun gleams into it from sea level, lighting up gold and pink flushes on the snow, and glinting on the opal of frozen becks, while the mist cuts off the tops, and leaves the imagination to create stupendous heights'.

With the upper valley clear of trees, walkers could look in wonder as each dramatic mountain feature was reached. At that time, above the farm of Gillerthwaite, it was said all trace of man disappeared. There was almost a primaeval landscape leading up to Gable. Apart from small scattered native woodland the landscape offered only mountains. The walker looked up into two fine combes; first the rushing waters of Low Beck where the water falls in a series of cascades then, in those days, through a deep, naturally wooded, ravine. A second combe where High Beck falls, half-way up the valley, begins life in a hollow below Wind gap. The best view of Pillar Mountain's north-side and its rock could be seen. The rough track bends slightly to the south and Great Gable comes fully into view, often described from this viewpoint in shape as a majestic dome, with its most precipitous face looking down the valley. The first sign of man's activity, a rough shepherds hut, is passed but the moraine heaps soon increase a sense of more desolation.

There are many valleys around the world where people travel up to the head waiting in great anticipation for a first, sudden sighting of a well-known mountain; for early walkers Ennerdale was one of these valleys where first a full sight of Pillar Rock came into view and then Gable.

In its wild state, Ennerdale was described by some as a valley so desolate it was said to deserve the epithet 'savage and remote' and a valley of great beauty with Gable as its crowning glory at its head.

The introduction of orderly trees has changed the true essence of the landscape.

The problems created by irresponsible forestation in Ennerdale helped save nearby Eskdale from a similar fate. So great were the protests at the disfigurement of Ennerdale, that the planting of upper Eskdale was abandoned. In June 1936 the Forestry Commission received a deputation from the signatories of a petition led by the Archbishop of York and included Bishops, Members of Parliament, University Professors and representatives of various bodies throughout the country.[12] *The Times* newspaper printed a picture of wild Eskdale without the alien trees alongside a picture of these trees on the Whinlatter pass to emphasise the difference. The Forestry Commission offered to screen plantations of conifers with broadleaf trees, not realising that looking from the valley the trees on higher slopes cannot be screened from view, and seen from the upper slopes the trees in the valley cannot be screened from view. This is an example of how the Commission did not appreciate or understand upland landscape. A letter-writer to *The Times* commented that 'ugliness cannot be hidden in Lakeland'.

Now that the Ennerdale forest is slowly being cut down the result is even worse with ugly scars all over the valley floor, clearly shown in an Ann Bowker photograph reproduced on page 133. When viewed from the summit of Gable it is a terrible blight upon an otherwise idyllic scene.

A common claim from supporters of various commercial schemes is that those who wish to preserve wildness come mainly from outside the district and have little concern about the jobs to be gained. In most cases claims about employment are exaggerated, while planting, and much later harvesting in the case of trees, there are jobs created, but not continuously in significant numbers. When a senior Forestry Commission Officer was travelling around Ennerdale and Eskdale incognito he was frequently asked, by locals, to sign a petition against forestation in the Lake District. Around 13,000 people did sign a petition in 1935 against forestation in Eskdale and Dunnerdale, but too late to save Ennerdale.

There are plans to create again a wild Ennerdale.[13] The three main bodies involved, the Forestry Commission, National Trust and United Utilities ('owners' of Ennerdale Water) are all too bureaucratic to display the sensitivity that is necessary. Ennerdale valley does not need any kind of forest design plan. They will set up rules and regulations for the 'management' of the area instead of simply leaving the valley to nature. If they truly want a 'wild' Ennerdale they should remove all non-native trees, remove all sign posts and notice boards, remove all forestry roads and picnic sites, and leave the valley alone.

Hopefully, sometime, future generations will be able to wander up to Gable alongside the singing water of the Liza in a way I and other fellow walkers have not been able to do in our lifetime. In years to come, my granddaughter Naomi and family may be able to enjoy Ennerdale as it was when Annie Armitt of Rydal penned these words in the late nineteenth century:

> *The place is very still and lone,*
> *A wilderness of grass and stone*
> *Save where the sweet lake fills the vale,*
> *And mirrors all the silent scene,*
> *Great mountain masses intervene*
> *Betwixt the world and Ennerdale.*

The thought that, one day, the experience could be possible, helps me to cope with the ravages of Ennerdale today. Dislike of alien trees is not a new response; Dorothy Wordsworth wrote how 'fir and larch plantations were a blotch or scar on the fair surface of the mountains'.

We have access to Pillar and Gable along the valley and through the dense forest but originally this access was to be denied by the Forestry Commission, only strong protests from members of the Fell and Rock Climbing Club in 1925 gained the right to walk the track. The Commission now attempt to be sympathetic towards walkers and provide amenities which, in themselves, are artificial and do this only after much protest from walker's groups. The commission members are responsible for creating tree slums not only in Ennerdale but in mountain country all over Britain. The romantic view of landscape leaves little room for functionality, order and rigid rules; there are numerous non-wild places where bureaucrats may exercise their trade. Ironically, one of the main reasons for repeated visits to the summit of Gable is to live for one short moment away from the outcomes of that trade yet to gain full benefit we must not look in the direction of the Ennerdale valley or further south to the nuclear reprocessing plant at Winscale-Sellafield.

Threat of 'being loved to death'
One possible threat to Gable is being 'kicked to bits' by numerous walkers. The term seems to be something of an exaggeration although some of the more popular routes have become ugly scars on the mountain. The term, 'being loved to death' is often quoted when talking about increasing numbers of visitors to the area. Gable has more than its fair share of visitors; in a year to be counted in thousands. The number of walkers would not be the cause of footpath erosion if each person knew how to walk over rough country. Unskilled walkers who kick and scramble their way over the paths cause considerable damage; carelessly placed feet is the main cause of footpath erosion. Skilled walkers in contrast place their feet

very precisely and leave hardly a stone overturned. Observing the movement of Swiss Guides in the Alps made me appreciate their careful, smooth flowing movement; from waist up it was as though they were sitting in an armchair at home. I copied their movement and eventually covered ground effortlessly in a slow rhythmic way. Watching many walkers on hills today the contrast could not be greater; they expend considerable energy swinging unwieldy sticks around and lunge their way along paths, steadily gouging out ruts in the ground. One of the biggest offenders seems to be charity walkers who race and kick their way over as many tops as possible with no concern for the mountain they are on and completely indifferent to their surroundings. There are numerous outlets for charity events, surely it is not too much to ask that they leave mountains alone. Lakeland photographer Ann Bowker, made the point that enough feet are eroding our hills for pleasure without adding those who have come to torture themselves in aid of some charity. The logical thing, she said, 'would be to sponsor me for every day I don't climb a hill and to give the money to a charity which is trying to preserve the wild areas of Britain'.

However much the mountain and valleys suffer from storming boots it is nothing compared to the indignity of having man-made pavements, laid by people who seem to have nothing better to do. They also cause damage to the environment by using helicopters to air-lift sacks of rock to a mountain side. Taking rocks to a mountain can be likened to buying water in bottles, an act crazy beyond belief.

When mankind has finally gone from the area all feeble attempts to pave over paths, as seen now above Stockley Bridge on the way to Sty Head, will be quickly obliterated. In other places, rather silly duck-boarding across wet areas will soon rot away and all other trifling impositions on nature will be gone. In wilder areas the modifications, without maintenance, will vanish quite quickly. The two legged creatures which have walked and climbed on Gable's sides will, in the end, seem only a minor irritation to the mountain.

Machines, masts and business
Wind turbines, euphemistically called 'wind farms' to give the impression that they somehow belong in the rural environment provide a threat to the overall view from Gable, in the same way that atomic-power installation and forestry do to the west of the mountain. One major difference is that current development of wind farms threatens to surround the Lake District with machines, in a band of steel. There are now turbines in operation on all four sides of the Lake District, with other sites under evaluation. Fortunately some applications have been turned down, but even if no further turbines are built, serious damage has already been done. Developers see no problem in building turbines immediately on the edge of a

National Park and there is little doubt that building would take place inside the boundary if permission was granted. There needs to be a new clause set into planning regulations about visual impact upon what has been called 'classic views'. Ecologist, Sir George Stapleton felt that any intervention by man on the outline of a mountain should be a criminal offence. The adverse impact created by these massive steel structures, some around 375 feet from ground to the vertical tip of a blade, upon skylines is as great when placed around wild landscape as it would be if placed inside the area. It is now difficult to walk the hills bordering north of Skiddaw without seeing turbines, as for example from Binsey where a mass of them at Wharrels Hill spoils the view.

There are close parallels with dam building and forestry described earlier; both were insufficiently viable to justify the damage caused and the same can be said of wind power; yet again lessons are not learned from past mistakes. There is not even a valid case for use of these turbines as an essential need, which could be used to offset any aesthetic considerations put forward. There is a reliable estimate of needing 800 wind turbines to replace one conventional power station. In the words of Sir Martin Holgate, ex-chairman of the Renewable Energy Advisory Group, 'the trouble with wind farms is that they have a huge spatial footprint for a piddling little bit of electricity'.[14] He also pointed out that renewable technologies need to be in the right place and on the right scale. There is a greater concentration of wind turbines on the west coast only a few miles from Gable and supporters claim that these can be justified more easily than on sites to the east because wind is stronger and more frequent. The only consolation to be found here is that the wind farms to the west simply add to the blight which is already there. However, as explained above, it is hoped Ennerdale will in time go back to its wild state. The reprocessing at Winscale-Sellafield to produce weapons-grade plutonium is morally indefensible. Hopefully, in time, this plant will be removed as far as is possible. The site poses a constant threat to the environment. There is risk of pollution, possible catastrophic damage from earth-disturbance or from operating failures, as in 1957. Between the early eighteenth century and the 1980s there were twenty-eight reported earthquakes in the north west of England.[15] The most severe was in Cumberland, on August 11, 1786, with the epicentre around Egremont. Thousands of tons of rock came down from Pillar, caused landslides on Red Pike and rock falls on Helvellyn. A more recent major earthquake near Carlisle in 1979 was yet another warning.

When Calder Hall was commissioned in the mid-1950s to serve the nuclear power industry, the station created some social upheaval in addition to bringing blight, aesthetically. The relatively well-paid work attracted people from the upper valleys and brought disruption to a settled way of life. It was not unknown for people dedicated to living only among the mountains to split their time between sheep farming and work at the site. Urban working practices, of existing for five days and looking forward to week ends or to days off when doing shift work, were unknown to farmers below Gable.[16] They do not look upon work as a necessary evil to be endured for so many hours each day, and the line between leisure and work is not so clearly defined. The result of such a social influence is that life at Wasdale Head has changed more in the past 50 years than it did in the past 500 years. Norman Nicholson, well-known Lakeland writer commenting on the change brought about by the atomic industry wrote, 'many of the atomic scientists from Winscale and Calder Hall now live in these villages, and it seems grimly appropriate that the rock formed in the deserts of the past should now house the men who are likely to turn the future into another desert'.[17] A major threat to valley around Gable come from the need to store high-level nuclear waste, that is material of no further use, as opposed to spent fuel. A White Paper in 2008 defines what needs to be stored and what consultation should take place,[18] but cannot establish a process to ensure that assessment and evaluation of potential storage sites, suitable for geological disposal, will result in a decision that is safe.

Now, with the possibility of closing the nuclear site there is an opportunity to clean up the west coast; unfortunately wind turbines will simply replace an earlier eyesore with a new eyesore. For some time, when looking west from Gable summit we will have the excrescences of nuclear plant buildings, wind turbines and possibly relay masts to add to the current mess that is the Ennerdale valley. The words of historian, G.M. Trevelyan come to mind 'until the end of the eighteenth century the works of man only added to the beauty of nature. But science and machinery have now armed him with weapons that will be his own making or undoing, as he chooses to use them; at present he is destroying natural beauty apace in the ordinary course of business and economy.'[19]

Finally, to add another threat to this sorry tale is the idea of 'corporate branding' of features in the Lake District. Great Gable could become a brand image and be within the clutches of some company executives who could see money-making possibilities. Unfortunately this idea seems to be supported by some members of the Lake District National Park Authority. No natural feature in the Lake District should be branded; the concept is alien to nature and abhorrent to all who love wild places. BBC Radio 4 presenter John Humphreys expressed alarm and distaste when interviewing a proponent of the idea. The Philistine who was proposing the use of branding in Lakeland seemed incapable of appreciating a view of nature expressed by Humphries. Possibly, the following example of what could happen, if branding was introduced, may bring some enlightenment.

A threat which has been raised by Friends of the Lake District is that a commercial body with investment in a branded image could be in a strong position when wanting to develop a business idea on or near that image. In practice, this could mean a mobile phone company 'adopting' Gable as a brand and being in a position to place relay masts on or near the mountain. The placing of mobile telephone relay masts on hills and moors throughout the country, especially on skylines, is a dreadful blight on our landscape and developers of appropriate technology have failed us by not devising more aesthetically acceptable relay points. Mobile telephone reception is poor to non-existent in Gable's upper valley, but if masts are the only option for relays long may this remain the case. There are numerous examples where business and wild places are not happy bedfellows. The general conclusion must be that they should be kept apart. Gable and its valleys must not fall into the clutches of people who have commercial gain as a main priority.

People who object to roads, railways, dams, alien trees and branding are heavily criticized for what is called their elitism and excess of nostalgia for the past. When walkers go in great numbers to hills and mountains they expect to find places where there is stability, a landscape which has remained unchanged for generations. Words of Lord Birkett, quoted by William Rollinson,[20] emphasise this point, 'national parks are for those who wish to enjoy beauty and are content to find their enjoyment in ways that do not injure it'. In attempting to protect beauty of wildness and not to injure, it is wise to resist change. John Muir, pioneer of nature conservation in the nineteenth century, stated simply, 'wildness is a necessity'.

Occasionally we may catch a glimpse of what life could have been like around Gable if all resistance to change had been successful. Peter Bicknell, architect and mountaineer, writing about Gable in the 1940s captures what it can be like to have one of the mountain's valleys to oneself and without the intrusions which come with change:

> 'I should like to leave Gable now as I left it one January evening during the war. I had spent a day of great peace alone in the hills and had come down to Rosthwaite in Borrowdale. After a very unwarlike Cumberland tea, I walked down the road towards Keswick in the dusk. I have often dodged the cars and inhaled the fumes of petrol on this road. But that evening it was a new experience. It was perfect, still, clear and frosty, and my walk was undisturbed by a single car or a single human being. For the first time in my life I was able to see the romantic beauties of the Jaws of Borrowdale, Lowdore and Keswick Lake in complete solitude. As I crossed the shoulder of the hill above Keswick to get to

Derwentfolds, I looked back to see if the fells were still visible, and there crowning them all was the familiar dome, velvet black, against the starlit sky.'

Around fifty years later I had a similar experience having crossed from Gable to Eskhause alone during midweek in February to reach Langdale. There was a covering of snow and the cloud was low; it was only when half-way down Rossett Gill that I could see into the Langdale valley. Suddenly I stopped and felt there was something unusual about the view. I walked further down and then realization struck; there was not a vehicle to be seen anywhere, not a coloured steel box in sight. So rare is this experience that it made a real impact on me and I could only sit down and stare in wonder. Eventually I reached the Old Dungeon Ghyll Hotel, walked around the side of the climber's bar, which was closed, and there hidden out of sight stood a white van belonging to a man doing fence work below Raven Crag. So good of him to park there, hidden, and allow me to have an experience of a lifetime.

Most of this chapter has focussed on threats mainly to our viewing and overall enjoyment of Gable and its upper valleys, rather than physically harming the mountain and its immediate surroundings. One exception is the proposed road over Sty Head Pass, which would drastically change the relative isolation of the mountain and must never be allowed to happen; constant vigilance is essential. Other threats which come from wind turbines, telephone relay masts, atomic establishments, artificial-path building and quarrying are also to be resisted but given the history of on-going degradation in Lakeland and elsewhere, there can be little hope of these threats being defeated.

William Wordsworth was around 100 years ahead of his time when, in the mid nineteenth century, he described the Lake District as 'a sort of national property' and the chapter began with the first two lines of a sonnet related to threats; it will end with the last two lines:

Speak, passing winds; ye torrents, with your strong
And constant voice, protest against the wrong.

References
[1]   Salt, H.S. 1908. *On Cambrian and Cumbrian Hills.* London: A.C. Fifield.
[2]   Clapham, A.R. 1978. *Upper Teesdale.* London: Collins.
[3]   Pennington, W. 1974. *The History of British Vegetation.* London: English Universities Press.

4   Wainwright, A. 2003. *Wainwright's Lakeland and England's North Country*. BBC Worldwide Limited.
5   *Cumberland Highway Committee Minutes*, CCH/1/4. July 13, 1896.
6   Oppenheimer, L.J.1908. *The Heart of Lakeland*. London: Sherratt & Hughes.
7   Street-Porter, J. 2004. *Keep these Motorised Prats off our Paths*. London: Independent Newspaper, March 18.
8   Marren, P 1990. *Woodland Heritage*. London: David & Charles.
9   Symonds, H.H. 1936. *Afforestation in the Lake District: A Reply to the Forestry Commisson's White Paper of 26th August 1936*. London: J.M. Dent & Sons Ltd.
10 Budworth, D. 2006. *The Benefits of Branching into Forestry*. London: The Sunday Times, July 2.
11 Tsouvalis, J. 2000. *A Critical Geography of Britain's State Forests*. Oxford: Oxford University Press.
12 Spence, K. 1936. Friends of the Lake District, Newsletter. December 1.
13 Browning,G and Yanik, R 2004. *Wild Ennerdale – letting nature loose*. ECOS (3/4) pp.34-37.
14 McCarthy, M. 2003. *Green Power and the Green Lobby*. The Independent, October 6.
15 Melville, C. 1986. *Historical Earthquakes in North West England*. Cumberland and Westmorland Antiquarian and Archaeological Society. pp.193-209.
16 Williams, W.M. 1998. *The Sociology of an English Village: Gosforth*, London: Routledge. pp.31-32.
17 Nicholson, N. 1972. *Portrait of the Lakes*. London: Robert Hale & Co.
18 *Managing Radioactive Waste Safely. A Framework for Implementing Geological Disposal: A White Paper*. London: Defra.
19 Trevelyan, G.M. 1929. *Must England's Beauty Perish?* London: Faber and Faber.
20 Rollinson, W. *A History of Man in the Lake District*. p.156. London: J.M. Dent.

Index

Also from Sigma Leisure:

The World of a Wainwright Bagger
Chris Stanbury

Chris Stanbury provides an insight into the world of a 'Wainwright Bagger', inspiring those new to The Wainwrights, to those who have done most of the fells with a series of essays giving a flavour of the enjoy- ment to be found in completing Wainwright's 214 fells.

£8.99

Lake District Wet Weather Walks
Chris Mitchell

There are hundreds of guide books on the Lake District but none of them deals specifically with the problem of where to walk and what to see in wet weather. After some of the wettest summers on record, 20 walks have been chosen to cover all regions of the Lake District so that you will be able to try them out wherever you happen to be when the weather closes in.

£7.99

Walking the Wainwrights
Stuart Marshall

This book links all 214 peaks in the late Alfred Wainwright's seven-volume Pictorial Guide to The Lakeland Fells. Clear route descriptions are presented with two-colour sketch maps.

"An excellent, concise manual on how to tackle the 'Wainwrights' in an intelligent way." – A. Harry Griffin MBE

£8.95

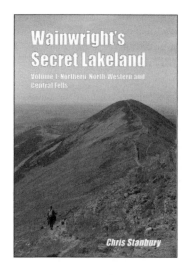

Wainwright's Secret Lakeland
Volume 1: Northern, North-Western and Central Fells
Chris Stanbury

Volume One of a trilogy covering approximately 200 walks of a secretive and secluded nature in the Lake District covering the Northern, North-Western and Central Fells as defined by Alfred Wainwright. 75 of Wainwright's ascent and ridge routes in Lakeland are described, selected for their secret and secluded nature. The routes are described from a modern perspective with a comparison where appropriate with how Wainwright described them in his day. Each walk is conveyed as a story with details along the way about features of geology, local history and associated literature.

£9.99 (available April 2012)

A Lakeland Saga
A Story of the Collingwood and Alounyan Family in Coniston and Aleppo
Jeremy Collingwood

The story of a family whose lives pivoted between the very English setting of the Lake District and the exoticism of Aleppo and Jerusalem. It touches on the family's connections with Arthur Ransome and his 'Swallows and Amazons', the Oxford world of Idealistic philosophy, and characters such as John Ruskin and Lawrence of Arabia.

£20 hardback (available April 2012)

All of our books are all available on-line at **www.sigmapress.co.uk** or through booksellers. For a free catalogue, please contact:

Sigma Leisure, Stobart House, Pontyclerc, Penybanc Road, Ammanford, Carmarthenshire SA18 3HP
Tel: 01269 593100   Fax: 01269 596116

info@sigmapress.co.uk   www.sigmapress.co.uk